PLANT BASED COOKBOOK FOR BEGINNERS

This Book Contains 4 Manuscripts :

1) <u>Plant Based Meal Prep</u>

2) <u>Vegetarian Meal Prep</u>

3) <u>Anti Inflammatory Diet</u>

4) <u>Anti Anxiety Diet</u>

Plant Based Meal Prep

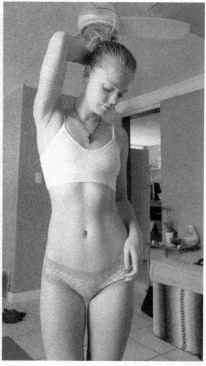

The Ultimate Book For Ready-To-Go Meals For a Healthy, Plant-Based, Whole Foods Diet With 4 Weeks Time And Money Saving, Easy And Quick Meal Plan.

PLANT BASED *Meal Prep*

NEW EDITION

"THE ULTIMATE BOOK FOR READY-TO-GO MEALS FOR A HEALTHY, PLANT-BASED, WHOLE FOODS DIET WITH 4 WEEKS TIME AND MONEY SAVING, EASY AND QUICK MEAL PLAN"

OLIVIA JOHNSON SMITH

Description

If you are looking for great ways to save money and at the same time eat healthy meals every day of the week, then this meal prep is your perfect companion. At times, preparing vegan meals may seem complicated and overwhelming. Fortunately, this list of vegan meal prep ideas will not only help you to prepare easy meals, but they will also be delicious.

It does not matter even if you are just starting on a vegan diet or you just want to try it out and see how it goes. Whichever your case, the point is that meal prep offers an amazing option to ensure you have healthy meals throughout the week.

The benefits you gain from Plant Based Meal Prep are quite encouraging. They give you the morale to do more. When you do meal prepping, you are guaranteed more time during the week to do other stuff.

You will not be pushed to create time from crazy schedules to go shopping. In fact, your shopping times will become fewer, less hectic and shorter.

Plant Based meal prep will save you the worries of what to cook every day. As much as you may be creative with your meals, there are those times your mind is just blank, and this can be very stressful. However, if you practice meal prepping, that can never be your portion.

It helps you to know what exactly you intend to make for breakfast, lunch, dinner, desserts, and snacks. As a result, you will be able to feed on healthy and nutritious meals every eating time without straining.

Would you love to prepare vegan for cheap?

It is the desire of every person to eat healthy and tasty food. The recipes and ideas in this book will help you meet your desires.

Is it possible to prepare your meals for 5 days in advance?

Yes. However, make sure you keep the meals in the refrigerator.

Are you on a diet and wants to learn how to prepare vegan meals for weight loss?

If you are on a diet or are planning to do so to lose weight, then vegan food can help you do just that. With a vegan diet, you will be able to replace unhealthy meals with foods low in calories and keep fuller longer.

Do you want to learn how to meal prep for a week of vegan lunches?

Perfect. This book entails all you need to know in regards to preparing healthy meals to take you the whole week.

The beauty of this book is that it contains informations that are beneficial to you and your loved ones.

You do not have to feed on junk and unhealthy meals just because time is not on your side. Whether you are a student or a committed worker, vegan meal prep allows you to prepare healthy meals for the whole week.

In this easy meal prep, you will learn the easiest way to prepare all your meals in super easy ways. You will have healthy and delicious vegan meals for you and your loved ones to feed on.

Why you need to read this awesome book

- This book is the only place you will learn how to prepare healthiest meals.
- The book is suitable for people of all walks of life.
- Assist students who need ready meals on the go.
- Enable busy parents to feed their families with healthy meals.
- Help you significantly reduce food wastage.
- If you are not the type who loves to cook every other day, you are well sorted with plant based meal prep.
- It will help you to save time, money and still feed on delicious healthy meals.
- The recipes are suitable for both adults and children.
- You will learn how you can prepare delicious meals even on a budget... and more...

First Book : Plant Based Meal Prep

Introduction

Chapter 2: Vegan lunch and dinner meal prep

Orange tofu chickpea bowls

Chickpea and lentil taco salad meal prep bowls

Curried chickpea salad meal prep bowls

Roasted Brussels sprout and chickpea meal prep bowls

Roasted summer vegetable meal prep bowls

Easy Greek salad meal prep bowls

Sheet pan tofu and vegetable bowls with ginger peanut sauce

Vegetarian mason jar burrito bowls

Tex-Mex sweet potato lunch bowls

Spiralized sweet potato enchilada bowls

Chapter 3: Dessert meal prepping

Helpful toolset for easy healthy dessert recipes

Bonus tips for making healthy desserts super tasty

Consider these tips;

Use seasonal fruits

Make it with nuts

Use real sweeteners

Use high-quality ingredients

Chocolate chip gingerbread

Healthy no bake cherry vegan cheesecake

Making the No-Bake Cherry Cheesecake

Vegan matcha coconut tarts

Doughy peach pie bars

No-bake blueberry custard pie (vegan and gluten-free)

Banana chocolate and peanut butter swirl bread with pecan praline

Dark chocolate almond oatmeal cookies with sea salt

3-ingredient guilt free brownies

Creamy lime and avocado tart

Vegan brown rice crispy treats

Chapter 4: Snack meal prepping

Healthy meal prep snacks

Chapter 5: Vegan meal prep high protein

Easy vegan chili sin carne

High protein salad

Mexican lentil soup

Black bean and quinoa balls

Chapter 6: Vegan meal prep weight loss

Tips to lose weight as a vegan

Conclusion

Description

Introduction

Congratulations on buying Book *"**Plant Based Meal Prep**"*, and thank you for doing so.

The following chapters will discuss how it is possible to eat healthy even when you are short on time. By being equipped this book all your meal prep will be budget-friendly, and you'll have assistance to stick to your diet, even when you have a busy week.

There are several books on this subject, thanks for choosing this book.

We made every effort to ensure that every piece of information is of use and importance to you, our reader. Please enjoy!

How to get started

What is vegan meal prepping?

Before you get started, it is better to understand what vegan meal prepping entails so that you will have an easy time when preparing these healthy meals. Vegan meal prep is about cooking some healthy meals ahead of time and then portioning them out throughout your week.

First of all, you begin by planning what you intend to eat and then prepare a grocery list based on the recipe you chose. This way, you will save time, money, and at the same time, feed on much healthier meals throughout the week.

Best tips for meal prepping

In everything you do, some basic guidelines go a long way, and plant based meal prep is not an exemption. Therefore, below are some important tips to help you start your vegan meal prep accordingly. Why is this important? It will help you to know the meals to cook in advance. You will also learn the best way to keep your food fresh for the longest time possible. There are also some equipment suggestions. All these are done to give you an easy time when preparing your meals.

Healthy, safety and storage tips

a) High protein foods

You need to be extra careful when it comes to high-protein foods. While plant-based foods tend to have a much lower risk or chance of food poisoning, it will still pose a certain level of risk.

The reason as to why foods high in protein need to be well taken care of is because bacteria tend to thrive more on food with high protein content in comparison to starches and sugars. For instance, it is advisable you take extra care when storing and reheating foods like rice and quinoa to eliminate any chances of food poisoning.

b) Fridge or freezer?

Any food you choose to store in the fridge should be consumed within 2 to 3 days. Hence, if you are not sure that you will have consumed some meals within that duration, then it is safe to store it in the freezer. Simply, remember to get it out of the freezer and maybe now put it in the fridge a day before the day you intend to have it.

c) Your Senses

Fortunately, your senses can help you decide if you can consume a certain meal or not. By using your sense of smell or sight, you can be able to determine whether the meal is safe to consume.

Note that tasting the meals to see if it is safe to eat is the last thing you should do if you care about your health.

d) Reheat properly

You do not have to be in so much hurry when reheating your food least you end consuming something that will lead to your next hospital visit. Make sure you thoroughly reheat your foods and consume them when they are still hot.

On top of that, always ensure that you keep cold meals at lower temperatures and hot meals at higher temperatures. You should avoid keeping hot and cold meals at room temperature.

According to the USDA, bacteria are more likely to thrive in temperature between 4 and 60 degrees Celsius. How do you tell your food is hot enough? Make sure you note some hot piping in the middle of reheated meals.

e) Do not put warm food in the fridge

When you decide to keep warm meals in your fridge, chances are the food will affect the fridge's overall internal temperature. This may put the other foods in the fridge at risk of spoiling. To avoid this, always ensure that the meal cools off first before placing it inside the freezer or fridge.

f) Defrost timely

As mentioned above, refrigerated meals should be consumed within 2 to 3 days. Frozen meals should be fully defrosted in the fridge or at room temperature before you even think of consuming them. Always remember this when preparing your meals for the entire week.

Suitable storage equipment to consider

Here are some awesome options for storing meals you prepared earlier.

Plastic food containers

When choosing a plastic container, go for the ones that are safe to use in the microwave and dishwashing machine.

Boxes/Glass Jars

If you do not prefer using plastic to store your food, then glass jars present a perfect choice. This should be your number one option for all your basic storage options.

Ziploc-style bags

You can use Ziploc-style bags in your freezer or fridge. They are also economical since you can use them multiple times.

Lunch boxes

Lunch boxes offer a perfect storage option, especially if you are storing the meals in portions to easily grab as you head out. You can also use them if you want to keep different foods separately.

What to consider when choosing a recipe

One amazing factor about meal prepping that you can enjoy a good number of delicacies throughout the week even when you have a lot to do in your workplace or school so long as you took your time to prep in the start of the week.

To help you get the most out of your experience with vegan meal preps, below are some awesome ideas to guide you. No worries, you don't have to grab everything. The point is, even if you fail to get the hang of things right away, with time, you will be able to tell what works for you and what does not. You will also be able to know the perfect portions for you at each meal time.

Begin with your favorite foods

In the beginning, go for recipes that contain foods you had eaten before and enjoyed. If you are not ready to try a new recipe or food combo, then ensure that all ingredients are paired with things familiar to you.

Plan out your recipe

Planning out your recipe is something you should never fail to do if you want to prepare meals you will enjoy eating for the whole week. Start by visualizing what you intend to prepare the day before you go for your shopping. Have a list of the foods you need to buy to avoid getting confused at the grocery store. This will also help you to reduce impulse buying, whereby you may buy foods that will not be eaten and end up going to waste.

Get to know the best ways to combine foods

Ideally, a good but simple meal prep combo has legumes, starches, vegetables/greens, and condiments.

Make your own condiments

Do you love salads? Then why not consider making dressings and sauces ahead of time and keep them in the refrigerator? They can even go up for a whole week.

By doing this, you are going to be able to add any type of raw veggie salad to your ideal legume or grain.

Then add your pre-prep dressing.

Frozen Produce

The impressive feature of frozen fruits and vegetables is that they are affordable, fresh, and usually pack a lot of nutrients with them. It is also possible to refrigerate them for a longer time, and even when you need to prepare them; you will not have a hard time doing so. This is because any trimming or chopping needed has already been done for you. The best foods to buy frozen are things such as berries, mangoes, cherries, broccoli, peas, cauliflower, and root veggies, including butternut and squash.

Chapter 1: Vegan breakfast meal prepping

Who does not love starting their day with some delicious breakfast? Whether you like your breakfast salty or sweet, this chapter has got your back. The truth be told, breakfast can be a bit tricky, especially to plant-based people. Oatmeal or smoothie recipes offer a great option, but this can get a little bit boring, especially if this has become your everyday meal.

There are those crazy mornings when you don't have time to apply makeup or even dry your hair. Cooking a full meal is not on the list, and healthy eating can easily feel like the last thing you want to consider while it is crucial to your overall health.

Good news, the power to solve this nightmare is in your hands, simply consider planning. If you do so, you will be able to prepare delicious meals that you can stock in the freezer and simply grab on your way out. Isn't that amazing?

Below are delicious recipes you can prepare ahead of time to enable you to have a healthy breakfast even when you are rushing out. They are not boring and not just that, they will make your mornings brighter.

1. **Vegan zucchini bread**

If you like it dense and moist and you do not want to add butter, the secret would be applesauce. You will love the results. The bread also freezes well. The perfect way to enjoy a full serving of veggies without realizing it is by treating yourself with this comforting baked treat. If you like, you can whisk up a mixture of sugar, cinnamon and coconut oil/butter and spread it on top.

2. **Berry beet acai bowl**

Try this earthy veggie with some tart berries and coconut flakes. Sure enough, you will want some more. This meal is not only sweet but also full of vitamins. Simply blend your beets with acai, mixed berries, and coconut milk. If you want to have it at its best, prepare it at night, and then store it in the fridge overnight so that the following morning you will just enjoy your delicacy as you head out. You can add your favorite toppings like hemp seeds and fresh berries, and the results will be something that is enough to brighten up your mornings.

3. **Freezer oatmeal cups**

No easier way to enjoy some oatmeal if not in this meal-prep hack. Cook enough of your morning oats, pour them into muffin tins and freeze them until they become solidified. In the morning, when you are ready to eat, simply get one of your frozen oats, put them on a bowl and microwave them. If you want to add more taste, just add your favorite milk and toppings of choice, and there is your awesome breakfast.

4. Vegan potato and bacon

Gone are days when special treats were left for the weekend and holidays when you have all the time you need to prepare your breakfast. You can also enjoy a tasty meal for your busy weekday mornings as well. This recipe provides you with an impressive solution. Here, you will need a diced potato, tofu, and vegan bacon. Wrap them in a flour tortilla. Alternatively, you can also try corn if you want it to be gluten-free. Although it is tempting to overstuff it, make sure you leave enough space to wrap if effectively for storage. In the morning, if time is on your side then take advantage of that and top with salsa and avocado.

5. Vegan freezer burritos

Seems like an awkward choice for breakfast? The good thing about this type of meal is that you can have it for breakfast and still enjoy it at any other time of the day. The good thing about burritos is that they are freeze enough to store for the longest time possible. Try this, your burritos, tofu scramble, roasted potatoes, veggies, steamed kales, beans, vegan cheese and anything else you would love to add. For instance, if you are eating the burritos fresh, avocado or guacamole does miracles. Overall, this meal is just tasty.

6. Peanut butter green smoothie freezer packs

This is what you do. Choose when you have time, maybe during the weekend, mix those ingredients and put them in the fridge. There are no rules here you can customize them just the way you like. Remember to subdivide them into portions before storing them. This will make things easier when you want to have some in the morning before heading out. When you are ready to use them, take one of the portions and blend it. If you are running out of time, put it in a portable cup, and you can have it on your way.

7. Banana quinoa breakfast

This option of breakfast is perfect for people with a sweet tooth. It will help them lead a healthy lifestyle. Another impressive thing about the banana quinoa breakfast is that it is naturally filling due to the fiber and protein in quinoa and nut butter. For that little extra crunch, add some coconut flakes.

8. Banana breakfast cookies

If you want to have granola in portable form, then consider this type of cookies. They consist of a combination of oats, chia seeds, and banana. To prepare it, whip the whole butch in about 30 minutes. You can then freeze it and then in the morning or whenever you want to enjoy this wonderful meal, microwave it. If you want them to be more filling, consider spreading some jam, coconut yogurt or nut butter on top.

9. Baked hash browns

Hash browns offer one of the best greasy brunch foods. They are not only crispy, but they are also carby. Those little slices are quite appetizing. If you want, runny egg or some zesty hot sauces do wonder. You do not need the sketchy oils they are normally fried in to make these hash browns. Just remember to freeze before you bake them. With this healthy meal in the freezer, you have no reason to leave the house in the morning with an empty stomach. You will need to pop them in the oven and if in not so much hurry, top with avocado.

Chapter 2: Vegan lunch and dinner meal prep

In this chapter, the book will guide you through super-simple ways to create delicious vegan lunches for a whole week. Incorporating a vegan diet or eating more plant-based meals has a lot of benefits to your overall health.

Healthy vegan meals will help you lower your risk of contracting diabetes, heart disease, and cancer.

Furthermore, you have higher chances of reducing weight or even maintaining a healthy weight because those filling fiber foods such as veggies, fruits, whole grains, and beans will ensure you are satisfied when you consume them.

Lunch and dinners are the most laborious meals of the day. You might be tempted to snack out unhealthy meals, especially if you are having a busy week. Thanks to the vegan meal prep ideas, you can make those meals a bit easier without compromising their quality.

Just a little meal prep goes a long way. You have the power to make lunch or dinner something everybody wants to have a share in by just some simple planning, slicing and dicing, and just a few strategic sauces. More so, even if these recipes are vegan, it will surprise you how tasty they can be.

Below is a prep plan to help you prepare healthy meals for the whole week. Interestingly, these tastier recipes will ensure you have an easy time throughout the week and still feed yourself and your loved ones healthy, tasty meals. They will thank you later. You may be required to adjust the recipes depending on the number of people you are preparing the meals for. Do not worry, if you happen to realize what you made is excess, then how about you use the leftovers to dinner this week?

Enjoy healthy, delicious and easy to make meals. By the end of this, you will have become a pro to all matters regarding vegan meal preps.

Orange tofu chickpea bowls

This is one of the healthiest and delicious meal prep for lunch. They also come in handy for a quick and easy weekday dinner. The orange tofu chickpea bowls are easy to make, full of flavor and filling as well. They offer a great option as a meal prep lunch that you can enjoy throughout the week.

Do you feel like this is something you would love to give a trial? Well, simply cook up the tofu and chickpeas, steam the broccoli, cook your rice and mix up the sauce.

You can use white rice for your grain, but you can still opt for other choices such as your favorite grain or cauliflower rice. The idea is to use your favorite or what you already have on your hands.

The same case, if you do not want to use broccoli, you can use other substitutes like sugar snap peas, carrots, asparagus and the like. If you like your sauce thicker, then cook it a bit longer but bear in mind that it will be lesser. In other words, the lighter it is, the more you will get.

If you are making for meal prep, then get good sized portions and put them in the freezer. It would be better to heat them before eating to avoid any issues of food poisoning.

How to prepare it:

Measure your ingredients depending on the number of people you intend to prepare the meals for.

What you will need;

- Rice or your favorite grain
- Broccoli
- Extra firm tofu (cubed)
- Sesame oil or cooking oil of your choice
- Low sodium tamari
- Optional toppings such as sesame seeds and sliced green onions

Orange sauce;

- Freshly squeezed orange juice
- Low sodium tamari
- Toasted sesame oil
- Pure maple syrup
- Grated garlic
- Grated fresh ginger
- Cornstarch

Preparation

Cook your rice the way you like or follow the package directions. Steam the broccoli to your desired tenderness.

Use a small bowl or jar to add all the orange sauce ingredients. Mix them thoroughly and ensure they are well combined.

Add some oil and heat a large skillet. Keep the heat at medium. Then add tamari, tofu and then sauté the connection until the tofu turns brown. Occasional stirring in about 7 to 10 minutes is recommended.

Then add your chickpeas and orange sauce to the pan. Allow them to cook until the sauce becomes thick enough to coat your cooking spoon. The longer it cooks, the thicker the sauce becomes. So, if you want to have more sauce, do not allow it to cook for too long.

In each bowl, add some rice, broccoli, orange tofu, and chickpeas. If there is extra sauce available, drizzle it over rice and broccoli. Then season it with some soy sauce.

For meal preps, divide the meal into ideal portions, put them in the refrigerator/microwave safe containers and store them in the fridge. You can keep them up to 5 days. Make sure you properly heat them in the microwave or on the stovetop before eating them.

Chickpea and lentil taco salad meal prep bowls

This meal prep plan of chickpea and lentil taco salad meal prep bowls are healthy, tasty and filling.

What you will need to prepare this awesome meal. Measure depending on the number of people and the days you intend to serve this meal.

- Olive oil or your favorite oil
- Cooked chickpeas
- Cooked lentils
- Ground cumin
- Garlic powder
- Paprika
- Salt
- Corn kernels
- Onion powder
- Mixed greens or chopped lettuce
- Diced tomatoes
- Diced red onion
- Optional toppings like salsa, jalapenos, cilantro or black olives

For crispy tortilla stripes;

- Corn tortillas
- Cooking spray
- Salt
- Paprika
- Garlic powder

Greek yogurt ranch;

- Greek yogurt or any other non-dairy yogurt
- Diced cucumber
- Chopped basil
- Chopped Dill
- Chopped green onion or chives
- Garlic powder
- Onion powder
- Salt

Instructions to prepare

Begin by preheating your gas or electric oven to around 375 degrees F. place the thinly sliced strips of tortillas and place them on a medium sized sheet pan. Use the cooking spray to spray and season with garlic powder, paprika, and salt to taste. In about 7 to 10 minutes, it should have become crispy and starting to turn brown. Allow them to cool and then separate them into equal portions. Put them in a Ziploc bag or airtight container and store them on the counter.

Get a blender, put all the dressing ingredients inside and blend them until they become creamy. Put your dressing into different containers in equal amounts and then refrigerate them.

Next, heat a huge skillet. Keep the heat at medium. Then add your favorite oil, lentils, chickpeas, and all the remaining spices. Stir until the mixture combines and allow it to cook until it is heated through for the spices to develop. This should happen in about five minutes.

Now, get your choice of prep containers and in each of the container add some chickpea/lentil mixture, corn, lettuce, tomatoes, and red onion. Whenever you are ready to eat, you can top with dressing, crispy tortilla strips or your favorite topping and enjoy your lunch and dinner throughout the week.

Curried chickpea salad meal prep bowls

If you are looking for super easy healthy meal prep for lunch or at times dinner, then these curried chickpea salad meal prep bowls have the solution you seek. Interestingly, they do not require cooking, and you can be able to prepare them in 20 minutes.

Curried chickpea salad is just amazing and can make you look forward to your lunches the whole week so long as you know you will enjoy eating such a hearty salad.

The sweetness of incorporating curry in your diet is the great flavor it comes with. It also really goes well with apples, dried cranberries and of course chickpeas. For those lunches, you just don't want to feel fuller and tired, opt for this salad for a perfect light lunch option.

There are times when no-cook meals come really in handy. They provide the easiest and quickest way to make a tasty salad. They are also healthy as they are prepared with lots of fresh ingredients. Although they are a favorite to many all year round, they tend to be more popular during summertime when everybody is avoiding heating their homes by turning the oven on.

If you want to separate your crackers and grapes/mixed nuts from the chickpea salad, simply use separate containers or store your salad in a plastic bag.

It is advisable you add your crackers and mixed nuts when you are about to have your meals. If you put them earlier, they might become a little bit soft on the third and fourth day. So, if you like to keep everything crispy and fresh, you know what to do.

If you do not want to have lettuce, feel free to exclude them. You can just scoop your curried chickpea salad with crackers and still enjoy your salad. You can include any fruits or sides of your choice such as grapes and mixed nuts, and you will be good to go.

What you will need

- Cans chickpeas, rinsed and drained
- Diced celery
- Diced apple
- Chopped red onion
- Dried cranberries
- Vegan mayo
- Dijon mustard
- Curry powder
- Salt
- Black pepper

- Lettuce
- Crackers
- Grapes or mixed nuts

How to prepare the salad

Add the chickpeas to a small bowl and slightly mash them using either a fork or a potato masher. Then add all the other remaining ingredients in the same bowl and mix them until they are super combined.

After that, line up your meal prep containers. Add a lettuce leaf and the chickpea salad mixture to all your containers depending with the portion you like. You can separate the crackers and grapes/mixed nuts with some liners if you want.

Roasted Brussels sprout and chickpea meal prep bowls

What a healthy meal is full of vegetables and protein! You can make this awesome meal ahead of time and enjoy it later over lunch or dinner. Quite convenient, right?

Roasting chickpeas makes them so crispy and spicy too. Although they tend to loose a bit of their crispiness once they are refrigerated, then still come out nicely when warmed up. What about roasting vegetables? Superb. Roasting veggies brings their perfect flavor even before adding any spices.

Some helpful tips to consider:

Instead of dressing the bowls and you are not yet ready to eat, it is better to store the dressing in another container.

When it comes to avocado, add it in the morning to avoid it turning brown. On the same note, squeezing a little lemon juice over it can help prevent browning.

You can enjoy these bowls, either cold or warm.

Things you will need:

- Uncooked quinoa
- Brussels sprouts
- Cooked chickpeas
- Olive oil
- Garlic powder
- Salt
- Paprika
- Dried cranberries
- Black pepper
- Avocado

Lemon tahini dressing:

- Tahini
- Lemon juice
- Salt
- Warm water

How to prepare it

Switch on the oven and preheat the oven to around 400 degrees F. Follow the instructions on the quinoa packaging, cook and set it aside.

Rinse the Brussels sprouts, cut off the stem, peel off the out leaves if you like and slice it in half. Get a large sheet pan and add the sliced Brussels sprouts and chickpeas.

Drizzle everything with some olive oil. Then season with pepper and salt. To the chickpeas, add the paprika and garlic powder. Toss each ingredient gently until all is well coated. Bake them until the Brussels sprout becomes tender and turns brown. The chickpeas should also be crispy. This should take about 30 to 40 minutes.

For the dressing ingredients, add them in a small bowl or a jar. Whisk them until they combine properly. You can put the dressing inside an airtight container until ready to use it.

Your meal is now ready. Assemble your bowls. Make sure each bowl contains quinoa, Brussels sprout, and chickpeas. On top of that, add some dried cranberries. For the avocado, consider adding it when ready to eat.

Roasted summer vegetable meal prep bowls

This is another meal filled with delicious summer vegetables. Make this healthy, filling and delicious meal at the start of the week and enjoy a whole amazing week of ready lunch or dinner.

If you like, you can leave your cherry tomatoes raw. However, you should try roasting them and enjoy the sweetness that comes with it. The good thing about these roasted summer vegetable meal prep bowls is that they can be enjoyed either warm or cold.

If you are not able to find fresh basil, then consider using parsley. Top it with a store-bought balsamic dressing or whatever kind of dressing you like and make things easy for you.

What you will need:

Get the ingredients depending on the portions you intend to make and the number of days you will be enjoying this delicious meal.

- Diced zucchini
- Diced summer squash
- Pint cherry tomatoes
- Diced red onion
- Olive oil or your favorite cooking oil
- Salt
- Pepper
- Dried Italian seasoning
- Rinsed quinoa
- Chickpeas
- Optional fresh herbs for garnish
- Balsamic dressing (homemade or store-bought)

How to prepare

Begin by pre-heating the oven to around 400 degrees F. Get a large baking sheet enough to hold the diced zucchini, summer squash, onion and cherry tomatoes. Pour some olive oil and then season with salt, Italian seasoning, and pepper. Make sure the vegetables are evenly coated. Then roast for about 30 minutes or until tender and then start to caramelize.

Add quinoa in a pot and cover it with some cold water. Bring them to a simmer. Make sure that quinoa if well cooked with no more water. About 12 to 15 minutes should be enough. After it's ready, set it aside.

Using safe refrigerator containers, assemble the meal prep bowls. In each bowl, ensure you add some quinoa, chickpeas and the roasted veggies.

Once through, top the meal with fresh herbs and balsamic dressing. No restrictions here, even your dressing of choice will be perfect.

The bowls can be refrigerated for up to four days. If you are re-heating these bowls, ensure that they are microwave/oven safe.

Easy Greek salad meal prep bowls

These super easy Greek salad meal prep bowls are not only flavorful, but they are also loaded with tons of healthy vegetables. If you are looking some healthy vegan meal prep recipes, this should on top of the list.

The good thing about this recipe is that it provides such a fresh and flavorful dish. In fact, it gives you a perfect excuse to eat all the veggies on your plate. You simply need a few extra minutes to meal prep these easy Greek salad prep bowls. They are a life saver. Just make them on Sunday, and you will have lunch and dinner ready for the next 3 to 4 days of that busy week.

If you love fresh tomatoes, peppers, and cucumbers, then do not fail to put them on your Greek salad meal prep bowls for that perfect sweet taste they bring. No worries, if these are not your perfect choices, then feel free to use your favorite vegetables.

Do you feel like using chickpeas and hummus in the same dish a bit redundant? Well, this should not be the case because the textures are a little different, and on top of that, it is never a bad idea to have more proteins. Just experiment with using different hummus flavors and you will love the results.

You can also serve this meal prep with some toasted pita bread cubes. It is good for your carbs. Further, it acts like a crouton and gives your salad a nice texture. Only add the pita bread when you are ready to eat because if you add it earlier, it might get soggy.

What you will need

- Your favorite greens such as romaine, spinach, baby kales and the like
- Diced cherry tomatoes
- Diced bell pepper
- Diced cucumber
- Kalamata olives
- Cooked chickpeas
- Hummus
- Pita bread
- Olive oil
- Salt
- Dried Italian seasoning

How to prepare

Start by preheating the oven to around 350 degrees F to make pita bread croutons. If you like, you can dice pita bread into bite-size pieces. Use a large baking sheet to toss together the pita bread with a drizzle of olive oil and salt. Add Italian seasoning to taste. Then bake the pita until it turns brown and crispy, flip it once. It should be ready in about 5 to 7 minutes. Store your pita croutons in an airtight container on the counter for no more than 4 days.

In each bowl, put a handful of greens, chickpeas, tomatoes, cucumber, bell pepper, kalamata olives, red onion, and hummus. Make sure you put them in airtight containers and refrigerate them for 3 to 4 days. If you happened to use a delicate green such as spring mix, then it is better you store it separately since it may not be able to hold up with all the other vegetables. When ready to eat and then top it with your favorite dressing and enjoy.

Sheet pan tofu and vegetable bowls with ginger peanut sauce

The idea of sheet pan meals comes really in handy, especially when you don't have enough time to clean every single dish in the kitchen. You can prepare this awesome meal and still leave your kitchen in good order. Basically, a sheet pan meals entail cooking the entire meal on a sheet pan in the oven. If washing dishes is not your thing, you will fall in love with this idea and end up doing it more often. If you want, you can add some rice but it is certainly not a must.

These sheet pan tofu and vegetable bowls offer a perfect healthy weeknight dial or meal prep lunch to be enjoyed by all family members.

What you will need (depending with the portions you intend to make)

- A packet of extra firm tofu
- Toasted sesame oil
- Tamari or soy sauce
- Garlic powder
- Diced red pepper
- Diced carrots
- Broccoli florets
- Snap peas
- Diced yellow onion
- Salt
- Ground ginger
- Black pepper
- Optional white rice or quinoa
- Optional garnishes

Ginger peanut sauce

- Creamy peanut butter
- Water
- Toasted sesame oil
- Tamari or soy sauce
- Pure maple syrup
- Rice wine vinegar
- Finely grated garlic
- Sriracha
- Salt

How to prepare

Pre-heat the oven to 400 degrees F. Then, drain any excess water from the tofu. Use a dish towel to press it for not less than 15 minutes if you can be able to press it for longer, the better.

After that, cut the tofu into bite-sized cubes, and then add them into a bowl. In the same bowl, add some sesame oil, tamari and garlic powder. Mix them properly and let the mixture settle for about 10 minutes or so.

In a sheet pan with non-stick mat, add all the vegetables. Toss the vegetables with sesame oil, garlic powder, ginger, salt, and pepper. Move the vegetables to one end of the pan to leave enough space for the tofu. Then dump the tofu onto the pan along with any other extra marinade.

Bake the tofu and vegetables for about 35-40 minutes. The tofu should turn brown while the vegetables should be tender. Remember to flip once. While this is going on, save time by making the peanut sauce. Simply add all ingredients to a bowl and whisk until combined.

Your dish is now ready. Assemble the bowls and in each of them add your favorite grain to the bottom of the bowl, top with vegetable mix and the tofu. Drizzle the desired amount of ginger peanut sauce on top. Then garnish with your choice of garnishes and enjoy.

Vegetarian Mason jar burrito bowls

The beauty about vegetarian Mason jar burrito bowls is that they are healthy, full of flavor and easy to assemble. They also provide an impressive make-ahead lunch for all family members.

Although it is not a must you enjoy this meal from a mason jar, this makes it super easy to store and portion your burrito bowls. It will be easier to take them off during meals time.

What you will need

- Dried white or brown rice
- Diced sweet potatoes
- Drained and rinsed black beans
- Corn kernels
- Salsa/Pico de gallo
- Olive oil
- Salt
- Pepper
- Chopped cilantro
- Lime juice
- Guacamole
- Lettuce

How to prepare it

Pre-heat the oven to 375 degrees Fahrenheit. Take the chopped sweet potato and toss with some olive oil, a pinch of salt and pepper. Bake the sweet potato for about 35 to 40 minutes or until fork tender.

Cook the rice the way you like it or better still follow the directions on the package. When rice is ready, stir in the chopped cilantro and lime juice.

In the assembled burrito bowls, put some rice, black beans, sweet potato, corn, salsa, a spoonful of guacamole and some lettuce. For best results, when you are making these burrito bowls ahead of time, consider leaving out the lettuce and guacamole until when you are ready to serve. If you intend to heat the burrito bowls warm, simply stick the Mason jar in the microwave for about 1 minute. Once warmed, add in the lettuce and guacamole and enjoy this tasty meal.

Tex-Mex sweet potato lunch bowls

There are those days you just feel tired for no apparent reason. Even when you think you have taken a long night rest, you still wake up feeling tired. It is on such days you want to grab the easiest and most convenient thing to eat. In that case, a perfect option would be Tex-Mex sweet potato lunch bowls.

Come to think of it, why would you not spend an hour or so making some Tex-Mex sweet potato lunch bowls and end up eating a healthy and filling lunch all week long? That would be amazing, and there will be no room to unhealthy snack foodstuff. You will always look forward to lunch time every single day of the week.

These bowls are perfect for people who struggle to eat healthy lunch every day or someone who feels like time is not on their side when it comes to preparing a healthy, tasty meal. In that case, simply make them on Sunday and the following week will be a special one to you and your loved one.

What you will need

- Sweet potatoes
- Dried quinoa
- Drained and rinsed black beans

Avocado dressing:

- Pitted avocado
- Juice of 2 limes
- Minced garlic
- Salt
- Ground cumin
- Black pepper
- Water

How to prepare it

Begin preparation by pre-heating your oven to around 4oo degrees Fahrenheit's. Line a medium-sized baking sheet with foil or parchment paper. Use a fork to pierce each of the sweet potatoes a few times until they become fork tender. This should take you about 45 to 50 minutes.

Cook the quinoa in your liking or according to the directions on the package. In a blender, put all the dressing ingredients and then blend the mixture until it becomes creamy. 30 seconds to 1 minute should be enough. Your meal is ready.

Then assemble the lunch bowls. Cut the sweet potato open, top with quinoa and black beans. Drizzle your desired amount of dressing on top and if you like, serve with greens and chips. If you are not ready to serve, then leave the dressing and any other additional toppings until when the times comes to enjoy your tasty meal.

Spiralized sweet potato enchilada bowls

If you want a make-ahead lunch or some quick dinner, the solution would be these delicious sweet potato enchilada bowls. If you do not have a spiralizer, no worries, these sweet potato enchilada bowls can also be made with grated sweet potato instead of spiralized. However, if you are in for a spiralizer, simply make then thin enough to cook pretty quickly in a frying pan. Your dinner will be ready in less than an hour.

Making recipes that double as quick and easy dinners and meal prep lunch are never a bad idea. These sweet potato enchilada bowls are just like that. They are perfect for a family dinner or make ahead lunches for a whole week. Alternatively, you can have some for dinner and the leftovers for lunch. Either way, you will have still enjoyed this Mexican food to the fullest.

What you will need

- Olive oil
- Diced yellow onion
- Diced red pepper
- Diced green pepper
- Pilled and spiralized sweet potato
- Corn kernels
- Rinsed and drained black beans
- Cumin
- Paprika
- Granulated garlic
- Salt
- Enchilada sauce
- Optional rice or quinoa
- Optional toppings such as diced avocado, tomato, cilantro or salsa

How to make it

Switch on the heat to medium heat. Then add the olive oil and onion. Sautee the onion for about 2 minutes and then add peppers and sweet potato. Cook the veggies until tender, but it should not go beyond 10 minutes least you spoil your delicacy.

Add the black beans, corn, and all the spices. Stir and allow to cook for about two minutes. Then pour enchilada sauce and mix until well combined. Cook for about 5 minutes to ensure everything is well heated.

If you like, you can serve over rice and top with your favorite toppings. If you are making them as meal prep lunch, portion the enchilada mixture into the desired portions and pair with rice or quinoa.

Chapter 3: Dessert meal prepping

You can still satisfy your sweet tooth without compromising your clean, healthy lifestyle if you are equipped with healthy dessert ideas. Funny enough, most people are afraid to embrace clean eating simply because they fear the change will stop them from enjoying their foods anymore.

As much as some certain sacrifices have to be made to lead a healthy lifestyle, it's never easy to let go off your favorite meals. Saying goodbye to desserts is even more challenging. Life without holiday desserts, birthday cakes, and all the sweet treats must sound horrible.

Fortunately, you do not have to go through all those nightmares in the name of eating healthy. You simply need to go for the real, whole ingredients and adjust your favorite recipe just a little bit. When it comes to desserts, things are not different, either.

Now, do you want to learn how to make healthy desserts? Perfect. In this chapter, you will come across the best tips you need and some delicious totes recipes you will love. They also include so many healthy alternatives such as light desserts, low-fat desserts, low-calorie desserts, quick healthy desserts and easy healthy desserts all in one chapter. After this, you will forget about stressful dessert time.

Now that you have your meal prep lunch and dinner ready, it is your high time you add another course to your weekly prepping sessions. What could that be if not the below mentioned desserts? They are super easy to make, totally tasty and better yet, they are sweeter than you can imagine.

Helpful toolset for easy healthy dessert recipes

To ease up things much further, here is a list of tools that you can use to make some easy healthy desserts for your loved ones.

Mixing bowls: You need this for sure. They are somehow mandatory in any kitchen. As much as you will need them for your healthy desserts, they are still useful for other types of foods. Hence, the more reason you need to invest in nice mixing bowls.

A loaf pan: This is another kitchen essential you need to own. It has many uses, but for this particular case, you will be using it for ice cream, slices of bread, bars, and cheesecakes.

Mixer: are you ready for some healthy desserts recipes? Well, if yes, then make sure your mixer is ready as well.

Kitchen blender and food processor: Still in the same topic of kitchen gadgets to help you make super healthy desserts, you will need these two kitchen gadgets.

A trimmed baking sheet: This one will allow you to freeze fruits, turn them into the sorbet and make baked goods.

Cookie sheet/cooling sheet: Who does not love cookies? You will need a cookie sheet when you bake those delicious cookies and a cooling rack for cooling them.

Popsicle mold: A popsicle mold will come in handy when making those numerous healthy popsicle recipes. Do not hesitate to try them out.

Bonus tips for making healthy desserts super tasty

Great news! Numerous desserts can be made healthy. Therefore, forget about those misleading ideas that unhealthy desserts taste less than the healthy ones. The truth is, healthy desserts are very tasty. Just try the recipes below, and you will agree with this statement.

Consider these tips;

Use seasonal fruits

There is no doubt to this, seasonal fruits taste better and hence make a notable difference in your dessert. Consider using them in your dessert recipes as often as possible.

Make it with nuts

Nuts can make your dessert taste better. You can even replace the classic base with a nut-base for healthier desserts. You surely need to make your desserts with nuts not unless you have a nut allergy.

Use real sweeteners

Some healthy desserts become unpopular because they are not sweet enough. People with a sweet tooth feel the difference, and that is understandable. To change this scenario and make healthy dessert sweet, use natural sweeteners like raw honey or maple syrup instead of refined sugar. You can also use ripe fruits; they tend to add a naturally sweet flavor to those healthy desserts.

Use high-quality ingredients

The quality of your dessert has a lot to do with the quality of the ingredients you have used. Therefore, make it your business to consider this and never compromise on quality.

Are you now ready for healthy ice creams, cheesecakes, healthy pies, healthy frozen yogurts, and other awesome healthy desserts? You do not have to wait any longer, here are some of the best healthy desserts you can make for you and your family.

Chocolate chip gingerbread

These flourless ginger blondies made with high-protein chickpeas are vegan and gluten-free snack bars. They can make the perfect healthy treat for both kids and adults.

What you will need

- Drained chickpeas
- Almond butter/ Cashew butter
- Pure maple syrup
- Ground ginger
- Vanilla extract
- Blackstrap molasses
- Ground flaxseed
- Cloves
- Cinnamon
- Nutmeg
- Baking powder
- Salt
- Baking soda
- Chocolate chips

For the maple glaze

- Cashew butter
- Maple syrup
- Cinnamon
- Coconut oil
- Ground ginger

How to prepare

Preheat your oven to 350 Fahrenheit. Spray your cooking pan with coconut oil and cooking spray.

In a large food processor, ass all the ingredients except the ones for glaze and process them until batter becomes very smooth. Two to three minutes should be enough, though.

Then spread the batter evenly in the prepared pan. Evenly press the mixture into the pan using a spatula sprayed with cooking spray. Then bake the mixture for around twenty-five minutes.

Place the glaze ingredients in a small bowl and stir with a fork until they become very well combined. Ensure the coconut oil slightly melts as you stir. Set the mixture aside and allow the bars to cool. Then cut the cooled bars. Drizzle glaze onto bars.

Healthy no bake cherry vegan cheesecake

There is nothing complicated in making healthier desserts. One big secret is to substitute bad ingredients with healthy ingredients. The results are amazing. For instance, this healthy no bake cherry vegan cheesecake is made with a cashew-based filling, glutted-free crust and some delicious cherry layer on top. This is among the better tasting low-fat desserts that are as good as the classic ones.

Health benefits of cherries

Cherries and cheesecake offer a perfect combination. Further, cherries make a healthier no-bake cheesecake that you will love. Cherries are nutritious because they contain the following elements;

Melatonin

Studies indicate that cherries are filled with melatonin. The ingredient that helps your internal clock which regulates your normal sleep pattern.

Natural sweetness

The ideal dose of sweetness without unhealthy sugars is found in dark sweet or Rainier cherries. The reason as to why cherries are unique when compared with other fruits is that they contain a lower glycemic index in comparison to other fruits as they tend to release the glucose slowly and evenly.

As a result, this helps you to maintain a more stable blood sugar level, which leaves you feeling full for a longer time. This is also a plus to people who want to maintain a healthy weight.

Fiber

Cherries contain fiber, and they can assist you in reaching the recommended current dietary of two cups of fruit per day. More so, it can contribute to healthy weight maintenance, prevent diabetes and improve cardiovascular health.

In addition to the above, cherries also contain vitamin A, vitamin C, calcium, antioxidants, iron, potassium and protein. Cherries are also fat-free, sodium-free, cholesterol-free and low in calories with just 87 calories in one cup.

In general, consumption of cherries is healthy, and they are good for you. They can also make a perfect yummy treat and a tasty topping for a healthy cheesecake.

Best way to preserve cherries

In this particular case, the healthy no-bake cherry vegan cheesecake has been made using frozen cherries. Henceforth, you do not have to wait for the cherry season to make it. Make sure next time during fresh sweet cherries season you will go to the stores and grab as much as you will need before the next season. If you do so, you must have ways to preserve them without them losing their quality.

This is very important since fresh cherries are rare to find during colder months. The best option is to preserve your cherries is to freeze them. However, before you consider buying frozen cherries in your local stores, be cautious since some are preserved with sugar and other unhealthy ingredients.

The only way to avoid this situation is to preserve them yourself. Do not worry, it is super easy to do so, and the results will excite you. You will also be able to control the ingredients used to preserve them. Nothing can be compared with taking control of what you feed yourself and your loved one with. On top of that, with all the outstanding cherry recipes, the meal can make all the year round if you decide to preserve the fresh sweet cherries, you have every reason to learn how to preserve them and enjoy all the benefits that come with it.

Here are a couple of basic options you can use to preserve cherries:

Frozen cherries

The good thing about freezing cherries is that they freeze well. They can be used to make sweet smoothies and of course, cheesecake. To freeze them, you should place the frozen cherries on a baking dish on a single layer. Place them inside the freezer and then freeze until firm. You should then transfer all the contents inside a Ziploc bag. Once inside store them in the freezer; they will wait for you patiently until you need them.

Dry cherries

If you do not want to freeze your cherries, then you can opt to dry them. They also offer an amazing option to several recipes like baked cherry goods or granola. If you want to dry your cherries, you have options.

You can always use a dehydrator or alternatively dry the cherries inside your oven.

Making the No-Bake Cherry Cheesecake

To make the no-bake cherry cheesecake, you will need to first get 3 ingredients, that is: crust, raw cashew filling and the sweet cherry topping with frozen cherries. Ideally, these are the basic steps one can use to in most cherry cheesecake recipes.

However, in this case, things will be a bit different since this particular case involves making healthy cheesecake. The most impressive thing about this specific cheesecake, is you do not have to keep on worrying about the cooking duration for the cheesecake.

Why? You will not have to do any cooking at all — no worries about oven heating issues and the like.

The ingredients required:

To pull out the crust you will need;

- Dates
- Raw pecans,
- Sea salt

To make the smooth, creamy filling you will need;

- Raw cashews,
- Lemon juice,
- Coconut oil,
- Pure maple syrup
- Coconut milk

The sweet cherry topping is made of;

- Frozen sweet cherries
- Water
- Lemon juice
- Pure maple syrup
- Arrowroot starch
- Lemon zest

Now that you know the ingredients, without further ado, let us learn how to make cherry cheesecake right away.

Begin by soaking the cashews inside boiling water for almost an hour. In the meantime, get your food processor, place the raw pecans, pitted dates and sea salt. Mix them until you create loose dough. Place it aside.

Next, take your loaf pan and then line it with parchment paper. Since this is a vegan no-bake cake, you will not be doing any baking. Just transfer your dough into a loaf pan.

Pack down the mixture using your fingers and there you have it. The cheesecake crust is now ready.

It is now time to check on the filling for the cheesecake. Drain all the soaked cashews. Then add them to the blender together with melted coconut oil, lemon juice, coconut milk, and maple syrup. Blend them until smooth. After that, pour your cheesecake filling on top of the cheesecake crust, then place it in the freezer.

You can now be working on the sweet cherry topping as your cheesecake settles in the freezer. To make it, simply begin by combining the cherries, water, lemon zest, lemon juice and the maple syrup inside a saucepan for around 12-15 minutes.

Then add the arrowroots starch and then whisk them together until the mixture turns smooth and then begins to thicken. Allow them to heat for another 2 minutes. Remove the mixture from the oven and then allow it to cool down to room temperature. Add it over the cheesecake. Feel free to taste what you just made!

Vegan matcha coconut tarts

Have you cooked with matcha before? If you have not yet, it is your high time you consider doing so. You should just roll up your sleeves and cook a tray of small matcha coconut tarts as soon as you can. This dessert is perfect for any season.

They are not only vegan but also gluten and refined sugar-free but better still; they are gorgeous and properly indulgent. They contain just the right amount of sweetness you need. If this is something you would love to give it a try, then why not, go ahead and make your matcha coconut tarts for your family.

What you will need:

Gluten-free pastry

Ingredients;

- Buckwheat flour
- Oats or oat flour
- Desiccated coconut
- Fine salt
- Tapioca starch or cornstarch
- Raw cacao powder
- Melted coconut oil
- Maple syrup

Matcha coconut filling

Ingredients;

- Soaked raw cashews
- Coconut cream
- Matcha powder
- Maple syrup
- Agar flakes or agar powder

How to make them

Use a coffee grinder or a food processor to grind oats and desiccated coconut into powder form.

Pre-heat the oven to 175/345 degrees F.

In a large bowl, put the ground coconut, buckwheat flour, oats, salt, tapioca, cacao, and starch. Stir them until they combine properly.

Add the melted coconut into the dry ingredients and rub it with your fingers. Add the maple syrup. Continue adding more oil and maple syrup until the mixture stops being too dry and comes together easily. Leave the dough for about 10 minutes.

Make sure you lubricate the ramekins with coconut oil. Once through with the greasing, you should then line the bottom of the pan with circles of baking paper. This will enable the tarts to come out easily after baking.

You should then divide the dough you just made into two equal portions and then press the dough into the sides and base of each ramekin. Ensure the dough is bound tightly together. Also, remember to press the dough gently to cover all the gaps.

After that, you can then bake it in the oven's middle shelf for about 16 minutes. Let the tarts cool down after baking and filling.

To make the filling, place the drained coconut cream, cashews, maple syrup and the matcha in a blender.

Then place the agar flakes inside a small pot, put some water and bring to a gentle boil. Simmer and then remember to stir frequently for around fifteen minutes or until the agar is almost dissolved. Leave it to cool down a bit. There is no point of adding the agar to the remaining ingredients.

Add the warm agar mixture to your blender and then process the mixture until it becomes smooth. Give it about 3o minutes to set in. Your filling should be ready now.

Doughy peach pie bars

These doughy peach pie bars should be your favorite because apart from them being a healthy dessert, they are also suitable for breakfast or snacks. In other words, these bars are multipurpose. If peaches are not delicious to you, you can use bananas instead.

Ingredients needed

Bottom crust layer

- Oat Flour
- Salt
- Egg
- Greek yogurt
- Small cubes butter

Middle layer

- Thinly sliced peaches or bananas

Streusel topping

- Old-fashioned oats
- Finely chopped walnuts
- Melted butter
- Honey
- Cinnamon
- Salt

Directions to make

To make the bottom crust layer, combine salt, oat flour, honey, egg, and the Greek yogurt inside a bowl.

Add the cold butter to the ingredients in the bowl. Use your fingers to incorporate the butter into the dough. Although the dough with not get crumbly likes sand, it instead is the consistency of the biscuit dough.

Grease a casserole dish and press your dough inside. Then place the sliced peaches on the dough.

Now it is time to make the streusel topping. In a medium-sized bowl, combine the walnuts, oats, butter, cinnamon, honey, and salt. Sprinkle the streusel on the peaches — Bake the contents for about 18 minutes.

You can enjoy it warm or keep it in the fridge and eat it cold. In both situations, you will like it for sure.

No-bake blueberry custard pie (vegan and gluten-free)

This easy no-bake pie will brighten up your days when you are not in the mood to heat the oven, especially during summer days but still, want something fancy and yummy at the same time.

The beauty of vegan pie crusts is that they are super easy to make. They also contain healthy fat and tastes great too. Plus, no baking is needed to enjoy this delicacy. As for the creamy vanilla custard filling, it is strictly vegan with almond milk.

Another interesting thing about this recipe is that you have the opportunity to make it a day or two ahead up to the crust/filling steps. Isn't it amazing? On the D-day, just throw the jam/blueberry mixture on top, and you are good.

You will not even believe its vegan and gluten-free when you finally taste it. All the growly goes to the crunchy crust, creamy vanilla filling and juicy blueberry topping. You just need to do your thing a few hours in advance, and everyone who tastes it will thank you a lot.

What you need for:

The crust:

- Raw walnuts
- Raw almonds
- Unsweetened shredded coconut
- Pitted dates

The filling:

- Vegan cane sugar
- Cornstarch
- Unsweetened vanilla
- Coconut oil
- Vanilla extract

The topping:

- Blueberry jam
- Fresh blueberries

Directions to make:

Process all the crust ingredients inside a food processor until they become finely ground. In a greased pan with a removable bottom, press the crust mixture inside. Set it aside.

Next, put sugar and cornstarch in a medium pot. Do so as you whisk to eliminate any lumps. Whisk the Almond Breeze inside the mixture.

Put the almond breeze mixture to medium to high heat and bring them to a gentle boil. Then adjust the heat from medium to low. Whilst the mixture vigorously until it thickens. This should take you about 3 to 5 minutes. Once the mixture is ready, remove the mixture from heat. Whisk in the coconut oil and vanilla extract.

Pour the filling onto the crust generously and gently, then leave it to cool. Once cool, use a plastic wrap to tightly wrap it and put it in the fridge for at least an hour, the longer, the better. If you don't intend on doing so much in just one day, you can always leave preparing the pie. It can always be consumed at this stage.

Next, melt the jam by warming it on the microwave. Spread all the liquid jam on the cooled filling. You can use a spatula or a spoon. Then top with fresh blueberries.

Banana chocolate and peanut butter swirl bread with pecan praline

Do you have overripe bananas in the house and are planning to throw them away? Please do not do that. Instead, consider giving this recipe a try, and you will love the outcome. The bread does taste so good that next time you will buy lots of bananas without the fear they will get spoilt.

What you will need:

- Gluten-free flour/All-purpose flour
- Baking powder
- Salt
- Baking soda
- Cinnamon
- Ripe bananas
- Creamy peanut butter
- Eggs
- Coconut oil
- Unsweetened applesauce
- Sugar
- Vanilla
- Semi-sweet chocolate chips

Pecan praline

- Brown sugar
- Butter
- Low-fat milk
- Chopped pecans
- Vanilla

How to make banana chocolate and peanut butter swirl bread

Preheat your oven to 370 degrees F. Use the cooking spray to spray the loaf pan and line it with parchment paper. The parchment paper makes the removing of the bread much easier.

Next, mix the baking powder, flour, baking soda, cinnamon, salt inside a medium-sized bowl.

In another bowl, mash the bananas until you see no chunks left. Then add in the sugar, eggs, oil, peanut butter, vanilla and applesauce. Gradually, mix gently the flour. Divide the butter into two bowls.

Put the chocolate chips inside the microwave to melt. The best way is to begin by heating it for around 30 seconds. Then continue heating the mixture at 15 seconds intervals. Do so, until all the chips turn glossy. You should then pull the chocolate chips from the microwave and immediately stir until you achieve a creamy-chocolate mixture.

Add the chocolate mixture to one half of the batter.

Take your loaf pan and pour the batter into it. Remember to alternate the dark and light batter. Swirl the batter on the top with the help of a knife, toothpick or a skewer. Simply create a pattern without overworking it.

Bake for about 55 to 60 minutes. You can test, using a toothpick. If it comes clean, then it's all ready. Allow the bread to cool for about 10 minutes. After that, you can remove it from the pan.

Then prepare the praline. Get a small saucepan and melt the butter. On the melted butter, add sugar and milk. Combine them thoroughly until you come up with something like a sauce. Remove from the heat and then stir in pecans and vanilla.

Now pour your sauce onto the bread. The praline tends to harden pretty faster.

In case it hardens before pouring it onto the bread, then you have to reheat it. However, this time around do it a bit faster. Any leftovers should be wrapped and refrigerated; they can last up to one week.

Dark chocolate almond oatmeal cookies with sea salt

Who said you must give up on your 3 pm cookie simply because you are **meal prep** for a healthier you? The truth is you do not have to, you just need to make a healthy recipe like this one, and all will be well.

These dark cookies are not something that you may want to overlook. They have got little extra protein and healthy fats thanks to the almond butter. They are also interesting and easy to make.

What you will need;

- Coconut oil
- Eggs
- Maple syrup
- Almond butter
- Rolled oats
- Vanilla
- Cinnamon
- Baking soda
- Dark chocolate
- Coarse sea salt

Instructions to make it

Begin by preheating the oven to about 350 degrees F. Line the baking pan with a parchment paper.

Use a bowl to mix the coconut oil, eggs, maple syrup, vanilla and almond butter.

Using a large bowl, mix the cinnamon, rolled oats, dark chocolate, and baking soda. Mix the wet ingredients with the dry ones inside a large bowl. Stir them to combine. Make sure the dry mixture is evenly coated.

Pour the dough into the baking sheet, leave some space between cookies. Then, sprinkle each with a few sea salt flakes. Bake the cake for around 12 minutes or alternatively until the cookies turn golden brown.

3-ingredient guilt free brownies

These brownies are gluten-free and vegan. Plus, they will take you not more than five minutes. No bake recipes are worth celebrating. Below are the 3 ingredients you will need;

- Dates pitted
- Cocoa powder
- Honey roasted vanilla
- water

If you like, you can add additional flavors such as vanilla, sea salt, chocolate chips, shredded coconut, seeds and the like.

How to make it:

Begin by placing the almonds in the food processor and coarsely chop. Remove and set aside.

Next, put the dates in the same food processor and coarsely chop. Add water and cocoa powder and process until combined like cookie dough. Add the almond and whisk until relatively combined. Transfer the mixture into a bowl and finish combining by kneading the dough into a bowl.

Get a piece of parchment on your counter top and roll dough into a 1/3 of an inch thick slab. Then cut them into square or your desired shape.

If you intend to keep them for longer, you can keep yours in a Tupperware in the freezer. You can do so by putting them on a baking sheet with a piece of parchment paper and freeze them. Then transfer them into the Tupperware. This way, they can last longer, and they taste sweeter when frozen. However, do not be restricted by this; you can also do it your way.

Creamy lime and avocado tart

You should try adding these tarts to your meal prep rotation. They are so tasty but healthy at the same time. After having a bite, you will wonder what you have been doing all this while without cooking these awesome creamy lime and avocado tart.

If you have opted to make a mini cupcake, make sure that the tarts are frozen when getting them out of the cupcake tin least you ruin them up.

The tarts are best served when frozen. After removing them in the freezer, you can allow them to thaw for around 10 minutes before serving. If you like the frozen texture, then go ahead and try them before the 10 minutes. You should test to see which form works best for your taste buds. However, if you leave the tarts unfrozen for some time, the filling will eventually get extremely soft, much similar to pudding. Henceforth, make sure you freeze any leftovers.

The beauty of these tarts is that they are made using natural ingredients. They are also full of healthy fats from avocados, pecans and coconut. They are vegan, gluten-free and creamy. Do you want to try them? Below are the ingredients you will need and how to make them.

What you will need:

Crust:

- Shredded unsweetened coconut
- Chopped pecans
- Dates
- Lime zest

Tart filling

- Avocados
- Freshly squeezed lime juice
- Coconut or honey
- Coconut oil
- Lime zest

How to make it:

Use a food processor to process the ingredients including pecans, coconut, lime zest, dates and sea salt. You can also use a mini chopper. The point is to ensure the dates have converted into a sticky paste so that they can hold the crust ingredients. Remove the mixture from the processor and evenly press it inside two mini springform pans. Place the pans in the freezer.

In the meantime, you can be making the tart filling. Blend the avocados, lime juice, agave, coconut oil and lime zest. Do so in a high-speed blender or better still a food processor until the mixture becomes creamy.

Pour the avocado filling over the crust in the two pans. Use a spoon or a spatula to evenly spread the mixture. Place the pans in the freezer for not less than 2 hours, overnight is best.

Take it out of the freezer, remove the pan and allow it to sit for 10 to 15 minutes. Then cut into the desired size and serve. Remember to store any leftovers in the freezer.

Vegan brown rice crispy treats

Healthy brown rice treats are not only vegan but also gluten-free. They are made using brown rice syrup, almond butter and coconut oil. Instead of feeding your loved ones with marshmallow based rice crispy treats, why don't you replace that with a healthier option?

To add a little bit of fun, you can always add a few dairy-free chocolate chips. However, if you prefer a lower amount of sugar, it is better you forego the chocolate chips.

The brown rice cereal is gluten-free since it's made using whole grain brown rice. You can find it in most health food stores. The brown rice syrup is a natural sweetener that has a much low glycemic index.

It is also available in your local healthy food store. Although you can use maple syrup, in this particular recipe, brown rice syrup tends to perform better. Its thick and sticky nature helps it to hold the treats together nicely. These treats are great for desserts or snacks. They can be enjoyed by both adults and kids. Without further ado, here is the recipe.

What you will need:

- Brown rice syrup
- Coconut oil
- Almond butter
- Vanilla extract
- Brown rice crisp cereal
- Sea salt
- Dairy-free mini chocolate chips (optional)

How to make it:

Place the brown rice crisp cereal onto a bowl.

Next, place brown almond butter, rice syrup and the coconut oil in a saucepan on medium heat. Heat and stir until the mixture is well combined and creamy. 5 minutes should be okay. Once ready, remove the mixture from heat and then add vanilla and a little bit sea salt. Pour the mixture onto the rice cereal and then stir until everything is well combined. Line your baking dish using a parchment paper. Press the chocolate chips onto the top. Put it in the fridge for about an hour. Remove and cut into desired shapes.

Chapter 4: Snack meal prepping

Snacks are those little meals you indulge in throughout the day between breakfast, lunch, and dinner. Snacking is a good thing, and it can help you to re-energize when you feel worn out. You need healthy and nutritious little snacks here and there throughout the day.

Snacks are sometimes forbidden for being sugary, salty and empty calories. However, snacks do not have to be unhealthy. For instance, carrots and hummus are popular snacks since they provide protein and easily fill a part of your veggie quota for the day.

Below are benefited your body gets to enjoy when you make it a habit to snack throughout the day. Therefore, go ahead and grab a snack and do not feel guilty about it.

1. Provides diverse nutrients

Apart from eating three square meals a day, snacking in between meals is a very healthy lifestyle choice. Snacking can help increase your nutrient intake and allow you to get many benefits from the different types of food you are taking. Adding healthy snacks to your regular meals can help your body to benefit from nutrients such as vitamins, proteins and fiber.

2. Prevents binge eating

One big mistake people do is an attempt to deny them something to snack for so long that when they eventually decide to eat, they end up reaching for something unhealthy. There is nothing wrong with snacking, and so you do not have to feel guilty when you.

When you deny yourself something to snack for a longer time, most probably you end up having unhealthy cravings. More so, it makes sustaining a healthy lifestyle seem like an unachievable task. Hence, it is better to snack on filling foods in between meals. It will keep you satisfied throughout the day.

3. Beats the afternoon slump

The late-afternoon slump is a difficult thing to defeat for sure. Fighting your fatigue until dinner time can be a nightmare as it leads to sluggishness and low productivity.

Fortunately, this is something you can avoid by treating yourself to something with something to eat in between meals. It will take your energy to the required level.

4. Raises metabolism

When your body is constantly busy processing food, turns into a well-oiled machine. Snacking on healthy snacks will also keep your ticker and bloodstream pumping away. This greatly improves your body from inside. So, next time you are told to eat fewer meals to keep fit, do not forget that your metabolism requires energy to function regularly and be the best it needs to be.

5. Increases concentration

When you snack on healthy snacks in between meals, your level of concentration also increases. As a result, learning in school or getting work done in the office becomes easier. Eating snacks helps you to feel full, sharp and alert throughout the day.

Healthy meal prep snacks

Although some planning and preparation are required to stay on the path of healthy snacking, the benefits are worth it. Meal prep is not about lunch and dinner only; it also involves snacks. If you find it hard to eat well during the day as you run errands, stay on track by knowing how to meal healthy prep snacks. The possibilities snack meal prepping are almost endless. Here are just a few ideas to help you get started.

1. Bananas and peanut butter

This combination is just amazing. They are a little sweet, a little salty and have a whole lot of potassium and protein. Do not underestimate them because of their small size. They have what it takes to give you a huge burst of energy to keep going throughout the day. To prepare them, remove the banana cover, cut it into medium sizes. Then apply peanut butter on one side of the banana and combine two pieces. If peanut butter and bananas are not your favorites, you can replace bananas with apples. This snack is equal parts crunchy and smooth. If you want more crunches, then consider putting apple slices and a smear of peanut butter on crisp bread. You can pack them to work or school.

2. Avocado hummus snack jars

There is nothing super convenient like having something nutritious and delicious you can easily grab out of the fridge. It helps you keep on track with your health and wellness goals even when time is not on your side. This is a healthy snack idea that can serve such a purpose.

What you will need to prepare it

- Rinsed and drained chickpeas
- Tahini
- Diced avocado
- Minced garlic
- Lemon juice
- Salt
- Water
- Sliced sundried tomatoes (optional)
- Carrot sticks
- Celery sticks
- Cucumber
- Assorted cracks

How to prepare it

Add all the ingredients except veggies, avocado, and crackers to your blender. Blend them on the lowest speed in intervals of about 30 seconds. Remove the lid and stir. Continue with the process until fully mixed. The whole process should take you about 5 minutes.

Pour into jam jars and top with avocado or sundried tomatoes. You can serve alongside cut up veggies, crackers, chips or any healthy snack you have been craving for.

3. Popcorn

There are so many benefits associated with making popcorn become your number one snack option. First of all, they are easy to munch on, light and whole grain can be extremely healthy. Not all popcorns are healthy, though. To know exactly what you are consuming, it is better you air-pop your own so that you can know exactly what is in it. Further, homemade popcorn is quick and easy to make. Make some on Sunday and have something to snack on the whole week ahead.

4. Vanilla cashew butter cups

This delicious easy to make vanilla cashew butter cups can serve as healthy desserts and snacks.

Ingredients needed:

- Dark chocolate chips
- Cashew butter
- Honey or maple syrup
- Vanilla sea salt
- Flaky sea salt for the tops

How to prepare

Begin by lining the mini muffin tin with liners

Place 2/3 of the chocolate in a pan over low heat. Then remove it immediately it becomes glossy and melted. Add the remaining chocolate and stir a few times as the residual heats the just added chocolate.

Add some of the melted chocolate to one of the cupcake liners. Make sure the chocolate comes goes up the side of the liner by tipping it on its side and rotating it.

Repeat the same to all the liners. Place them in your fridge to harden.

Add the honey/maple syrup, cashew butter, vanilla, and salt to a bowl and gently combine them.

Once the chocolate cups have hardened, divide the cashew butter between the cups. Press it into the cup with your fingers or a spatula.

You can pour the remaining chocolate over the tops of the cashew butter cups and put them into your fridge until they harden. Finally, sprinkle a little flaky sea salt on top to make them irresistible.

Important things to note

If you have a microwave, you can use it to melt the chocolate. 20 to 30 seconds should be enough.

If you follow a vegan diet, make sure you read the label on the chocolate to see if it is okay for you to eat it.

Cashew nuts can be pricey. Save your cash by making your own using a food processor or a high powered blender.

Chapter 5: Vegan meal prep high protein

Are you wondering where vegans get their protein? Well, you are not alone. Most people ask this question a lot. What they do not know is that there are tons of protein sources in a vegan diet. Getting the amount you need is also easy. Plus, you do not have to achieve it by eating copious amounts of beans.

Below are a mixture of breakfasts, lunches, dinners, desserts and snacks recipes. They are most suitable to all those who are looking for proteins, healthy and gluten-free diet options.

Easy vegan chili sin carne

This is very easy to make delicacy as it will take you less than an hour to cook it. Further, if you are running out of time and want to make it extra easy, you can buy ready-prepared soffrito mixes at the food stores in the fresh veg or frozen section.

This recipe involves a mixture of pre-chopped onion, celery and carrots. It is a very handy mixture to have in your fridge for soups, veggie Bolognese and the like. It is also packed with plant-based protein. You can make it in big portions for later servings.

Here is the recipe.

What you will need:

- Olive oil
- Minced garlic
- Thinly sliced red onion
- Finely chopped celery stalks
- Peeled and finely chopped carrots
- Roughly chopped red pepper
- Ground cumin
- Chili powder
- Salt and pepper
- Tinned chopped tomatoes
- Red kidney beans
- Split red lentils
- Frozen soy mince
- Vegetables

How to make it:

Begin by heating the oil inside a saucepan.

Using medium heat, onion, sauté the garlic, celery, carrots and pepper for a few minutes. Then add cumin, chili powder, salt and pepper. Stir the mixture.

Pour in the chopped tomatoes, kidney beans, lentils, soy mince and vegetable stock. If you want to use any extra flavoring, this is the time to add it.

Simmer for 25 minutes. You can then serve it with rice, some freshly torn coriander and a squeeze of lime juice. You can also keep it in the fridge for up to 4 days.

High protein salad

This salad is the answer you seek if you have been looking for high protein, healthy salads recipes. The question of how vegans get protein is well answered. It is a great recipe for home snacks. You can also take with you to work, college or school.

What you will need:

For the salad;

- Canned green kidney beans (you use red ones as well)
- Canned lentils
- Arugula
- Capers

For the dressing

- Caper brine
- Tahini
- Peanut butter
- Tamari
- Hot sauce
- Balsamic vinegar

How to prepare it:

Add all the ingredients inside a bowl and whisk together until they combine to form a smooth dressing.

To make the salad, mix beans, lentils, arugula and capers. Top the meal with dressing and then enjoy your healthy meal.

Mexican lentil soup

The Mexican lentil soup is a tasty, nourishing, vegetarian and heart-healthy meal. It is indeed a complete one-pot meal. Both green and red lentils are a great protein source. You can then top the soup with several ingredients to add lots of flavors. Try it and who knows, it could be your new way to enjoy lentils.

What you will need:

- Extra virgin olive oil
- Diced yellow onion
- Peeled carrots
- Celery diced
- Diced red bell pepper
- Minced garlic
- Cumin
- Smoked paprika
- Oregano
- Diced tomatoes
- Diced green chilies
- Green lentils
- Vegetable Broth
- Salt
- Hot sauce
- Fresh cilantro, for garnish
- Avocado, peeled, pitted and diced

How to make it:

Inside a large pot, heat olive oil on medium heat. Then add carrots, onions, bell pepper and celery. Sauté for about 5 minutes or until they soften. Add cumin, garlic, oregano and paprika. Sauté for a minute.

Add tomatoes, chilies, lentils, broth and salt. Bring to simmer until lentils become tender. 30 to 40 minutes should be enough — season with pepper.

You can serve your lentil soup topped with avocado, fresh cilantro and dashes of hot sauce.

Black bean and quinoa balls

The quinoa balls are rich in flavor and delicious. Plus, you just need a few ingredients, and they are super easy to make. They go well with pasta or spiralized zucchini. You can also have them as snacks with your favorite dip.

This recipe is easy, quick, oil-free and healthy.

What you will need:

For the quinoa and the black bean;

- Quinoa
- Sesame seeds
- Black beans
- Oat Flour
- Sriracha
- Tomato paste
- Nutritional yeast
- Chopped fresh herbs
- Garlic powder
- Pepper
- Salt

For the sun-dried tomato sauce

- Sun-dried tomatoes
- Halved cherry tomatoes
- Garlic
- Apple cider vinegar
- Nutritional yeast
- Toasted pine nuts
- Oregano
- Fresh basil
- Pepper
- Salt

How to make it:

Add quinoa and water in a pot. Cook them for 15 minutes. You then drain any excess water and allow it to cool down for sometimes.

In the meantime, add a handful of black beans to the bowl and then mash them coarsely. Use a fork or a masher. Add sesame seeds, quinoa, oat flour, Sriracha, tomato paste, spice and nutritional yeast. Mix them well together. Make it into moldable dough.

Then roll the dough into small, tiny balls. Place the tiny balls on a baking sheet that is lined with baking paper — Bake for 35 to 40 minutes or until crispy.

Prepare your pasta the way you like it or according to the directions on the package.

For the tomato sauce, place the ingredients inside a food processor and then blend the ingredients until they turn creamy.

To serve, pasta with a few balls on each serving and then sprinkle them with fresh basil.

Chapter 6: Vegan meal prep weight loss

To maintain optimal health as a vegan is achievable.

Begin by ensuring you select fresh, seasonal unprocessed, locally sourced organic foods.

Here are the key ingredients that you will need to include to your healthy vegan plan;

1. Whole grains

Oats and brown rice are a great source of iron, and they can also keep you satisfied for longer as compared to the processed options. Foods made in grains are full of fiber. Hence, consider increasing your intake of millet, amaranth, barley and faro. They will keep you full and reduce your intake of unhealthy snacking.

2. Vegetables

Vegetables such as collard greens, kale and spinach are widely known to boost one's iron levels. Further, you squeeze some fresh lemon juice; your body will receive enough vitamin C to accelerate your iron absorption.

Sweet potato and butternut squash are rich in the element calcium and with them, you can forget about consuming dairy products. As for broccoli, cauliflower and Brussels sprouts, they are part of cruciferous family best known as cancer superheroes.

3. Legumes (soy, beans, and lentils)

Legumes form the base of a vegan meal plan. Legumes will deliver more than enough plant-based protein to your body, and this keeps your metabolism running. You also get strong muscles and most importantly, you do not feel the urge to grab any processed treats since you will not feel hungry.

Soy products such as soy milk or tofu tempeh are foods that greatly supports your weight loss efforts. However, they give the best results when consumed in their unprocessed and unsweetened state.

4. Healthy Fats

Who said you enjoy intake of fats if you are losing weight. So long as they are healthy fats, you do not have to feel guilty indulging your favorite dish or snack. For instance, avocado and olive oil contain high levels of vitamin E, which is beneficial to healthy skin. Besides, they also have high levels of monounsaturated fats. Walnuts and Ground flaxseeds are high in omega-3 fats, an anti-inflammatory whose task is to assist the body release excess water or toxins.

5. Nuts, nut butter, and milk

If you want healthy snacks to grab as you head out, then go for walnuts, peanuts, almonds, cashews, pistachios and hazelnuts. They are not only super tasty, but they are also high in protein and calcium. When you consume them, you fill full for a longer time and so you will not eat too much.

6. Berries, apples, and bananas

Berries are very beneficial to your body. They protect you from inflammation and cancer. Moreover, they assist your skin to stay young-looking and supple. As for bananas, they form a great component for a vegan meal plan either for sweetening or baking.

Although bananas are high in soluble fiber, control your intake as they are still high in sugar. Apples are also essential to your weight loss journey as they contain pectin, a substance which tends to feed on the healthy bacteria found inside the gut. A healthy gut often translates to a much healthy weight.

Tips to lose weight as a vegan

According to research, individuals who follow a vegan diet can loose weight having a higher chance in comparison to those who are animal-based diets user. If you also want to loose some weight, below are tips that can help you do just that.

1. Eat greens

An addition of greens such as broccoli, spinach, chard, swiss, bok choy, zucchini and Brussels sprouts to your meal is crucial. Their greens are ideal for weight loss since they are extremely low in calories and high in fiber. The high-content in fiber makes sure you feel full for a longer time, and this helps you to avoid unhealthy snacking. Other high-fiber options you can consider are fruits and raw tree nuts such as walnuts, almonds and cashews. They can also help lower cholesterol.

2. Increase your protein intake

If you intend to lose some extra pounds, then up your protein intake. Foods rich in protein helps you to feel full up faster. Thus, with just a little food, you will feel satisfied. Because proteins are readily available in different forms, it is convenient to incorporate them into your meals since you can have them in their row forms or cooked.

For breakfasts and mid-day smoothie, you can have protein powders. The other plant-based proteins like beans, tempeh lentils oats and quinoa can be used to serve the main elements of a burrito, veggie, stir-fry or salad.

3. Limit processed soy

When a transition to a vegan diet, soy products comes in handy as they are the easiest and most convenient items you can grab on your way. This does not mean soy is unhealthy, not at all. However, it is important you limit the processed soy. For instance, instead of a tofu scramble for breakfast, soy veggies burger for lunch and a pad Thai with tofu for dinner, why can't go for vegan cheese made with nuts, a black bean burger or even a pad Thai with veggies?

4. Prepare healthy meals

Meal planning has a lot to do when it comes to proper nutrition and weight loss. If time is not on your side, you can prepare easy dishes such as quinoa bowls; a mixed stir-fry blend of carrots, broccoli and mushrooms, vegan cheese, eggplant cutlets with a little bit of marinara sauce and soba noodles. Plus do not be limited to this; you can also get more easy-to-follow recipes that are dietitian approved.

5. Stay hydrated and exercise.

The key components of a successful weight loss program must incorporate healthy meals, water and exercise. To burn calories and lose weight, you should engage in 150 minutes of moderate aerobic activity or 75 minutes of vigorous aerobic activity in a week.

Conclusion

Thank you for making it through to the end of **_Plant Based Meal Prep_**, let's hope it was informative and able to provide you with all of the tools you need to achieve your goals whatever they may be.

The next step is to highlight the best parts of the book that you would not want to miss.

Here's what you learned:

- Knowing what exactly is vegan meal prepping
- Best tips for meal prepping
- Safe and healthy tips for storing your food
- Vegan meal prepping for breakfast
- Vegan meal prepping for lunch and dinner
- Vegan meal prep for weight loss
- Things to consider when choosing a recipe
- Dessert meal prepping
- Snack meal prepping
- How to save time while meal prepping
- Best ways to feed yourself and loved ones with healthy meals the whole week

This book will greatly help you to make maximum use of the free time you have on weekends to prepare healthy and delicious meals that will be eaten throughout the week. The book is meant to help you cope with tight schedules like a pro.

Life becomes much easier and interesting when meals are ready and what is required of you is just a few minutes to serve dinner or breakfast. Plus, you can also have readily available snacks to grab on the go. All these things are possible, and you can make life much enjoyable if you take your time to go through this Book.

In general, when you read this book and learn different *vegan meal prep* recipes, the results will be impressive. The ideas will help you save time. After a day of *meal prep*, things will be much easier the following days. There will be fewer dishes and plates to clean and less time to spend in the kitchen as dinner can be ready in minutes.

It will also help you create healthy eating habits for you and your family. Healthy eating is about being prepared, and if you have readily prepared meals for the week, nothing will stop you from eating healthy. It will also be easier for you to eat a balanced diet and this is very beneficial to your overall health. This book will also help you reduce stress. When you know that your family has something to eat for dinner, you will be able to relax and concentrate more on what you are doing.

Finally, if you found this book useful in any way, a five star review is always appreciated !

DISCLAIMER :

The author is not a licensed practitioner, physician, or medical professional and offers no medical diagnoses, treatments, suggestions, or counseling. The information presented herein has not been evaluated by the U.S. Food and Drug Administration, and it is not intended to diagnose, treat, cure, or prevent any disease. Full medical clearance from a licensed physician should be obtained before beginning or modifying any diet, exercise, or lifestyle program, and physicians should be informed of all nutritional changes.

The author/owner claims no responsibility to any person or entity for any liability, loss, or damage caused or alleged to be caused directly or indirectly as a result of the use, application, or interpretation of the information presented herein.

Vegetarian Meal Prep

A Complete Vegetarian Meal Prep Book, For Weight Loss And Increase Energy. Top Foods For Breakfast, Lunch, And Dinner. Easy To Be Made And Great Taste.

VEGETARIAN *Meal Prep*

NEW EDITION

A COMPLETE VEGETARIAN MEAL PREP BOOK, FOR WEIGHT LOSS AND INCREASE ENERGY. TOP FOODS FOR BREAKFAST, LUNCH, AND DINNER. EASY TO BE MADE AND GREAT TASTE

OLIVIA JOHNSON SMITH

TABLE OF CONTENTS

Description

If you want to create a healthy, sustainable vegetarian lifestyle and not break the bank or lose your free time while doing it, then keep reading!

- Do you want to save time and money at the grocery store each week without compromising quality and taste of your food?

- Are you tired of cooking and want to free yourself from being chained to the stove every day while still enjoying tasty meals that are great for you?

- Do you wish you had a guidebook to help you learn how to do this without spending hours looking for recipes?

- Our fresh, hot, delectable meals something you want to have for every occasion instead of having to depend on the drive-through because you are tired after a long day?

This book will teach you everything you need to know to get started and prepare scrumptious vegetarian meals that are good for you without having to spend hours to do them! Learn about what meal prep is, how it will help you save time and money, and how to get started doing it today. If you want to get healthy, lose weight, and feel great while keeping up with a vegetarian lifestyle, this book is for you!

Inside this book you will find

- Lists of all the equipment you will need to get started preparing meals and a bonus list of items to invest in that will make your life easier.

- Tricks on how to save yourself time in the kitchen so you can have more free time to do the things you love.

- A guide to make grocery shopping simple, easy, and fast instead of the boring chore it once was.

- Tips for customizing your meal prep to work best for you, your lifestyle, and the type of foods you like to eat.

- Recommendations on how to create unique flavor combinations that make your taste buds water and let eat at home instead of eating out.

- Recipes for breakfast, lunch, dinner, and snacks that are ready to go, easy to make, and taste great.

Never tried a vegetarian diet? No problem! This book provides plenty of great vegetarian recipes for every meal and snacks. If you want to lose weight and live a healthier lifestyle, this book is where you need to start!

Even if your week is already swamped and you feel like you have no more time to devote to a new routine, you can quickly and easily learn how to turn your daily cooking grind into a once per week event that will give you the time to focus on the things you care about. With this simple, ready to use the guide you can transform your food from being boring and exhausting to prepare into the delight of your day and something you were looking for!

Introduction

Congratulations on buying : **"Vegetarian Meal Prep"**

The Exclusive Guide for Ready-to-Go Meals for a Healthy Plant-Based Whole Foods Diet with a 30-Day Time- and Money-Saving Easy Meal Plan.

Thank you for doing so and for your decision to pursue a sustainable and healthy vegetarian lifestyle. Your body, wallet, and the weekly schedule will thank you for it!

The chapters included in this book will teach you all about how to make meal prep work for you to reduce the amount of time you spend in the kitchen each week while still eating good vegetarian food that tastes great.

This book starts by discussing the basics of meal prep, including descriptions of what meal prep is, different options for how to prepare meals to best suit your lifestyle and the type of foods you like to eat, and the equipment you will need to get started with prepping meals.

As a bonus, you will also receive a list of life-changing items for the kitchen that will make preparing meals an absolute breeze.

After that, you will learn about how to plan your menu to include healthy vegetarian meals all week long, tips for making grocery shopping a cinch and how to save money while at the store, and a list of suggestions that will save you time in the shopping and prepping process.

Finally, you will receive a plethora of tasty recipes for every meal and snacks that can easily be made once a week (or sometimes less!) that will provide you with hot, delicious food whenever you want it.

There are plenty of books on this subject on the market, so thanks again for choosing this one! Every effort was made to ensure it is as full of as much useful information as possible! Please enjoy!

Everything you need to know about getting started and what you'll need to start saving time and money on healthy meals that taste great

Why to prepare meals?

Do you come from work and dread cooking after an exhausting day? Do you find yourself reaching for whatever is quick and easy rather than healthy food options? Are you constantly running out of time or feeling rushed? Have you tried eating a healthy vegetarian diet but had trouble sticking with it?

If the answer is yes, then meal prep is perfect for you! By prepping meals in advance, you can save yourself time and money, eat better, and take the stress out of the question, "What's for dinner?" Meal prep is the key to making healthy, homecooked, and tasty meals every day!

Prepping meals for the week all at once saves you time in the kitchen every day. Instead of spending 30 minutes to an hour cooking daily, you can get everything done at once and relax in the evenings! Not only that, but you will save yourself hundreds of dollars on your grocery bills by only buying what you will use in your meals throughout the week. By taking charge of your menu, you make it easier on yourself to stick with healthy vegetarian options instead of turning to what's quick and easy (which means it's probably not good for you!). By freeing yourself of the constant need to make decisions about meals, you can focus more time and energy on more important things!

How do I do it?

Meal prep can look scary or intimidating when you're first getting started, but it's very simple! There are several different methods you can use:

- Preparing ingredients: This is the most basic method, where you would chop, slice, and dice all your veggies, proteins, and garnishes. You can also make marinades, sauces, or spice mixes to make your food taste great. Then everything you need is ready to go for a fresh, hot meal every day.

- Single-serve meals: Cook a big batch of something tasty and divvy it up into single-serving containers. This also works great for chopping veggies for salads or portioning out healthy snacks and desserts.

- Full meals in advance: Enjoy variety? With this method, you make your meals all at once and store them in containers for each day. Then you aren't limited to a single option.

- Freezer-ready: If you enjoy foods that are easy to make in large batches, this is the way to go! It is perfect for soups, stews, rice, and curries, or for freezing fruits that are in season for smoothies or just to munch when you're craving something sweet.

What do I need?

Meal prep supplies come in two varieties: must-haves and time-saving extras. You probably have almost all of the must-haves in your kitchen already, so getting started should be a breeze. It's always a good idea to invest in high-quality equipment, especially for something you do often. While cheaper options can get you started and get you by for a little while, they tend to break or dull a lot sooner than the equipment you spend a little more money on. Using high-quality equipment will also reduce the amount of time you need to spend doing things like cutting veggies or grating cheeses.

Must-haves:
- **Containers:** Containers are the cornerstone of meal prep. Since you're portioning out food for an entire week, you need to make sure you have enough containers for every meal. Choosing containers that can stack or are similar in size or shape will help you fit everything into your fridge or freezer. There are several different options as far as containers go:

    o **Glass jars:** These babies are amazingly versatile! They are fantastic for layered salads for lunches, storing chopped ingredients with an airtight seal so they don't brown or go bad, or for freezing (just make sure you leave enough room at the top for any liquids to expand!)

    o **Silicone:** Silicone containers are microwavable, so you can heat an entire meal in a jiffy. These are also often collapsible, which makes packing up after lunch or storing them a breeze!

o **Divided BPA-free containers:** This is your go-to for dinners! Using divided containers makes it easy to ensure you're eating a balanced diet and getting enough protein, vegetables, and whole grains at every meal.

o **Reusable bags:** Also great for anything that needs an airtight seal or to go in the freezer. But these bags also have the benefit of taking up less space, so you can store more.

- **Knives:** Never overlook the importance of having good kitchen knives! A sharp, high-quality knife will cut down the amount of time and effort you need to put into cutting, chopping, and dicing. Having special knives for specific purposes will make this even easier.

o **Chef's knife:** This is your all-in-one knife that can do just about any job in the kitchen. If you can only invest in one knife, make it this one! It can slice, chop, and make fine cuts and is great for any fruit, veggie, or protein you come across.

o **Paring knife:** Smaller than a chef's knife, a paring knife is perfect for removing the peels or rinds from veggies and fruits. You can also use it to create garnishes to go with your meals.

o **Kitchen shears:** These are not your ordinary scissors! Kitchen shears are used for snipping fresh herbs, dicing veggies fast, or even cutting pizza!

- **Cutting boards:** Cutting boards are an often overlooked yet vital component to every kitchen. When you are preparing ingredients for an entire week's worth of meals at once, they become even more important. They will save your kitchen counters, your knives, and your food from damage. It's best to have at least 3 in different sizes, preferably small, medium, and large so that you can fit anything from a carrot to an entire watermelon on one!

- **Mixing bowls:** Along with blending ingredients, mixing bowls are essential for marinating veggies before they go in the oven. You will want a variety of sizes so you can have multiple bowls going at once and accommodate foods of any size and shape. Glass bowls are best, but metal bowls are also good choices.

- **Measuring cups and spoons:** You can't make a recipe if you don't know how much of something to add! The more sizes you have of these, the easier your life will be. You can also find collapsible silicone versions to save space in your drawers.

- **Baking sheets:** Using the oven is one of the best ways to cook veggies that taste great. Once you pop the tray in the oven and set your timer, you can move onto other things without having to constantly stir. A large baking tray will fit enough veggies at once for an entire week's worth of dinners, or you can use two smaller trays side-by-side to cook multiple veggies at the same time.

- **Cooling rack:** It's important to let your food cool before packing it up and storing it in the fridge or freezer. The fastest way to do this is to use a cooling rack. It's also the best way to prevent excess moisture from building up on your food.

- **Grater:** Grating your fresh cheese instead of buying packaged is the first thing that comes to mind, but a grater is so much more versatile than just this. You can use it for veggies to go on salads or adding zested lemons or another citrus to kick the flavor of your meals up to a notch. Once you use your grater to utilize fresh spices like cinnamon and taste the difference yourself, you'll never go back to jars again.

- **Time-saving extras:**
  - **Rice cooker:** This one piece of equipment will save you hours! Rice is a wonderful and filling staple to add to any meal, but it can take so long to cook. Using a rice cooker instead of having to constantly stir and check to make sure it is not burned or hard in the middle will take the headache out of cooking rice once and for all.

  - **Crockpot:** A crockpot is a fantastic way to cook a large batch of stew or curry. You can also use this piece of equipment to make sure you have a fresh, hot meal ready to go when you get home at the end of the day. By adding prepared ingredients and leaving on low temperature for several hours, you can start dinner first thing in the morning before you leave and not have to wait for it once you get home. Crockpots are not just for dinners, either! You can make some tasty treats, like cakes, puddings, or cobblers in a crockpot.

  - **Food processor:** A food processor will cut the time you spend chopping down to nothing. Most food processors have several different blades, which can provide a variety of results. You can do anything from creating veggie noodles to dicing onions (without the tears!) to pureeing salsa.

  - **Blender:** Not just for smoothies or milkshakes. Blenders are great for creating homemade marinades or sauces. You can even make your peanut or almond butter in one! Bullet-style blenders are an especially good choice for meal prep. They come with large and small blender jars, as well as lids and shaker tops!

- **Food scale:** A scale is a more precise way to measure ingredients than measuring cups or spoons. It is also handy for separating proper portion sizes or if you happen to find a European recipe you want to try.

- **Mandolin:** No, not the instrument! A mandolin is a quick, easy way to slice fruits and veggies. Like a food processor, most come with a variety of different blades to produce different types of cuts. A good mandolin will also have a high adjustment knob so you can create slices as thick or as thin as you want them.

- **Garlic press:** Just about any food tastes better when you add a bit of fresh garlic but mincing it can be tedious and time-consuming. A garlic press takes a task that seems to take forever and make it happen in an instant.

- **Hand blender:** Also known as a stick mixer, this bad boy can mix anything from smoothies to soups. It's great for use with smaller pots and bowls since it is more compact than your traditional hand mixer. You can also quickly and easily blend spices.

- **Vegetable peeler:** Instead of painstakingly using a knife to peel potatoes, just use a vegetable peeler instead. A few quick motions will remove any peel without having to press very hard.

- **Food dehydrator:** Dehydrated fruits and veggies make great healthy snacks, but they can take a long time to make in the oven since they require low temperatures and take up precious oven space you need for roasting veggies. A food dehydrator accomplishes this easily, and you can stack several different fruits, veggies, or both in as many or as few trays as you want.

- **Vacuum sealer:** This gadget is helps creat an airtight seal around any food, even ones that are too large or oddly shaped to fit in a regular sealable bag. Vacuum seals guarantee freshness and will help packages of prepared foods fit more easily in the freezer.

- **Hot water kettle:** Rather than having to wait around for water to boil on the stove, a water kettle makes the process go so much faster. This is great for making foods like hardboiled eggs or for pouring into a larger pot to cook noodles fast.

- **Plastic tubs:** These go in your fridge and pantry for easy storage and sorting. You can have one for snacks, one for seasonings, another for pasta... Your imagination is the limit!

- **Fatigue reduction kitchen mat:** Prepping meals can mean standing in one spot for a while. A fatigue reduction mat makes this easier on your body. Your feet, knees, and back will thank you for this addition to your kitchen.

Tips and tricks for creating a sustainable, healthy vegetarian lifestyle

Planning your menu

Menu planning is probably the single most important part of prepping healthy, great-tasting meals. Without a menu, it's hard to know what ingredients to buy and you are more likely to be tempted by options that are not very good for you.

Planning a menu ahead of time helps you make sure you are getting enough of all the macronutrients you need and will save you money once you're at the store. Ensuring you are getting your macronutrients in the right proportions is especially important for vegetarians since it can sometimes be challenging to make sure you are eating enough protein and not eating too many carbohydrates.

How to start planning your menu:

- Begin with plans for dinner options. This is where the majority of people like to have the most variety in their meals, so it can be the most difficult one to plan for. Dinners also usually require the most ingredients, so having a plan for this can give you an idea of things you can buy in bulk and use for breakfast or lunch to save money.

- Take care of lunch ideas after planning for dinners. If you enjoy cooking food in bulk to reduce the amount of cooking you have to do, many of your dinner options can double for lunch, but in smaller portion sizes. You could also use specific elements of your dinner ingredients, such as the veggies, to make some spectacular salads that won't get boring.

- Think about breakfast next. Breakfast is the most important meal of the day, so you should never skip it! Treat it as the vital start to the day that it is. Breakfasts can be sweet or savory, so you have no end of tasty options.

- Finally, plan for snacks and desserts. This is a step that many people forget to do, but it can make or break a healthy diet. Everyone gets cravings or can become hungry outside of mealtime, so having prepared, healthy snacks is the secret to success for sustaining good eating habits.

When planning out your menu, make sure to include exactly the number of meals you will need. If you plan to have a night of eating out, you need to make sure to consider that when preparing your menu so that you don't buy too much food when you go shopping. Snacks can be the hardest to plan for the right amount with, so this may take some experimentation before you know what works best for you. Until then, it's a good idea to keep packets of slices fruits or veggies handy since they are good to eat anytime.

There is more than one way to plan your menu, so this is where you can add some of your styles into meal prep.

- Dinner options
  — Plan a different meal every night. If possible, ensure this something you can make extra to use for lunches as well.
  — Choose one meal to make in a large batch, like a curry, and eat this for 3-4 nights in a week. Alternate this with nights of different meals to keep variety in your diet.
  — Pick two recipes that can make large batches and alternate them. This option is the most budget-friendly, but you will want to make sure you choose recipes you enjoy so you don't get bored with them by the end of the week.

- Lunch options
  — Lunches should be quick, easy, and simple, so the best option here is to choose one recipe for the entire week. You can change things up by having something a little different on the weekends as a treat.
  — If you make different meals every night for dinner, you can plan to cook a little bit more than absolutely needed and use the "leftovers" for lunch. This will ensure that your midday meal stays interesting.
  — Like with dinners, choose two options and alternate them during the week, even on the weekends.

- Breakfast options
  - Pick a theme for the week and make variations on that theme for every day. For example, have toast or oatmeal every day, but change the toppings you add to it for different flavor profiles.
  - Choose one sweet and one savory recipe for the week and alternate throughout the week. This gives you the best of both breakfast worlds.
  - Choose one recipe to eat during the week and another recipe for the weekends. This way you can plan something that's a bit of a treat for your relaxing weekend days.

- Snacks
  - Choose at least 3-4 snack recipes for a week. This is the area you are most likely to "cheat" on, so having a variety can help you stay on track.
  - The one exception to this rule is dessert. Plan to make one dessert or sweet snack that you will eat all week long, but make sure to portion properly!
  - Ensure that you have snacks on hand with different flavor profiles to combat any sort of craving you may have. These include savory, salty, sweet, and spicy. Spicy snacks will also help give your metabolism a boost, keeping your body in top calorie-burning shape.

Grocery shopping

Once you start prepping meals in advance, grocery shopping is no longer the headache it was before! It will take less time to complete and you won't come home with ingredients or foods you don't end up using that just clutter up your cabinets. As you are writing down your recipes for the week, start a grocery list based on the ingredients. By writing your grocery list as you plan your menu, you will eliminate the need to go back through your recipes again and save yourself time in the process.

Decide on which grocery store you will shop at before you leave the house to go shopping. Then order your list based on how the store is arranged. This will reduce the amount of walking you do in the store and is another way to save yourself time, which is what meal prep is all about. This way you can also check sales brochures and look for coupons to save yourself even more money than you already are.

One trick to ensuring you have plenty of healthy ingredients for your meals is to focus on the ones around the edge of the store and ignore the shelves in the middle. The foods on the outside of the store tend to be the freshest and healthiest, while the foods in the center aisles are usually packed full of chemicals, preservatives, and other additives that are not very healthy or good for you.

Try to focus on fruits and vegetables that are ripe at the time you are shopping. These will be the freshest, taste the best, and will usually be the least expensive options for your meals. By planning your ingredients by season, you will also be able to rotate through different recipes regularly(but not so often that it gets overwhelming!) to keep variety in your meals and continue making prepared meals interesting.

Shopping at a store that has a bulk foods section will save you a TON of money. This way you can get as much or as little of specific ingredients as you want to minimize waste or maximize your savings. This is a great way to stock up on essentials like rice, flour, oats, and granola. You can also find a wide variety of nuts in bulk food sections, which are a wonderful source of protein for vegetarians and make fantastic snacks. You can eat them plain or toss them with your favorite seasonings to have a variety of flavors on hand during the week.

Don't go grocery shopping on the same day that you plan on prepping your meals if you can help it. Both tasks can take up at least an hour or two of your day, so trying to both on the same day can become tiring. Spreading them out will make you more likely to stick with the habit of preparing meals instead of becoming frustrated with how much time it takes to do.

Similarly, don't go grocery shopping when you're hungry. If you are already thinking about food, you are more likely to buy impulsively and add items that are not on your list. This will cost you extra money and your food choices when you are hungry are likely not going to be focused on what is healthy and good for you, be whatever you are craving at the time. By eating even a small snack before going shopping, you can prevent this from happening and stick with your list.

The time of day you go shopping also make a big difference in how long it takes to accomplish. Most grocery stores are busiest in the middle of the day or after work. The best time to go shopping is early in the morning right after breakfast. The store will be less crowded so you can be in and out in a flash and save yourself time. You will have also just eaten, so you will be less likely to impulsively buy foods that are not on your list from being hungry. Later in the evening can also be a good time to shop if you are willing to go out then. Most people will be home by that point, so you will have most of the store to yourself.

Time-saving suggestions

Here are some tips and tricks that will make preparing meals a sustainable habit that you keep up with the long term:

- Use a single ingredient in multiple meals. This way you are having to chop and cook fewer things, cutting down the time you spend prepping your meals.

- Play music or your favorite movie or television show while working on your meals. Having something to entertain you will make the time seem like it flies by instead of dragging from boredom.

- Prepare larger amounts of a certain ingredient that you need in a week and freeze the rest. This works especially well for anything with a marinade because the extra time will give the flavor time to soak into the food as it is defrosting. This is also something you can do to regularly cut down the amount of time you spend preparing ingredients in a week. Your future self will thank you!

- If you have food that will take a long time to cook, start with that one first! This usually includes rice or potatoes. While that ingredient is cooking, you can work on preparing others that will not take as long. This way you will finish faster.

- Put labels on your meal containers. This is a good idea so that not only do you know what is in each container and what meal it is for, but you can also know when you cooked it. This will ensure that food does not stay in your refrigerator longer than it should.

- Have fun with your menu. By creating interesting ideas that play with words or planning a theme for your meals for the week, you can ensure you stay interested in what you're eating. This is also a good way to encourage yourself to try foods from different regions of the world or ones that you might not have thought of trying before.

- Have a consistent day where you prepare your meals. Choosing one day of the week that you will always prep meals on makes you more likely to stick with the plan and makes it easier to schedule the time to do it into your busy week.

- Know yourself. If you already know you don't like an ingredient or a type of food, then don't choose a recipe that includes it. Doing this makes you less likely to eat the meals you prepare and more likely to make unhealthy choices as a replacement. This defeats the purpose of prepping meals in the first place! Likewise, if you know you like an ingredient, then use it as much as possible in your menu.

It's the most important meal of the day, so make it great.

Oatmeal while you sleep

What you will need

- Yogurt (.5 C)
- Milk (.25 C) – you can use almond milk to increase the amount of protein you are getting
- Cinnamon (a sprinkle)
- Nutmeg (a sprinkle)
- Vanilla flavoring (as much as you like)
- Traditional oatmeal (.5 C)

What to do

- Stir yogurt, cinnamon, nutmeg, and vanilla together
- Add in oatmeal to the mixture
- Pour in milk slowly until a good consistency is reached. You may decide to use a little more or less than recommended, depending on how thick you like your oatmeal
- Store in your refrigerator overnight. The oatmeal will soften in the yogurt mixture for a filling breakfast you don't have to spend a lot of time making

Make it yours

The toppings are where this recipe shines. The best combinations include fruit and nuts for a good balance of protein, healthy carbohydrates, and essential nutrients. Whenever possible, choose seasonal fruits for a fresh, delightful breakfast. Use natural products, such as honey or maple syrup, to sweeten instead of sugar if you desire.

Flavor suggestions:

- Walnuts and pears
- Peanuts and bananas
- Hazelnuts and strawberries
- Macadamia nuts and pineapple
- Almonds and mandarin oranges
- Pecans and cherries

Make your freezer burritos

What you will need

- Cooked rice
- Eggs, scrambled (can be replaced with soft tofu)
- Tortillas (flour)
- Peppers and onions (one of each), sliced and sautéed
- Protein source (will depend on the theme)
- Fillings (will depend on the theme)

What to do

- Cook rice and let cool completely
- Cut up peppers and onions. Sautee in olive oil, then set aside to cool
- Cut and cook fillings and protein source (see below for details), then let cool
- Put your burritos together
    — Start by laying out a tortilla onto a cutting board
    — Then spread approximately .25 C of cooked rice in a line along the middle, leave space at both ends of the tortilla for folding
    — After this, spread approximately .25 C of scrambled eggs or tofu on top of the rice
    — Add a layer of sautéed peppers and onions on top of the scrambled eggs or tofu
    — Finally, spread protein and fillings on top of peppers and onions
    — Fold the top and bottom of the tortilla (the areas you left space while assembling the burrito) onto the fillings. Then fold one side onto the fillings and tuck around them. Finally, roll the burrito along the last side of the tortilla to complete

Make it yours

These burritos can be refrigerated to eat over a week, or they can be made in large batches and frozen to keep on hand for up to 3 months. They are easy to make in large batches, so freezing them is a perfect solution for long-term breakfast planning and will save you time in your meal prep. It is also very easy to use different flavors or themes in your burritos to keep breakfast interesting. Choose spices and seasonings that are appropriate to the theme you are working with. **Some suggestions:**

- Mexican: black beans, corn, salsa
- Greek: chickpeas (also known as garbanzo beans), spinach, feta cheese
- Ethiopian: lentils, stewed tomatoes (make sure to drain well before using), cauliflower

French toast from the oven

What you will need

- Eggs (8 large)
- Milk (1 C)- you can use almond milk for an extra protein boost
- Cinnamon (1 tsp)
- Nutmeg (a sprinkle)
- Vanilla flavoring (1 tsp)
- Bread (about 12 slices or 1 loaf)
- Maple syrup (2 Tbsp)
- Fruit and nut fillings of your choice (about 2 C combined)

What to do

- Start by making sure your oven is set to heat to 375 degrees Fahrenheit.

- Then coat a glass cooking dish with oil to prevent your French toast from sticking. This is easiest if you use cooking spray.

- Prepare your eggs by putting them in a bowl and using a whisk to mix until thoroughly combined. Then combine in the cinnamon, nutmeg, vanilla, and milk while continuing to use the whisk. Set aside for later use.

- Tear your bread into bite-sized cubes. Try to get about 9 pieces per slice. Your French toast will be healthiest if you use whole grain bread instead of white bread.

- Take about half of your bread chunks and use them to create the first layer of your French toast in your glass cooking dish.

- Then take your fruit and nut mixture and spread about half of this on top of the first layer of bread.

- Finish creating your layers by adding the rest of the bread chunks followed by the rest of the fruit and nut mixture.

- Take the bowl containing the egg and milk mixture and spread this across the entire baking dish. Coat as much of the bread, fruit, and nuts as possible and try to avoid an uneven coating. If you want, sprinkle a bit more cinnamon and nutmeg on top after coating.

- Place your baking dish in the heated oven and set a timer for 35 minutes before checking to see if your French toast is done. Do this by taking a toothpick and inserting it into the middle of the dish. If it comes out clean, then it is finished! If not, cook for another 5 to 10 minutes at a time until the toothpick is clean.

Make it yours

Like with the oatmeal overnight, you can come up with endless flavor combinations for your French toast by trying different fruit and nut mixtures. You are only limited by your imagination and palate. You can use the same recommended flavors as for the oatmeal or try some new ones. Suggestions:

- Macadamia nuts, pineapple, and coconut
- Walnuts, raisins, and apples
- Pecans, persimmons, and plums
- Almonds, blueberries, and bananas

Muffin tin eggs

What you will need

- Cheese, shredded (cheddar is best)
- Tomato (1 large)
- Pepper (1 large)
- Onion (1 medium)
- Eggs (6 large)
- Spinach (1 bunch)
- Muffin liners

What to do

- Start by making sure your oven is set to heat to 400 degrees Fahrenheit.

- Take your spinach and remove all stems. Then roll leaves into a bundle (this makes them easier to cut) and slice into thin ribbons.

- After this, take your onion, pepper, and tomato and chop into small pieces. Combine these into a medium-sized mixing bowl with the spinach.

- Prepare your eggs by putting them in a bowl and using a whisk to mix until thoroughly combined. Add a sprinkle of salt to them to enhance their flavor.

- Combine the eggs with the chopped veggies and stir until everything is well blended and coated.

- Insert the muffin liners into a regular-sized muffin tin (usually makes 12 muffins). If you do not have muffin liners, then spray the tin with cooking oil so that your eggs don't stick to the sides during cooking.

- Spoon the vegetable and egg mixture into the muffin liners. Make sure you don't overfill or underfill any of the cups.

- Take the shredded cheese and add a little to the top of each cup.

- Put the muffin tin in the oven and set the timer for 15 minutes before checking to see if they are done. To do this, take your fingers and test the top of each egg cup. If they are firm, then they are done. If they are not done, put them back in the oven for 2 minutes at a time until they are firm

Make it yours

You don't have to stick to only one vegetable combination with these eggs. You can choose different themes and add appropriate vegetables to create new flavor combinations. However, when you are doing this make sure you are aware of how long the vegetables you are using take to cook. If they take a while (like potatoes), then you may need to precook them before adding to the muffin tins so that they do not come out hard by the time the eggs are finished.

Suggestions:

- Shredded carrots, green onions, zucchini
- Sweet potatoes, corn, and peas
- Butternut squash, green beans, and onions
- Green, red, yellow, and orange bell peppers
- Asparagus, chives, leeks, and potatoes

Make-ahead whole wheat pancakes

What you will need

- Milk (.6 C)- use almond milk for added protein
- Egg (1 large)
- Whole wheat flour (.3 C)
- White flour (.3 C)
- Cinnamon (a sprinkle)
- Toppings of your choice

What to do

- Separate egg yolks from whites. Set the yolks aside.

- Use a whisk to beat the egg whites until they are aerated. When this happens, they will be firm and produce peaks. Set aside.

- Combine cinnamon, whole wheat, and white flours using a sifter or fine-mesh strainer to avoid any lumps you may find.

- Add the egg yolks into the combined flours, stirring constantly. Slowly add the milk and stir well to prevent lumps from forming.

- Carefully add the egg whites into the flour mixture. You do not want to remove the air from them, so folding in with a spatula is the best way to do this.

- Set a stove burner to medium and place a small pan with a nonstick coating over the burner. Let it heat up until it is hot.

- Pour about .25 C of batter into the pan and let cook on one side

- It is time to flip the pancake when you see bubbles come through the batter and create small holes. This means the first side is done the cooking.

- Flip the pancake to cook the other side. Be careful as you do this since you do not want to break the pancake or fold it over onto itself.

- Let the other side cook for several minutes. You can flip the pancake over again to see if it is done. When it is ready, it will be brown on both sides (but not too dark). After the first flip, it should be easy to flip again if either side needs to cook longer.

- Once they are cooled, you can freeze your pancakes for up to a month. To reheat, just pop in the toaster!

Make it yours

The toppings are where you can add some creativity to these pancakes. Top with yogurt, fresh berries, nuts, and a sprinkle of granola for a healthy, complete breakfast. Conversely, you can create a savory pancake by using yogurt, granola, nuts, and shredded veggies such as carrots or zucchini. It is important to make sure you add nuts so that you are getting enough protein with your breakfast, but otherwise, the toppings are up to you!

Scrambled chickpeas with potatoes and crispy kale chips

What you will need

- Olive oil
- Potatoes (3-4 large)
- Onion (1 medium)
- Pepper (1 large)
- Chickpeas (1 can)
- Avocado (1 sliced)
- Kale (1 bunch)

- Feta cheese
- Garlic (2 cloves, diced)
- Salt (as much as you like)
- Pepper (as much as you like)
- Paprika (as much as you like)

What to do

- Take the potatoes (you can peel them or leave the peel on depending on what you like) and cut them into small cubes.

- Set a stove burner to medium and place a large pan over the burner. Let it heat up until it is hot.

- Add the olive oil to the pan and then add the potato cubes.

- Cook the potatoes until they have softened but are still slightly firm. Make sure you stir often so they do not stick to the pan or burn on one side.

- While the potatoes are cooking, chop the onion, pepper, and garlic.

- Once the potatoes start to soften, add the onions, peppers, and garlic. Continue to stir frequently.

- As the veggies are cooking, open the can of chickpeas and let most of the liquid drain out from them.

- Add the chickpeas to a bowl with the salt, pepper, and paprika. Use a fork to mash them all together. Don't mash too much, because this dish tastes better with chunks of chickpeas left with the mashed.

- Mix the chickpeas in with the potatoes and other veggies. Cook until the potatoes are soft enough that a fork goes all the way through them and remove from heat.

- Take the kale and tear from the stalks. Toss in a bowl with some olive oil and salt, pepper, and paprika.

- Place the kale on a baking sheet and put in an oven that has been heated to 425 degrees Fahrenheit.

- Set a timer for 8 minutes and take the kale out of the oven when it goes off. Stir it up on the baking sheet and place it back in the oven for another 5 minutes.

- When the kale is cooked, top a portion of the mashed chickpeas and potatoes with the kale chips. Add the feta cheese to the bowl as well.

- Cut the avocado into slices and add them to the bowl. It is best to do this right before you plan to eat it so that the avocado does not brown

Make it yours

Seasonings are where this recipe shines and stands out. You can change the flavor profile dramatically by changing which seasonings you use. This is a great place to experiment with regional flavors and spices. If you are portioning this out to eat over several days, do not add the kale until the morning you plan to have this for breakfast, otherwise, it will not stay crispy. Store the kale in an airtight container to retain its crunchiness.

Deconstructed smoothie in a bowl

What you will need

- Yogurt (2 Tbsp)
- Banana (1 medium)
- Fruit (1 C, frozen)
- Nut-based butter (2 Tbsp)
- Milk (2 Tbsp)- use almond milk for extra protein
- Granola
- Fresh fruit
- Chia seeds

What to do

- Using a blender, puree the frozen fruit and peeled banana until thick.

- Add the yogurt and nut-based butter and blend again. The mixture should be thick.

- Then add the milk to the blender and blend until it is a consistency you like. You may use a little more or a little less, depending on how thick you like your smoothie.

- Pour the smoothie into a bowl. Top your bowl with sliced fresh fruit, granola, and chia seeds

Make it yours

There is no end to the number of flavor combinations you can come up with for your smoothie bowls. You are only limited by what you can imagine. The key is to make sure that you use fresh and frozen fruits that go well together. Your smoothies can be stored in the fridge for up to a week or can be frozen after blended for up to a month.

When storing, do not add the toppings until right before you plan on eating it for breakfast. This is especially true of the granola. If you refrigerate your smoothie bowls with the granola, it will become soggy and mushy.

Suggestions:

- Frozen mixed berries with slices of fresh strawberries and coconut.

- Frozen peach slices with fresh whole blueberries and banana slices.

- Frozen strawberries with fresh sliced mango and raspberries.

- Frozen tropical fruit with chunks of fresh pineapple and passion fruit.

- Frozen bananas with peanut butter, banana slices, and strawberries.

You won't even think about stopping at the drive-through with these fabulous lunch options.

Tuna replacement salad

What you will need

- Bread (sliced whole grain)
- Tomato (1 medium)
- Lettuce (several leaves)
- Celery (1 stalk)
- Mayonnaise (2 Tbsp)
- Chickpeas (1 can)
- Onion (1 medium red)
- Brown mustard (1 Tbsp)
- Pickle (1 large dill)
- Salt (as much as you like)
- Pepper (as much as you like)
- Garlic (1 clove, chopped)

What to do

- Take the celery, onion, and pickle and chop into fine pieces.

- Drain the water from the can of chickpeas, leaving a little bit in the can. Put the chickpeas into a bowl. Using a fork, mash them into a paste. This recipe tastes better and more closely.

- resembles tuna if you leave a few chunks of chickpea in the paste.

- Add the mayonnaise, brown mustard, salt, pepper, garlic, and any other seasonings you want to the smashed chickpeas. Mix until everything is combined completely.

- Combine the chickpea mixture with the chopped veggies and stir until everything is well blended.

- Refrigerate the tuna replacement salad for at least 1 hour until it is chilled.

- When you are ready to make lunch, slice up the tomato.

- Take a slice of the whole grain bread and layer it with the lettuce and tomato. If you want, you may want to add some extra sliced red onion and sliced pickles.

- Top the lettuce and veggies with approximately .25 C of the chilled, not tuna salad mixture and finish with the other slice of bread.

- This recipe can also make a great snack if eaten with vegetable slices or crackers.

- If you have the opportunity, you can make this lunch even better by taking time to toast the whole grain bread before you assemble your sandwich

Easy lunch burrito in a bowl

What you will need

- Olive oil
- Black beans (1 can)
- Corn (1 can)
- Salsa (3 Tbsp)
- Vegetable stock
- Quinoa
- Shredded cheese
- Avocado
- Cilantro (1 bunch)

What to do

- Start by cooking the quinoa. This is very similar to cooking rice. Measure out as much quinoa as you want into a large pot (2 C will make enough for a weeks' worth of lunches). Then add twice as much vegetable stock as quinoa to the pot. Cook the quinoa over medium heat until all the liquid has been absorbed and the quinoa is not hard.

- Take the can of black beans and drain the liquid from them. Then rinse them with water until the water is clear. Also, drain the corn at the same time.

- Set a burner on the stove to medium. Place a medium pan on the burner and heat until hot.

- Add the olive oil to the pan. Then add the black beans and corn. Season them with salt, pepper, garlic, and anything else you like. Cook until hot.

- Once the quinoa is cooked, add the black beans and corn. Stir them together until they are well mixed.

- When portioning out, top each lunch with a bit of shredded cheese, some cilantro, and the salsa.

- On the day you plan to eat this lunch, cut the avocado into slices and add them to the burrito in a bowl. Do not do this too early to prevent the avocado from turning brown.

Vegetarian lunch fajitas

What you will need

- Rice
- Vegetable stock
- Pepper (2 large)
- Onion (1 medium)
- Sweet potato (2 large)
- Garlic (2 cloves, chopped)
- Salt (as much as you like)
- Pepper (as much as you like)
- Cumin (a sprinkle)
- Chipotle pepper (.5 tsp)
- Paprika (1 tsp)
- Olive oil

What to do

- Start by making sure your oven is set to heat to 375 degrees Fahrenheit.

- Cook the rice. Measure out as much rice as you want into a large pot (2 C will make enough for a weeks' worth of lunches). Then add twice as much vegetable stock as rice to the pot. Cook the rice over medium heat until all the liquid has been absorbed and the rice is not hard.

- Peel the sweet potatoes and cut them into strips that resemble thin French fries.

- Place the sweet potato strips into a bowl with some olive oil. Add about half of the seasonings and coat the sweet potatoes with oil and spices.

- Pour the sweet potatoes onto a baking sheet and place your baking sheet in the heated oven. Set a timer for 10 minutes.

- While the sweet potatoes are baking, cut the peppers and onion into slices. It is best if you have two peppers of different colors.

- Places the peppers and onion into a bowl with some more olive oil. Add the other half of the seasonings and coat the peppers and onion with oil and spices.

- Pour the peppers and onions onto another baking sheet. When the timer has gone off for the first time, add this baking sheet to the oven with the sweet potatoes.

- Set the timer for 15 minutes. When it has gone off, take both baking sheets out of the oven and stir the vegetables. Place them back into the oven for another 15 minutes.

- For lunch, start with a bit of rice in a bowl and add the roasted veggies on top of it.

Turkish cannellini salad

What you will need

- Lemon (1, juiced)
- Olive oil (2 Tbsp)
- Salt (.5 tsp)
- White wine vinegar (1 tsp)
- Eggs (4, hard-boiled)
- Green onions (1 bunch)
- Cannellini beans (2 cans)
- Pepper (2 large)
- Dill (1 bunch)
- Cucumber (1 medium)
- Parsley (1 bunch)
- Tomato (1 large)

What to do

- Start by creating a dressing to go on the salad. Stir the vinegar, salt, olive oil, and lemon juice together. The best way to do this is with a whisk so that it will be thoroughly combined. Put this in the refrigerator to get cold.

- Take the peppers and chop them up into small pieces. They do the same thing for the tomato. Add both of these to a mixing bowl.

- Cut up the green onions, parsley, and dill until they are chopped finely. Add them to the bowl with the peppers and tomato.

- Open the cans of beans and let the liquid drain out from the cans. Wash the beans in water.

- Add the beans to the mixing bowl with the herbs and vegetables. Mix them until they are combined well.

- Take the dressing out of the refrigerator and use it to coat the bean and vegetable mixture. Make sure the dressing is evenly spread across everything.

- Slice the hard-boiled eggs into thin sections. Add a couple to each portion of the bean salad.

- This salad tastes good by itself, or you can eat it with crackers. It is also great spread across whole-grain toast slices.

Pocket salad sandwiches

What you will need

- Spinach (1 bunch)
- Tomato (1 large)
- Onion (1 medium red)
- Chickpeas (1 can)
- Cucumber (1 medium)
- Feta cheese
- Tahini dressing
- Lemon (1, juiced)
- Pita pockets

What to do

- Open the chickpeas and pour the water out of the can. Place these into a mixing bowl.

- Take the tomato, onion, and cucumber and chop into small chunks. Add these to the mixing bowl with the chickpeas.

- Coat the vegetables and chickpeas with the lemon juice. Mix them all in the mixing bowl to ensure they are all coated and well combined.

- Cut a pita and open each half up to reveal the pocket.

- Take the stems off the spinach. Line the pita on both sides with spinach.

- Fill the rest of the pita with the vegetable and chickpea mixture.

- Add some feta cheese to each pocket and drizzle with tahini.

Cucumber hummus rolls

What you will need

- Hummus
- Avocado (1 large)
- Cucumber (2 large)
- Tomatoes (1 jar, sun-dried)
- Garlic (1 clove, chopped)
- Basil (4 Tbsp)
- Salt (as much as you want)
- Pepper (as much as you want)
- Toothpicks

What to do

- Start by cutting the avocado in half and removing the pit. Spoon the contents out into a bowl and mash with a fork until creamy. Add the garlic and some salt and pepper. Cover and set aside in the refrigerator.

- Spoon the hummus out into another bowl. Add the basil and stir until well combined.

- Open the jar of tomatoes and let most of the juice pour out. Keep a little bit in the jar.

- Add the tomatoes and juice to the hummus. Stir again until combined well.

- Cut the ends off the cucumbers and slice long way into thin ribbons. This is easiest if you use a vegetable peeler or mandolin set to a thin slice.

- Lay the cucumber slices out. Spread a bit of the hummus mix onto each one. Then spread a bit of the mashed avocado on top of the hummus.

- Be gentle and roll the cucumbers up into spirals. Be very careful not to roll too tight and squeeze the fillings out as you are making your spirals. Skewer each spiral with a toothpick through both sides to keep them from unrolling before you have a chance to eat them.

Pasta-based garden salad

What you will need

- White wine vinegar (.5 C)
- Italian seasoning (2 Tbsp)
- Olive oil (.5 C)
- Garlic (1 clove, chopped)
- Salt (as much as you like)
- Pepper (as much as you like)
- Small tomatoes (1 package, cut in quarters)
- Corn (1 can)
- Pepper (1 large)
- White beans (1 can)
- Parsley (1 bunch)
- Tortellini (1 package)

What to do

- Heat a burner to high. Fill a large pot with water and set onto the stove. Add a sprinkle of salt and olive oil to the water and boil.

- As you are waiting for the water to heat up to boiling, mix the vinegar, salt, pepper, Italian seasoning, olive oil, and garlic. The best way to do this is to put everything into a jar and shake it until it is all completely combined. Set this in the refrigerator.

- Cut the pepper up into small pieces. Put this in a mixing bowl with the tomato quarters. Open the can of corn and pour the water out. Add this to the bowl as well.

- Open the can of white beans. Pour out all the juice from the can. Wash the beans in a strainer before combining them in the bowl with the vegetables.

- Take the stems off the parsley and roll into a bundle for easy cutting. Slice this into small ribbons. Add to the vegetables and mix until combined well.

- Once the water boils, cook the tortellini. This should take between 5 to 8 minutes if it is fresh. If it is dried, this will take about 15 to 20 minutes.

- Once the tortellini are finished, place into a large strainer. Use cold running water to reduce the heat until cold.

- Place the tortellini into the bowl with the vegetables, beans, and parsley. Stir them all together until you have an even mixture.

- Take the dressing out of the refrigerator and use to coat the tortellini, beans, and vegetables. Mix thoroughly so that everything has an even layer of dressing on it.

- Refrigerate the salad until cold before eating for lunch.

Vegetable tortilla spirals

What you will need

- Mushrooms (1 package)
- Alfalfa sprouts (1 package)
- Carrots (2 large)
- Zucchini (2 large)
- Cucumber (1 medium)
- Onion (1 medium red)
- Pepper (1 large)
- Broccoli (1 head)
- Hummus
- Whole wheat tortillas
- Toothpicks

What to do

- Begin by cutting the onion into thin slices. Cut these in half so you have very thin onion strips.

- After this, slice the pepper into very thin strips as well. This recipe is best if you use a colored pepper. Then cut the cucumber into very thin round slices. This is easiest to do if you have a mandolin to use.

- Use a cheese grater to shred the carrots and zucchini. Make sure to remove all the water from both vegetables by squeezing over the sink. Then separate the squeezed clumps into piles of shredded vegetables.

- Cut the mushrooms up into small pieces. Do the same thing with the broccoli, focusing on the top parts. If you use the stem of the broccoli, make sure this is chopped very finely so that it does not tear up the tortillas or become too chunky to eat easily.

- Layout the tortillas. Take some of the hummus and use a knife to coat the tortilla evenly across the whole face.

- Sprinkle the alfalfa sprouts on top of the hummus. Ensure a good covering of the tortilla face.

- After this, sprinkle the onions, peppers, mushrooms, and broccoli on top of the alfalfa sprouts. Then layer this with the shredded carrots and zucchini.

- Finally, arrange the cucumber rounds across the tortilla face on top of the rest of the vegetables. Try to only overlap slightly and take care with how you arrange the rounds.

- Once this is finished, roll the tortilla into a spiral. Place 8 toothpicks evenly across the tortilla spiral so that they go all the way through. Cut the tortilla into spiral slices in between the toothpicks.

Jar salad constructions

What you will need

- Chopped vegetables (as many as you like- see suggestions)
- Nuts
- Grains
- Salad dressing
- Green leafy vegetables
- Protein source (beans, lentils, tofu)

What to do

- Start with a clean glass jar. Pour approximately 2 Tbsp of salad dressing into the bottom of the jar.

- Chop up your vegetables into small pieces. Separate these into crunchy vegetables and soft vegetables. Add the crunchy vegetables on top of the salad dressing in the jar.

- After this, add a layer of whatever protein source you are using on top of your crunchy vegetables.

- Place your grains on top of your protein source into another layer. It is okay if the layers end up mixing a bit. You will be eating it all anyhow!

- Then add your softer vegetables in a layer on top of your grains. Be careful not to pack these too tightly so that they get smashed up. You will want to combine any cheese you use with your softer vegetables.

- Your leafy green vegetables will go on top of your soft vegetables. Again, be very careful not to pack your jar too tightly. It will likely be getting full by this point!

- Finally top the jar off with your nuts, seeds, and other toppings before sealing and placing in the refrigerator until you are ready to eat it for lunch.

- Before you eat your jar salad, make sure the lid is tight on the jar. Then shake your salad enthusiastically to mix the dressing onto the contents and to hopefully mix the contents. This part will be a lot harder if you packed your jar tightly with food.

Suggestions:

- Mexican: chipotle ranch dressing, corn, peppers, black beans, quinoa, avocado, tomatoes, cheddar cheese, lettuce, tortilla strips.

- Sushi roll: wasabi soy dressing, shredded carrots, cucumber, edamame, rice, avocado, rocket, sesame seeds, almond slivers.

- Greek: Greek dressing, cucumber, red onion, chickpeas, orzo, tomato, olives, feta cheese, spinach, sunflower seeds.

- Middle Eastern: lemon Zaatar vinaigrette, onion, cucumber, radish, lentils, tomato, Romaine lettuce, chopped mint, pita strips.

Why order takeout when you can wow yourself with quick and easy home-cooked meals?

Chinese style chickpeas

What you will need

- Rice, cooked
- Cornstarch (1 tsp)
- Brown mustard (1 tsp)
- Sesame oil (1 tsp)
- Chili sauce (2 tsp)
- Coconut sugar (4 tsp)
- Rice vinegar (1 Tbsp)
- Soy sauce (1 Tbsp)
- Creamy peanut butter (.5 Tbsp)
- Tomato paste (1.5 Tbsp)
- Vegetable stock (6 Tbsp)
- Chickpeas (1 can)
- Pepper (1 large)
- Broccoli (1 head)
- Onion (1 small)
- Olive oil (1 Tbsp)
- Garlic (2 cloves, chopped)
- Sesame seeds

What to do

- Start by cooking the rice. Measure out as much rice as you want into a large pot (2 C will make enough for a weeks' worth of dinners). Then add twice as much vegetable stock as rice to the pot. Cook the rice over medium heat until all the liquid has been absorbed and the rice is not hard.

- While the rice is cooking, you can start working on the sauce. Put the cornstarch, brown mustard, sesame oil, chili sauce, coconut sugar, rice vinegar, soy sauce, creamy peanut butter, tomato paste, and vegetable stock together in a bowl. Combine them until completely blended. The easiest way to do this is with a whisk. Place to the side once combined.

- Cut up the onion, pepper, and broccoli into small pieces.

- Set a burner on the stove to medium. Place a large pan on the burner and heat until hot.

- Add the olive oil to the pan. Then combine with the garlic and onion pieces. Cook the onion until it becomes a little see-through. Make sure to mix often as the onion is cooking.

- Once the onion has cooked a little, combine the pepper and broccoli with it in the pan. Let them cook until the broccoli and peppers begin to be soft.

- Pour the sauce into the pan with the vegetables. Mix them until well combined and stir regularly while cooking.

- Open the can of chickpeas and pour out the liquid. Wash the chickpeas in a strainer after pouring out the liquid.

- Add the chickpeas to the pan and mix. Let the vegetables, chickpeas, and sauce cook until everything is hot.

- When serving or getting ready to store, place the rice in bowls or containers and put the vegetable and chickpea mixture on top. Sprinkle with some sesame seeds on top.

Squash-a-Roni and cheese

What you will need

- Cheddar cheese (1.5 C)
- Milk (.75 C)
- Vegetable stock (.5 C)
- Paprika (1 tsp)
- Butter (2 Tbsp)
- Butternut squash (3.5 C)
- Macaroni (1 box)
- Salt (as much as you want)
- Pepper (as much as you want)

What to do

- Make sure your oven is set to heat to 425 degrees Fahrenheit.

- Start by working on the butternut squash. Start by taking the peel off and removing both ends. Then cut it in half. Take the seeds out. The easiest way to do this is with a spoon. Chop the butternut squash into medium-sized cubes.

- After this, put the butternut squash into a mixing bowl. Add a little bit of olive oil and any seasonings you may want. Mix the squash and oil until it is even across the contents of the bowl.

- Pour the butternut squash onto a baking sheet. Put the baking sheet in the oven and set a timer for 30 minutes before checking to see if the squash is done. You can tell it is cooked when a fork goes all the way through it. If it is not ready, set the timer for another 5 minutes before checking again. Do this until it is cooked.

- Use a cheese grater to turn the cheese into ribbons.

- Heat a burner to high. Fill a large pot with water and set onto the stove. Add a sprinkle of salt and olive oil to the water and boil.

- While you are waiting for the water to heat, add the butternut squash, vegetable stock, milk, paprika, salt, and pepper into a food processor or blender. Puree until there are no lumps and everything is smooth.

- After the water has started to boil, you can cook the macaroni. This will take about 15 to 20 minutes. After it is done, place it in a strainer to remove the water.

- Set another burner on the stove to medium. Place a large pan on the burner and heat until hot.

- Put the butter in the pan and melt it. Then combine the macaroni in the pan with the butter and mix.

- Pour the butternut squash mixture into the pan with the pasta. Also, combine the cheese with the rest of the ingredients. Mix until everything is well combined and there is an even coat on all of the pasta. Keep the pan on the burner until the cheese is melted and everything is ready to serve.

Curried mixed vegetables

What you will need

- Rice, cooked
- Curry paste (2 tsp, whichever color you prefer)
- Maple syrup (1 Tbsp)
- Coconut milk (1 can)
- Vegetable stock (1 C)
- Onion (1 large)
- Frozen mixed vegetables (1 bag)
- Frozen peas (.5 C)
- Small corn (1 can)
- Ginger (2 tsp)
- Vegetable oil (2 Tbsp)

What to do

- Start by cooking the rice. Measure out as much rice as you want into a large pot (2 C will make enough for a weeks' worth of dinners). Then add twice as much vegetable stock as rice to the pot. Cook the rice over medium heat until all the liquid has been absorbed and the rice is not hard.

- Cut up the onion into small strips and place to the side.

- Set a burner on the stove to medium. Place a large pan on the burner and heat until hot.

- Put the vegetable oil in the pan with the ginger and onion. Cook the onion until it becomes a little see-through. Make sure to mix often as the onion is cooking.

- After this, you can combine the frozen vegetables with the onion in the pan. Cook for about 5 to 7 minutes.

- While the vegetables are heating you can open the can of small corn and pour the liquid out. Cut the corn into small chunks.

- Add the corn and peas to the vegetables and onion. Heat for another 5 minutes.

- Lower the heat on the stove burner before pouring in the coconut milk and vegetable stock. Cook until the liquid begins to bubble lightly. This should take around 10 to 15 minutes.

- Once the liquid is bubbling, combine the maple syrup and curry paste. Continue to let the mixture bubble lightly until it becomes slightly thick. Once it is thick, the curry is ready to serve.

- When serving or getting ready to store, portion the rice out into containers or bowls and add the curried vegetables on top.

- If you enjoy the taste, you can sprinkle some cashews or peanuts onto the curry to give it a bit of a crunchy texture.

Deconstructed lasagna bake

What you will need

- Pasta sauce (1 jar, either red or white- whichever you like better)
- Mozzarella cheese (2 C, shredded)
- Egg (1 large)
- Parmesan cheese (.5 C, grated)
- Ricotta cheese (1 container, 15 oz)
- Frozen spinach (1 package, 10 oz)
- Lasagna noodles (1 package)
- Salt (as much as you want)
- Pepper (as much as you want)

What to do

- Heat a burner to high. Fill a large pot with water and set onto the stove. Add a sprinkle of salt and olive oil to the water and boil.

- Make sure your oven is set to heat to 350 degrees Fahrenheit.

- Until the water heats, warm the spinach from frozen. You can do this by placing it in a bowl and heating in the microwave for 1 minute at a time. Ensure all the water is removed from the spinach by squeezing it over the sink. Then separate the spinach clumps until you have a pile of warm spinach.

- Place the spinach into a mixing bowl. Mix in the egg, parmesan cheese, ricotta cheese, pepper, and salt. Combine until well mixed.

- After the water has started to boil, you can cook the lasagna. This will take about 15 to 20 minutes. After it is done, place it in a strainer to remove the water. Ensure the noodles are cooled by adding cold water from the tap into the strainer.

- Spread out the lasagna noodles. Place .3 C of the spinach combination on top of each noodle. Then roll the noodle into a spiral.

- Take a large glass baking dish and add 1 C of pasta sauce to the bottom. Be sure to coat it completely. Place the lasagna spirals into the baking dish with the end of the noodle at the bottom.

- Add more pasta sauce to the top of each spiral. Once they are covered, sprinkle the mozzarella cheese on top of the sauce.

- Cover the glass baking dish with a sheet of aluminum before putting it in the oven. Set a timer for 40 minutes before checking to make sure they are done. You will tell this because the cheese will be melted and slightly golden.

- When serving or getting ready to store, coat the bottom of each plate or container with a little bit more pasta sauce before adding the lasagna spiral.

Stewed Spanish-style chickpeas with spinach

What you will need

- Rice, cooked
- Spinach (2 bunches)
- Chickpeas (1 can)
- Tomato paste (1 Tbsp)
- Tomatoes, canned (2 cans, 28 oz)
- Brown sugar (2 tsp)
- Onion (1 medium red)
- Salt (as much as you want)
- Paprika (1.5 tsp)

- Powdered hot pepper (.25 tsp- you can add more if you like spicy food)
- Cumin (3 tsp)
- Garlic (3 cloves, chopped)
- Olive oil (2 Tbsp)
- Sliced almonds (.25 C)

What to do

- Start by cooking the rice. Measure out as much rice as you want into a large pot (2 C will make enough for a weeks' worth of dinners). Then add twice as much vegetable stock as rice to the pot. Cook the rice over medium heat until all the liquid has been absorbed and the rice is not hard.

- Cut up the onion into small strips and place to the side

- Set a burner on the stove to medium. Place a large pan on the burner and heat until hot.

- Put the olive oil in the pan with the garlic and onion. Cook the onion until it becomes a little see-through. Make sure to mix often as the onion is cooking.

- Mix the paprika, powdered hot pepper, cumin, and salt into the onion and garlic combination. You can leave the powdered hot pepper out of the recipe if you do not like spicy food. If you do this, then increase the amount of paprika and cumin by .5 tsp each to retain enough flavor. Continue to heat and stir regularly

- Combine the tomato paste into the pan and heat until it starts to thin slightly.

- Open the can of tomatoes and smash them with their liquid still combined. This is easiest if you pour them into a bowl and use a potato masher. Combine them into the rest of the ingredients with the sugar in the pan. Let the mixture cook until lightly bubbling. Make sure you mix it up from time to time so that nothing sticks to the pan.

- Once the tomato stock has turned slightly thick, open the can of chickpeas. Pour the liquid out and wash the chickpeas before mixing them into the pan. Heat until the chickpeas are hot.

- Finally, remove the stems from the spinach. Add the leaves of spinach to the pan and add a lid to it. Let the mixture heat until the spinach is no longer firm. This should take about 5 to 10 minutes.

- When you are ready to serve or store, place some rice in the bottom of the bowl or container you are using. Put some of the stewed chickpeas on top of this. Finally, sprinkle with the almond slices.

Spicy vegetable Cajun stew

What you will need

- Rice, cooked
- Parsley (1 bunch)
- Cilantro (1 bunch)
- Paprika (1 Tbsp)
- Thyme (2 tsp)
- Cajun seasoning (2 Tbsp)
- Powdered hot pepper (2 tsp)- you can leave this out if you do not like spicy food
- Tomatoes (1 can dice)
- Zucchini (1 medium)
- Kidney beans (1 can)
- Mushrooms (1 package)
- Celery (2 stalks)
- Pepper (2 large)
- Onion (1 medium red)
- Okra (12-15 pieces)
- Olive oil (.25 C)

- Flour (.25 C)
- Liquid smoke
- Worcestershire sauce (make sure to check the ingredients label to find a vegetarian version)
- Salt (as much as you want)
- Pepper (as much as you want)

What to do

- Start by cooking the rice. Measure out as much rice as you want into a large pot (2 C will make enough for a weeks' worth of dinners). Then add twice as much vegetable stock as rice to the pot. Cook the rice over medium heat until all the liquid has been absorbed and the rice is not hard.

- Then cut the mushrooms, peppers (this recipe tastes best if you use two different colors), zucchini, celery, okra, and onion into small pieces.

- Set a burner on the stove to medium. Place a large pan on the burner and heat until hot.

- Put the olive oil in the pan and heat until very hot and ready to bubble when other ingredients are added. Then add the flour in small amounts at a time and combine well. The best way to do this is with a whisk. Keep adding flour and mixing until you have combined all of it with the oil. Continue to mix and let the flour and oil for about 8 to 10 minutes until it turns brown to create a roux. Be very careful not to let this burn.

- Pour the vegetable pieces into the pan. Combine the vegetables and roux with the liquid smoke and Worcestershire sauce. Heat the vegetables for approximately 10 minutes until they are no longer hard.

- Sprinkle the vegetables with the paprika, powdered hot pepper, thyme, Cajun seasoning, salt, and pepper. Then remove the stems from the parsley and cilantro and roll them into a bundle. Cut them into thin slices and add to the vegetables as well.

- Open the can of kidney beans and pour out all the liquid. Wash the beans in a strainer until the water you are using becomes clear.

- Pour the kidney beans into the vegetable mixture. Open the can of tomatoes and pour out a little bit of the liquid but keep some of it. Add this to the pan also.

- Let the mixture of vegetables, beans, and tomatoes heat until the tomato stock becomes slightly thick. This should take approximately 20 minutes.

- When you are ready to serve or store, place some rice in the bottom of the bowl or container you are using. Then add some of the Cajun stew on top of this. You can sprinkle with a bit more of the fresh parsley and cilantro if you like the taste to accentuate the flavor.

Chapter Six - Snack Attack

Catch those cravings before they hit!

Oatmeal pizza with fruit

What you will need

- Fruit mixture (2 C)
- Oatmeal (3 C)
- Cinnamon (1 Tbsp)
- Eggs (2 large)
- Vanilla flavoring (1 tsp)
- Maple syrup (.5 C)
- Salt (.5 tsp)
- Apple sauce (.3 C)
- Greek yogurt (2 C)

What to do

- Make sure your oven is set to heat to 375 degrees Fahrenheit.

- Take a glass pie dish and coat it with spray oil to prevent sticking.

- Place salt, cinnamon, and oatmeal into a large mixing bowl. Stir to make sure it is all well mixed.

- Combine the vanilla flavoring, maple syrup, and apple sauce with the eggs. Mix until well combined. The easiest way to do this is with a whisk.

- Create a hole in the middle of the cinnamon, salt, and oatmeal combination to pour the egg, applesauce, vanilla, and maple syrup combination into. Mix them until well combined and there are no dry, flaky spots or lumpy areas.

- Pour the bowl contents into the glass pie dish. Use the back part of a spoon or your fingers to pat the mixture down until it is firm and holds together.

- Put the dish into the oven and set a timer for 10 minutes before checking to see if it is cooked. You will know this when the mixture is a little brown but not too dark. If it is not done, set the timer for another 2 minutes at a time before checking again.

- Once the pie dish comes out of the oven, place it onto a wire rack to let heat dissipate. Leave it there and set a timer for 10 minutes.

- Once the timer goes off, take the oatmeal mixture out of the glass pie dish and set it back onto the wire rack to let more heat dissipate. You need to leave it there until it is not hot at all anymore. You can make this happen faster by putting the entire rack into the refrigerator and set a timer for about 10 minutes.

- Once the base is not hot anymore, pour the yogurt onto it. Use the back of a spoon to push it evenly around the entire surface.

- After you have added the yogurt to the base, put it back into the refrigerator for an hour or longer so that it becomes cold and starts to keep its shape.

- Once the yogurt is cold, cut up any fruit that needs to be cut. If it does not need to be cut, like blueberries or raspberries, you can leave it complete. Make sure to use as many of your favorite fruits as possible to make this pizza taste great. Decoratively put the fruit on top of the yogurt. Try to make sure that each slice will have a little bit of all the different fruits you use.

- Use a knife to make separate slices of your pizza. If you want, you can add dollops of whipped cream on top of each piece for an extra treat.

Sweet and spiced pumpkin cupcakes

What you will need

- Coconut oil (3 Tbsp, melted)
- Eggs (2 large)
- Vanilla flavoring (1 tsp)
- Whole wheat flour (3 C)
- Maple syrup (.5 C)
- Milk (1 C)- use almond milk for an added protein boost
- Salt (.75 tsp)
- Baking soda (1.5 tsp)
- Pureed pumpkin (1 C)
- Cloves (a sprinkle)
- Nutmeg (.25 tsp)
- Cinnamon (1 Tbsp)
- Ginger (1 tsp)
- Allspice (a sprinkle)
- Muffin liners

What to do

- Make sure your oven is set to heat to 375 degrees Fahrenheit.

- Insert the muffin liners into a regular-sized muffin tin (usually makes 12 muffins). If you do not have muffin liners, then spray the tin with cooking oil so that your cupcakes don't stick to the sides during cooking.

- Put the cinnamon, allspice, ginger, nutmeg, cloves, baking soda, salt, and whole wheat flour into a bowl. Combine until well mixed. The easiest way to do this is with a whisk.

- Put the pureed pumpkin, maple syrup, coconut oil, vanilla flavoring, milk, and eggs into a different bowl. Combine until these are well mixed also.

- Pour the flour combination into the milk combination and mix until there are no lumps and all the ingredients are completely mixed. Be careful not to stir too much. This will make your cupcakes tough and not taste as good.

- Pour the combination into the muffin cups. Try to make sure that each cup has an even amount of mixture in and that some are not too full or not full enough. If you think you would like the taste, you can sprinkle a little bit of coconut sugar on the top of each muffin cup.

- Put the tin into the oven and set a timer for 15 minutes before checking to see if they are cooked. Do this by taking a toothpick and inserting it into the middle of the dish. If it comes out clean, then it is finished! If not, cook for another 3 minutes at a time until the toothpick is clean.

- When the cupcakes are cooked, take them out of the oven and put the pan on top of a wire rack to dissipate heat. Set a timer for 5 minutes. Once the timer has gone off, take the cupcakes out of the pan and put them back on top of the wire rack until they are not hot anymore.

Once there is no heat left in your cupcakes, you can keep them fresh in the refrigerator for a week. If you want to make a lot of these at once, you can put some of them in the freezer. They can stay frozen for 3 months before they are no longer good.

Make your healthy whole wheat and grain bread

What you will need

- Oatmeal (2 Tbsp)
- Sunflower seeds (2 Tbsp)
- Salt (.5 Tbsp)
- Whole wheat flour (2 C)

- Water (1.5 C, warm)
- Yeast (.75 Tbsp, or 1 envelope)
- Maple syrup (2 Tbsp)
- Salt (.5 Tbsp)
- White flour (1.75 C)

What to do

- Use a big mixing bowl to add the maple syrup, water, salt, whole wheat flour, yeast, and white flour. Mix these ingredients until well combined. The result will be very sticky and coarse. When a spoon is no longer strong enough to move through the sticky mixture, use your hands to continue combining inside the bowl.

- As you are combining the ingredients with your hands add extra flour until it does not stick to you or the bowl anymore. Do this by mixing in .5 C at a time and alternate between white flour and whole wheat flour.

- Spray another bowl with cooking oil so that your bread batter doesn't stick to the sides. Move the batter from the first bowl into the new bowl that has been sprayed with oil. Add a sheet of plastic to the top of the bowl and leave it on the counter so that the batter can get bigger. You want it to be two times as big as when you put it in the bowl.

- Once the batter has become big, open a hole in the middle of it to put the oatmeal and sunflower seeds into. Sprinkle flour onto your kitchen counter and move the batter from the bowl to the counter. Mix the batter by hand again until it is stretchy and bounces back a little bit. This will take you around 20 minutes to accomplish.

- Once your batter is stretchy and the oatmeal and sunflower seeds are well spread out throughout the entire mixture, use your hands to create a round shape with it.

- Spray a baking sheet with cooking oil so that your bread batter doesn't stick to it while it is cooking. Move the shaped batter from the counter to the baking sheet and sprinkle a little bit of flour on the top. Cover it with another sheet of plastic and set a timer for 45 minutes before checking to see if it has gotten bigger again. You want the shaped batter to be twice as big as when you put it in the baking sheet. If it is not, set the timer for another 15 minutes before checking again.

- While you are waiting for your batter to get bigger, make sure your oven is set to heat to 425 degrees Fahrenheit.

- Before you put the baking sheet in the oven, cut the shaped batter with a knife in a diagonal pattern 3 times. Only cut about .5 deep and be careful not to cut too far into the batter.

- Put the baking sheet in the oven and set a timer for 25 minutes before checking to see if it is done. You will know this when the entire shape is light brown but not too dark. You can also test whether or not your bread is done by lifting the shaped batter and tapping the bottom of it with your fingers. A hollow-sounding knock means it is cooked in the middle.

- When the bread is cooked, take it out of the oven and put the baking sheet on top of a wire rack to dissipate heat. Set a timer for 5 minutes. Once the timer has gone off, take the bread off of the baking sheet and put it back on top of the wire rack until it is not hot anymore.

- Once there is no heat left in your bread, you can keep it fresh in the refrigerator for a week. If you want to make more than one bread at once, you can put some of them in the freezer. They can stay frozen for 3 months before they are no longer good.

- Your bread will be perfect for so many uses in your healthy diet. You can create fantastic sandwiches, tasty toasts, or eat it on its own with a little bit of honey or nut-based butter. This is a recipe that can do anything!

Cookies that are good for you

What you will need

- Egg (1 large)
- Salt (.5 tsp)
- Baking powder (1.5 tsp)
- Honey (.5 C)
- Oatmeal (1 C)
- Cinnamon (1.5 tsp)
- Vanilla flavoring (1 tsp)
- Whole wheat flour (.75 C)
- Any nuts, flavored chips, or other ingredients you want to mix in (.5 C)

What to do

- Make sure your oven is set to heat to 375 degrees Fahrenheit.

- Spray a baking sheet with cooking oil so that your cookies don't stick to it while they are cooking.

- Use a big bowl to combine the cinnamon, baking powder, whole wheat flour, salt, and oatmeal. Mix until well combined. The best way to do this is with a whisk.

- Heat the butter until it is melted. Pour this into a different bowl with the honey, egg, and vanilla flavoring. Mix these until well combined, also using the whisk.

- Pour the butter mixture into the oatmeal mixture and combine with a spoon. Mix until there are no lumps and all the ingredients are completely mixed. Be careful not to stir too much. This will make your cookies tough and not taste as good.

- Pour your nuts, chips, or other ingredients into the mixture and combine until they are completely mixed in and even in the entire batter.

- Move the bowl to the refrigerator and set a timer for 30 minutes before taking it back out.

- Form your cookies into balls using your hands. You should be able to create about 15 balls with one single recipe. You can easily make more at a single time if you want without needing to use a lot of extra effort to do so. If you do this. You can separate the batter into different types of cookies and add different fillings to each batter.

- Arrange the batter balls onto the baking sheet. Make sure to leave space in between them so that they do not run together while cooking. 2 inches should be enough to prevent this.

- Put the baking sheet into the oven and set a timer for 12 minutes before checking to see if they are done. You will know this when the sides of the cookies at the bottom are a little brown but not too much. If they are not cooked, set a timer for 2 minutes at a time until they are.

- When the cookies are cooked, take them out of the oven and put the baking sheet on top of a wire rack to dissipate heat. Set a timer for 5 minutes. Once the timer has gone off, take the cookies off of the baking sheet and put them back on top of the wire rack until they are not hot anymore. If you want. You can add more fillings to the top of the cookies as soon as you take the baking sheet out of the oven.

Crunchy chickpeas in the oven

What you will need

- Your favorite spice flavor(s) (4 tsp)
- Chickpeas (1 can)
- Salt (1 tsp)
- Olive oil (2 Tbsp)

What to do

- Make sure your oven is set to heat to 425 degrees Fahrenheit.

- Open the chickpeas and pour the liquid out of the can. Wash the chickpeas in a strainer until the water is clear.

- Set out two sets of paper towels that have been layered. Pour the chickpeas onto one set and cover with the other. Rub vigorously to remove all the water from washing. If any shells have come off during this, you can throw them away.

- Pour the chickpeas into a mixing bowl. Combine with the salt and olive oil. Blend until well combined and the chickpeas all have oil covering them completely. If you want, you can add a little bit of your spice flavor into the mixture before cooking. If you do this, make sure you save the listed amount for later as well.

- Pour the chickpeas onto a baking sheet. Move them around to make sure they are not clumped up in one area and are spread across the entire baking sheet so that they cook evenly.

- Put the baking sheet in the oven and set a timer for 10 minutes. When the timer goes off, take the baking sheet out of the oven and move the chickpeas around on it.

This will prevent only one side from cooking and make sure they bake evenly all around their entire surface.

- Once you have moved the chickpeas around, put the baking sheet back in the oven and set the timer for another 10 minutes before doing the last step over again. You will want to do this 3 times before taking the baking sheet out of the oven for the last time when the chickpeas are finished cooking. You will know they are done when they are dark brown all over but not black and all of the oil has been cooked off. They will feel soft inside but be crunchy outside.

- Once the chickpeas are cooked, pour them into a mixing bowl with your favorite seasoning. Blend the chickpeas and spices until well combined and the chickpeas all have spices covering them completely.

- These crunchy chickpeas are great by themselves as a snack instead of eating potato chips or something else unhealthy. You can also add them to lunches or dinners to add extra flavor and crunchiness to whatever you are eating. They are never a bad addition since they are good to get protein from and can increase this in any meal. This can be difficult to get enough of when eating vegetarian food, so it's always good to have tasty ways to eat more of it.

Conclusion

I hope you enjoyed your copy of Vegetarian Meal Prepping:

The Exclusive Guide for Ready-to-Go Meals for a Healthy Plant-Based Whole Foods Diet with a 30-Day Time- and Money-Saving Easy Meal Plan. Let's hope it was informative and provided you with the tools and knowledge you need to get started prepping healthy vegetarian meals all week.

The next step is for you to start implementing what you learned from this book into your diet! Your time and money are valuable, so save both of them by using this guide to start prepping your meals once a week instead of cooking every day, or even worse- going back to the drive-through!

Start by deciding which type of meal prep described inside you want to start with and is the best fit for you. Then schedule when you will make time to go grocery shopping and when you will prepare your meals. From there, choose your favorite recipes from this book to get started with and create your menu. Keep in mind which fruits and vegetables are currently in season for the freshest possible options. Then make your grocery list and go shopping. Finally, get started with prepping your meals! As long as you stick to this easy to follow the guide, you can make meal prep and a vegetarian diet a sustainable lifestyle that takes little to no effort to keep up with!

Finally, if you found this book useful in any way, a five star review is always appreciated !

DISCLAIMER

The author is not a licensed practitioner, physician, or medical professional and offers no medical diagnoses, treatments, suggestions, or counseling. The information presented herein has not been evaluated by the U.S. Food and Drug Administration, and it is not intended to diagnose, treat, cure, or prevent any disease. Full medical clearance from a licensed physician should be obtained before beginning or modifying any diet, exercise, or lifestyle program, and physicians should be informed of all nutritional changes.

The author/owner claims no responsibility to any person or entity for any liability, loss, or damage caused or alleged to be caused directly or indirectly as a result of the use, application, or interpretation of the information presented herein.

ANTI INFLAMMATORY DIET

A Complete Book To Reduce Inflammation Naturally, With a Plant Based Diet. Healthy Vegan And Vegetarian Meal Planning. Top Anti-Inflammatory Foods.

ANTI INFLAMMATORY *Diet*

A COMPLETE BOOK TO REDUCE INFLAMMATION NATURALLY, WITH A PLANT BASED DIET. HEALTHY VEGAN AND VEGETARIAN MEAL PLANNING. TOP ANTI-INFLAMMATORY FOODS

NEW EDITION

OLIVIA JOHNSON SMITH

DESCRIPTION

If you want to learn how to significantly improve your health and well-being and fight inflammatory disease, simply by changing your eating habits, then keep reading and you will be amazed by what new information you'll learn!

We Are Here to Answer Some of Your Most Important Questions :

- Do you want to get health and wellness from an <u>anti inflammatory diet</u>?

- Do you want to know what <u>inflammation</u> and <u>inflammatory</u> disease are?

- Do you want to know how to combat prolonged inflammation simply by changing your eating habits?

- Do you want to learn how you can avoid years of joint pain and muscle stiffness?

- Do you want to increase your energy levels?

- Do you want to increase your mood?

- Do you want to learn how to avoid chronic illnesses?

- Do you want to learn about delicious vegan and vegetarian meal plans?

- Do you want to learn how you can travel and still eat healthily?

- Do you want to improve your overall quality of life?

Imagine waking up every morning and barely being able to get out of bed. Your morning consists of taking multiple medications for various illnesses that you have.

You head to work and whatever breaks you can get are spent making appointments for various doctors that you have to see on a regular basis. This is your life every day, filled with chronic pain, chronic illnesses and being at the mercy of poor health and pharmaceuticals.

Now imagine that you can avoid all of this and have a significantly better quality of life.

With a quality, anti-inflammatory diet, chronic illnesses like heart disease, kidney failure, stroke and even cancer, can be avoided. Chronic Inflammation can lead to a wealth of health problems. Proper eating habits can reduce and even prevent these problems from occurring and give you a lifestyle you will enjoy. This is not hyperbole; it is a reality. By reading this book, you will obtain the knowledge you need to:

- Understand the inflammatory process and inflammatory disease.

- Understand the further health risks of prolonged, untreated inflammatory disease.

- Avoid or correct prolonged inflammation.

- Avoid chronic pain and many serious illnesses.

- Incorporate the **inflammatory diet** into your everyday life.

- Learn about delicious meal plans that follow the *anti inflammatory diet*.

- Learn about meal plans from all over the world, in case you love to travel.

Ready to learn more about the "**Anti Inflammatory Diet**" and its amazing benefits? Everyone can truly enjoy and get something out of this book.

- This book is for you if you are not currently on a healthy diet plan.

- This book is for you if you suffer from chronic pain and illness.

- This book is for you if you are relatively healthy, but still, want to learn more about diet and avoiding chronic disease.

- This book has something new for everybody, no matter what age, to learn because we touch on so many topics related to the **anti inflammatory diet.**

TABLE OF CONTENTS

Chapter 4

The Diet and You

Chapter 5

Tasty meals

Chapter 6

Traveling with the Anti-Inflammatory Diet

Mediterranean:
India:
Mexican/Hispanic Food/Latin:
Asian Food:
Italian:

Chapter 7

Setting Up A Schedule: Taking Action

Sunday:
Monday:
Tuesday:
Wednesday:
Thursday:
Friday:
Saturday:

Chapter 8

The Popular Diet:

Mike Tyson:
Kevin Smith:

Introduction

Congratulations on buying "**Anti Inflammatory Diet**": Healthy Vegan and Vegetarian Meal Planning and thank you for doing so.

A common Ailment which has become a serious problem for people's health and well-being is an inflammatory disease. Dangerous on its own; dangerous when left unchecked.

Inflammation is a common process and protective mechanism for our bodies, however, when inflammation gets out of hand, it can lead to inflammatory disease, which can have detrimental health consequences for all us.

It is a disease that can ravage the body and create permanent issues and even be fatal. For this reason, it is important to understand the disease and how to deal with it by eating a proper **anti-inflammatory diet**.

It is crucial to our daily well-being. While there are many medical and lifestyle changes a person may make in order to improve or even resolve inflammation, in this Book, we will mainly be discussing diet and its effects on this particular disease process. We will be discussing what causes inflammation, the signs and symptoms to look out for, and what dietary steps one can take in order to minimize, prevent and even resolve the effects of inflammatory disease.

The information provided will give a solid understanding of how the food we ingest has a positive or negative impact on the inflammatory disease process and our health. Simple, everyday changes to our routine can improve our overall health and well-being in ways we can't even imagine.

Diet can be used as a very strong tool in order to put those affected by this often-debilitating disease on the right path.

The inflammatory diet is a diverse diet which can improve the health and livelihoods of many people suffering from a painful and often deadly disease. With this particular diet, we may have to skimp on some ingredients, but hopefully not on taste, and definitely not on nutrients. A healthy diet which still satisfies our palate is what we will be discussing.

Through this book, we hope to be able to answer any questions or concerns about what inflammatory disease is, as well as what steps people can take in order to prevent or improve the signs and symptoms through a well-balanced diet. With the information provided, people suffering from **inflammatory** disease can still live relatively normal and active lives as long as they are willing to make the effort.

The first step is in knowledge; the second is in making the changes that are necessary. After all, knowledge without action is ultimately meaningless. Knowledge is power. Action is essential. Let's learn about some great eating habits and then go out there and enjoy what the world has to offer.

With plenty of books on the market about this we thank you again for choosing this one! All effort was made to ensure it is full of as much useful information as possible, so please enjoy!

Chapter 1

What Is Inflammatory Disease

Before we can fully appreciate the anti-inflammatory diet and what it does, we must understand what it is used to prevent, and that is the process of chronic inflammation.

Chronic inflammation is basically a normal body process that goes unchecked. Inflammation, on its surface, is not a bad thing. In fact, it is essential for our bodies in order to maintain health and prevent being overcome by ravaging disease.

It is not an illness in and of itself, but a natural response by our immune system to illness, infection and foreign substances that enter the body. When our own immune system feels threatened by something it does not recognize, it jumps into action with an inflammatory response, which results in an increase in white blood cells, immune cells and cytokines to the affected area. When the immune system feels threatened, it jumps into action.

This response is a normal way for the body to protect itself. Basically, like our own army fighting off an outside invader.

The fact is that inflammatory responses are occurring inside of us constantly and we don't even realize it. It is amazing how our bodies have multiple metabolic processes going on inside of us to keep us healthy and to keep us running. All without us even knowing. The human body is truly a specimen of great functions in and of itself. For this reason alone, we should treat our bodies with the very best care that we can. Our bodies truly are a temple, to recite an old adage.

Think about when you get a cut. The affected area can become red, swollen and warm. Our body temperature may also rise. These are the result of various immune cells and body processes helping us fend off an attack from a foreign substance that does not naturally occur in our bodies.

When injuries to our body occur, such as with a cut, the damaged cells release multiple chemicals that cause blood vessels to leak fluid into the tissues, which in turn, causes swelling. The chemicals released during this whole process also attract white blood cells and other immune cells to the area which basically eat up and eliminate the injury-causing substance and also eat the dead cells.

The white blood cells that eat up everything are called phagocytes. Phagocytes eventually die after completing their job. In most circumstances, the inflammation is short-lived and goes down after the threat has been subdued. If you experience mild inflammation, know that your body and immune system are doing their job to keep you protected from harmful diseases.

An external wound and the swelling we witness is a much more visual representation of inflammation that we can actually observe. Similar operations are going on inside of us that we can't physically see. It is a complicated and in-depth process, indeed. But our immune systems are designed to take care of it.

Think about it this way: An unwanted and dangerous person walks into your house, with the intent of doing severe damage. Imagine also that there is some type of security system in the home. Everyone inside is alerted of the breach and they immediately jump into action.

The vicious guard dogs pounce on the person, the people come in and subdue the culprit and then throw them out of the house. The police come and take them away.

A couple of household items get damaged in the process, but as a whole, the dangerous threat has been taken care of. The people and the dogs stop fighting when they no longer need to, and things begin getting back to normal.

The small damage that was done to the house will slowly get repaired by the people inside. No harm, no foul.

What the heck is the point of this story? It illustrates our own immune system protecting us from harmful invaders. The dogs and the people in the home represent the immune cells pouncing on and fighting off the unwanted substance, represented by the unwelcome intruder. Just like with the story, once a threat to our bodies is eliminated, under normal circumstances, our internal body processes go back to normal. The inflammatory process is complete. We hope that in the situation with the home, nobody dies. Believe it or not, the inflammation that occurs in our bodies is much more violent.

Cells are actually dying. Someone should make an animated action movie about this whole process. Perhaps it can be called "Inflammation Army". Well, that's not too creative, but it could become the next big thing.

In more extreme situations, the inflammation may be misdirected, and this can lead to inflammatory disease, which is a serious illness. This is when the inflammatory response can become a problem. In these cases, the immune system will begin attacking healthy tissues and organs, rather than diseased ones. Our internal immune cells will jump into action, but there is nothing to fight. If there is no pathogen, then what gets attacked? Our own body, and if it's not dealt with early, it can cause severe damage. Rheumatoid arthritis is an example of a result of chronic inflammatory disease.

This disease can be characterized by painful, warm, stiff and swollen joints. In most cases of mild inflammation, this is temporary. With rheumatoid arthritis, it is long term and can become permanent. Other examples of chronic inflammatory disease include asthma, tuberculosis, Crohn's disease, lupus, and periodontitis, which is major gum disease. Remember when your dentist told you that oral disease might be indicative of overall health? Well, they weren't lying. No matter how much we want to avoid it, it is important to go to the dentist for regular checkups.

While the inflammatory disease is most often associated with the joints, in more extreme cases, other organs, including vital internal organs, of the body can be affected. Signs and symptoms are based on which part of the body is under attack. Long term and untreated inflammation can lead to detrimental health consequences.

It is important to understand that chronic inflammation that can be assessed on the outside, can also be indicative of internal inflammatory disease. This is the point we really want to drive home, and we will be doing it constantly, because it is our health, after all. We don't just want to increase our longevity in life, but our quality of life also.

Let's go back to the story from earlier. In that scenario, there was an unwanted intruder, and everyone inside the home jumped into action to subdue and eliminate the threat. This is inflammation at its finest. A threat was perceived, the proper alarms were initiated, and everyone involved jumped into action and did what they were supposed to do.

Our immune system army is probably the most organized team we can imagine. Not only that, it works around the clock and never takes a break. If it ever does, that's when we are in trouble. Now, imagine that the same thing occurs as far as the people and the dogs in the home. The difference now is, there is no intruder. For whatever reason, everybody inside the home rushes to the front door area and begins fighting and attacking the area. There is nothing to attack though.

They just keep going and start damaging the home and all of the items inside of it. Also, since there was no threat in the first place, there is nothing to indicate to anyone, to stop fighting.

So, everyone just keeps going and continues to damage the home, until there is literally nothing left. There was no reason for them to do what they did, and no one to stop them either. The home is destroyed, maybe even beyond repair. This is what can happen to our bodies with chronic and uncontrolled inflammatory disease.

With enough time, our bodies can be completely damaged. Let's make sure this does not happen to us. Let's figure out ways to stop this. We are here for you and your health. We hope you enjoyed this story. There are plenty more to come.

Inflammation and Overall Health:

Chronic Inflammation, no matter where it is, can affect our overall health and well-being. First of all, let's discuss the physical impacts of the pain and swelling, as with rheumatoid arthritis. This can severely limit our physical capabilities, impact our work and our hobbies and just create a miserable day to day experience.

When we wake up in pain, it puts a damper on the rest of our day. When we experience pain throughout the day, it limits our movement, our work ethic, our relationships and our overall ability to enjoy life. It is difficult to deal with this kind of pain for a day, let alone day after day with no improvement in sight.

Imagine being a grandparent and you just want to wake up in the morning and take your grandkids to the park. You would love to just be able to wake up get ready and go have some fun.

When you wake up though, your knees, your hips, and your back are aching to the point that you can barely move, let alone go anywhere. This creates a huge impact on our lifestyle.

Many peoples' mobility becomes so poor that they cannot get around without the aid of a device, like a wheelchair or a walker. Other people can barely get out of bed and become sedentary. Pain and swelling, indeed, wreak havoc on our everyday lives, no matter how tough we think we are. Some pain and immobility are a result of natural aging. However, a lot of it can be avoided by making simple lifestyle changes.

Some things in life are beyond our control. It is best that we do not waste time worrying about them and deal with things as they come. Worrying about a problem is often worse than dealing with the problem itself. However, as far as the things we can control, we should try our best to do so.

With illnesses like rheumatoid arthritis, pain can hit from anywhere at any time with little to no warning. You could be asleep in the middle of the night, cooking in the kitchen or working at your job. Suddenly, out of nowhere, debilitating pain hits you and takes you out of commission.

This pain can become so bad for people that they have to be rushed to the hospital. Sometimes, the pain is localized to a certain area, other times it is widespread throughout the body.

It is a debilitating pain beyond what we can imagine unless we have personally dealt with it.

It may sound like hyperbole, but it is anything but that. Pain and immobility from chronic inflammation is nothing to take lightly.

Furthermore, inflammatory disease can impact our health depending on which part of the body is being impacted. All of the organs and organ systems are at risk. Here are some examples.

- Inflammation of the heart, which is called myocarditis, can lead to fluid retention and difficulty breathing. This will ultimately lead to a lack of perfusion of oxygen-rich blood, and excess fluid in the body will eventually have a detrimental effect on other vital organs. Widespread swelling throughout the body, often called edema, creates pressure and excessive workload on the heart and many other vital organs. If prolonged, extreme wear and tear will occur. Our heart can only function under these conditions for so long before the muscle starts shutting down. Heart disease, congestive heart failure, heart attack, poor contractility, sudden cardiac arrest and risk of stroke all increase in probability with unchecked inflammatory disease. Who would have ever thought that chronic joint pain could also be indicative of heart disease? The truth of the matter is, it can. So, take it seriously.

- Inflammation of the airways can lead to difficulty breathing and damage to the lungs. This will, in turn, decrease the oxygen-rich blood available to peruse the rest of the body. Pneumonia, pulmonary (lung) edema, chronic obstructive pulmonary disease, respiratory failure and a wealth of other respiratory system illnesses will result from an inflammatory disease that is not taken care of early. When your breathing is affected, your life is affected. Oxygen is a life force, and we need it all of the time.

- Inflammation of the kidneys, nephritis, can lead to kidney failure and impact many functions of the body, including blood pressure regulation, and fluid and electrolyte balance. Our kidneys are often not given the credit they deserve, like the brain, heart or lungs. However, the Kidneys perform a lot of functions beyond what was just mentioned earlier. When our kidneys fail, our bodies cannot properly eliminate excess fluid and toxins that come from what we eat and drink and through normal metabolic functions. Almost everything we ingest gets processed by our kidneys. There is also a lot of breakdowns that occur in our bodies through various metabolic processes. If these broken-down substances remain in our bodies for too long, they can become toxic. All of these waste products are eliminated by our kidneys. To bring it full circle, when our kidneys cannot eliminate waste, which is essentially what urine is, then the buildup in our bodies will impede on our heart, lungs, brain and other organs. Our bodies will not utilize calcium properly, leading to bone disease. And our red blood cell production will go down too. If we go into kidney failure, immediate medical response is needed, up to and including, dialysis or a kidney transplant. Poor kidneys equal poor health. The most frightening part is, symptoms from kidney disease may not manifest until it is way too late. That is why the earliest signs and symptoms must be taken seriously. Fatigue, muscle stiffness, pain, and swelling are all early warning signs that there could be a problem. See how important our kidneys are?

- Inflammation of the digestive tract can lead to severe issues such as diarrhea, bloody stools, fatigue, and unintended weight loss. Yes, unintended weight loss is not a good thing, no matter how you want to spin it. The digestive disease should not be a diet plan. Digestive tract health is often overlooked, but it is essential to our well-being. This might get a little gross for some but think about when you have been constipated for days. You feel fatigued, bloated, irritable and just plain miserable. Then one day, you have a huge bowel movement. Suddenly, you feel so much better. It is a pretty amazing feeling to have after the fact. This is a simple example, but yes, digestive tract health is very important. The digestive system breaks down the food that we eat and absorbs and assimilates it into our bodies. Food that is not absorbed eventually gets eliminated. This process of digestion is very in-depth and very important to the functionality of our bodies. Also remember, the digestive system is not just our stomach and intestines. It also includes many ancillary organs like the liver, gallbladder, and pancreas. A poor functioning digestive system will affect a multitude of other body processes. For chronic digestive issues, seek the help of professionals to see if there is anything concerning going on. It may be a simple solution, or it could be something more complicated. Make sure to find out. Take the time you need for your health.

Remember that all of our organs and systems work in conjunction with one another. They have their own unique functions, but the functions of one intensely affect the others. Some have a much more mutualistic relationship, like the heart and lungs. Others have a more secondary or tertiary relationship. In the end, if one is affected, they can all become affected.

This is especially true if inflammation persists for an extended period of time. It is important to recognize the early signs and symptoms of inflammation and seek help immediately. Let's not wait until we need a heart transplant or dialysis to begin taking our health seriously. This may sound extreme, but in the end, it is still a reality. Remember the house that got destroyed?

Don't let yourself be that house. We don't want to provide this information to scare you. We don't want you to get up each day and be terrified of what can happen. On the contrary, we want you to have more peace of mind knowing that your health is being taken care of. Don't worry about the things you can't control and work hard on the things you can. Your personal health is something you have control over.

Distinguishing Inflammatory Disease from Other Illnesses:

While the inflammatory disease may have distinct signs and/or symptoms. It can also mimic other illnesses as well. With inflammation, people may experience flu-like symptoms like a headache, chills and muscle stiffness.

Many of the signs/symptoms we spoke about earlier may or may not be caused by inflammatory disease. With continued research though, it has been determined that many of our illnesses are caused by chronic inflammation. Whatever the case, seek medical attention for any of these health concerns. Chronic, or extended, inflammation is not something you want to take lightly.

Diagnoses of Inflammatory disease and Your Next Steps:

Various diseases that occur can produce similar signs and symptoms for a person. We never truly know what illness we have until we have certain diagnostic exams performed on us. Before we go there though, let's get more in depth about the various manifestations of inflammatory disease. If you are experiencing these on a regular basis, then it's time to make some serious changes.

- One of the most common symptoms of inflammatory disease is swelling. With the influx of white blood cells, the fluid from these cells needs to go somewhere, so it begins pooling in certain areas of the body. More often than not, this will be in the joints and extremities. Due to gravity, a lot of the time, the swelling will occur in the feet or lower extremities. Walking long distances can have a major impact on this. In addition, fluid collection swelling may occur in the neck, back and shoulder area and cause chronic pain here as well. This can also be related to lifestyle or stress and injury, but it is important to get confirmation if it is chronic pain. If chronic pain can be avoided, then why live with it? In many cases, you may not have to deal with it at all.

- Headache, fatigue, chills, weakness and muscle soreness or stiffness are common symptoms of inflammatory disease. They may mimic a cold or flu, but it is important to get it diagnosed for sure. Especially if they are chronic issues. If a person has these symptoms regularly, but otherwise healthy, it is a strong indication of inflammatory disease. These are also some of the earlier warning signs, so a good time to get checked out.

- There has been much research in the past that inflammation can directly affect our mood, resulting in mood swings and depression. For example, people with heart disease who also appeared to be depressed generally had higher inflammation levels with lab testing. Feeling down and don't know why, maybe it's not your fault, but something you can control physically. And let's be real, when we feel healthy, we often feel happier. Continued research is coming out that shows the correlation between physical health and mental health. Many clinicians and mental health professionals are working together to determine some of the correlations between the two. For example, the disciplines of neurology and psychiatry are merging together in many ways to understand the strong relationship between mood and physical health. There is strong support to even merge these two disciplines together completely. Whatever the case, just realize that a poor daily mental outlook may be indicative of poor physical health. If you are always in a poor mood, seek the help of a professional and find ways to correct/fix any underlying issues.

- Inflammatory disease can commonly cause issues with the skin. Skin inflammation will manifest with itchiness, redness, rashes and even chronic conditions like dermatitis. It may be as simple as needing a better moisturizer, or it could be something much more concerning. Skin issues are another thing that is taken lightly. There have been many sitcoms in the past that have even insulted the specialty of dermatology. The jokes are actually pretty funny. However, nothing could be farther from the truth. Our skin is our largest organ. It covers our whole body and has so many different layers. It serves more functions than we can imagine. It is also usually the first line of defense from outside invaders. Skin health can also be a strong determinant in assessing general health. Chronic illnesses may manifest themselves on the skin first. For example, Lupus, which is another inflammatory/auto-immune disease, may manifest itself on the skin with certain types of circular rashes. Furthermore, dry and itchy skin can be indicative of kidney disease. These may be an extreme example, but one of the goals of this Book is to help the reader understand how inflammatory disease can present itself. Do not take skin conditions lightly. They are a strong indicator of our overall health and wellness. Some good news regarding the skin as it relates to the anti-inflammatory diet, which we will discuss later on. Many dermatologists maintain that an anti-inflammatory will give you smoother and younger looking skin. This may sound like a commercial for moisturizer, but it is true that various types of food have an effect one way or another on the skin.

- Inflammation can create very painful and uncomfortable symptoms in the digestive tract. Acid reflux, bloating and diarrhea can occur due to inflammation. Abdominal pain and cramping can also become very severe. Crohn's disease is an anti-inflammatory bowel disease that affects the lining of the digestive tract. If left unchecked, it can cause life-threatening complications. We talked earlier about not taking digestive tract health lightly. Not only can so many diseases affect the digestive tract, poor digestive health heavily weighs down on our lifestyles. Imagine sitting at a ball game and having to get up every few minutes to use the restroom. Imagine being at a restaurant or other gathering and not being able to sit still due to digestive problems. This is certainly no way to live. A proper diet can really have a positive result for our digestive tract. We will discuss this later. For now, let's continue further with inflammatory disease.

- Heart and lung disease are associated with inflammation. Studies from top universities have found that coronary artery disease risks have a strong connection to inflammation. Many different cardiac diseases will result from inflammation. As well, asthma, chronic obstructive pulmonary disease, infections, and many other pulmonary diseases are associated with lung inflammation. This can also lead to fluid accumulation, which will result in breathing difficulties. We discussed earlier the correlation between inflammatory disease and the heart and lungs. We really want to emphasize the severity of its impact. The heart and lungs also have a strong mutual relationship with each other as they are constantly feeding each other blood and other substances directly. The heart sends blood to the lungs to receive its oxygen supply, and then the lungs send the oxygen-rich blood back to the heart for it to pump to the rest of the body. Their relationship is truly symbiotic. Do you have chest pain, difficulty breathing, fatigue, swelling in the feet or other symptoms of concern? Get checked out immediately.

- Chronic inflammatory disease can also lead to a decrease in bone density. Higher risks of osteoporosis and fractures will result from a lack of bone growth. It may be hard to recognize the signs and symptoms here, but often times, it can be excessive back pain, loss of height or fracturing a bone with even mild trauma.

We hope that if you fracture something, you will go to the hospital anyway. Upon arriving at the hospital, a healthcare provider should ask you how you received a fracture. If it was from a trauma that was not that severe, then further tests for inflammation can be done. We touched on the effects of inflammatory disease as it relates to the musculoskeletal system with the swelling of the joints and extremities. Let's delve more into how it can affect the system overall. Inflammatory disease can cause any of a group of diseases called myopathies. In short, myopathy is an umbrella term used to describe a multitude of conditions affecting the muscles. There are several different types of myopathies, but the primary symptom with all of them is muscle weakness. Myopathies may produce simple effects like weakness, fatigue or mild pain. However, in a more extreme case, severe debilitation may occur, and things can also become fatal, such as when it affects the muscles that help us swallow or help us breathe. Take even the mildest forms of musculoskeletal disease seriously. Especially if they are chronic.

While many of these signs and symptoms are indicative of inflammatory disease, we cannot be certain until certain diagnostic exams are completed. While many advanced clinicians would most likely be able to tell by the signs and symptoms you are having, they cannot be sure until further testing is done.

As we said, many types of diseases can produce similar symptoms. Word of advice: do not go to your healthcare worker friend and ask them to diagnose you by what you tell them. They will not be able to tell you for sure. First of all, a thorough examination by a healthcare provider is essential.

They will do a physical assessment to check on the swelling, plus ask in-depth questions about lifestyle, symptoms of pain, what you have been experiencing and how long your current issues have been going on. The physical assessment will really be focused on your joints and extremities. Likely, they will check your mobility, doing a neurological assessment and check your vital signs. By doing a thorough examination, the healthcare provider can help to distinguish between inflammatory disease and other ailments.

One of the biggest indicators of chronic illness as related to joint pain and swelling is by knowing how long it has been going on and if the signs and symptoms are getting worse.

Furthermore, diagnostic tests such as scans, which include x rays, ultrasounds, CT scans, or MRIs may be needed to assess internal issues related to inflammation. An MRI, especially with some type of contrast agent, is the most in-depth of the scans. Also, certain blood tests will likely be performed to check for certain markers related to inflammatory disease.

A common blood test used to assess inflammatory disease is C-Reactive Protein, a major marker indicative of inflammation found on blood tests. We will talk more about C-reactive proteins later on. All of these assessment strategies will work in congruence with one another to get the most comprehensive information needed to make a proper diagnosis. Without these, there is truly no way of knowing for sure what ails us.

As you can see, inflammatory disease can have detrimental effects on the body, including many vital organs. For this reason, it is important to recognize the signs and symptoms and seek treatment immediately. Many people may call you a hypochondriac, but it is ultimately your health and not theyrs. Care must be taken in order to get the correct diagnosis and start a proper treatment plan, the backbone of which is a proper diet.

We hope that this chapter has given you a solid understanding of the inflammatory disease. While the inflammatory disease can be damaging to our health, with proper care and recognition, the negative results can be minor or even nonexistent.

The main thing though is to intervene before things become too bad. In those cases, more extreme measures may be necessary. Understand what inflammatory disease is, recognize the signs and symptoms and seek help when needed. Next, we will be discussing diet and its relationship to inflammation.

CHAPTER 2

Resolving Anti-Inflammatory Disease

We have spoken extensively about the inflammatory disease. It is important to shine a light on chronic inflammation in order to truly highlight the risks associated with the illness.

To fix something, you must first understand what it is. Now that we have gone over the disease in-depth, we will start getting to the heart of this Book.

The main reason why we are here and that is to talk extensively about a major lifestyle change that can create very positive results. We are referring to the anti-inflammatory diet. You may have heard about this diet before. However, if you have not, we are here to tell you more about it.

An important thing to remember is that each person's body is different. A strong consideration to make when altering your diet and overall lifestyle. Do your research and understand yourself. Assess thoroughly whether or not something is working well for you. Especially based on how it makes you feel. This may not be conclusive, but a strong indicator of the benefits of something. Don't be afraid to speak up if you don't feel right. Don't be afraid to ask for help.

Anti-Inflammatory Diet:

Mild inflammation is a necessary process for the body to protect itself. But prolonged and misguided inflammation is when things get out of hand. How can we resolve chronic inflammation or inflammatory disease? There are many ways. For this Book, we will be focusing on the anti-inflammatory diet. Furthermore, we will focus specifically on vegan and vegetarian foods. These are really the meat, pardon the pun, of the diet as a whole. The vegetarian diet really encompasses more than we may think. There are actually different levels of vegetarianism and we hope to stay within those lines. Let's get started.

Let's begin with a couple of stories, shall we? Yes! More amazing stories. Just bear with us. "Tommy is dealing with painful arthritis. He has been for a few months now and things are getting worse instead of better. It started in his hands but is now traveling to his neck and back. Also, it is becoming more difficult to walk long distances.

Tommy eats a steady diet of cheeseburgers, pizza, fries, chocolate cakes, and sodas. This is what he likes, and this is what he eats. It is so delicious, so why would he stop? He heard about the anti-inflammatory diet, but he was not interested. He did not care for what this diet had to offer. Trading in burgers, pizza, and fries for whole grains, fish, fruits and vegetables was not that appealing to him. He was a meat eater through and through and he was not planning to change anytime soon. He wanted all of the fat, cholesterol and sugar filled foods.

He kept eating and eating, until one day, he developed extreme chest pain. It was excruciating to the point he could not breathe. His feet were also starting to swell.

He was sent to the hospital via emergency ambulance and is now diagnosed with heart disease and is also developing a digestive tract illness call Crohn's disease. The staff was also concerned about his labs that were showing early stages of kidney disease. The doctor informed him about the inflammation that had been going on for a very long time at this point.

The chronic condition leads to more severe health consequences and Tommy will now need more aggressive therapies for his various ailments. Tommy is a busy guy running his business, taking care of his family and needing to travel on a regular basis. Now he is incapacitated to a degree with these various illnesses. He will have to start taking several different medications for blood pressure, cholesterol, pain, and diuretics to help excrete excess fluid.

He will also have to make serious lifestyle changes immediately, or things will continue to spiral out of control. He was literally weeks away from having a heart attack or something much worse. The damage has been done, but with a little help, things can still improve tremendously."

There's a strong chance that if Tommy would have listened to the warning signs earlier, he would need less drastic interventions. There were definitely plenty of warning signs. He either did not recognize them or did not care. Let's talk about what they were. The chronic pain was becoming worse and having difficulty walking long distances.

These were some early signs that something was wrong. If the inflammation was affecting him outwardly like this, imagine what it may have been doing to him internally. Those whole grains and vegetables probably seem a lot more appealing than before.

Now Tommy will need to take many medications and receive extensive therapies. Would an improved diet have fixed all of his problems? It is hard to say. There is no way of predicting this. The chances are, things would not have become as extreme as they did. You can run a red light, and nothing bad may happen. However, the chances of something bad happening increase dramatically. Same thing with our health. We can do everything right, and things can still go wrong. The chances of things going wrong though decrease dramatically if we do things right.

Hopefully, Tommy can get his health together and make the necessary improvements in his life. Lucky for him, he was rushed to the hospital when he was. Things could have still turned out much worse for him. Let's talk about another story.

"Bobby loved eating high salt, high fat and high sugary foods. His favorite thing to do was grease his eggs with a lot of extra butter. A few extra pieces of bacon on the side, plus some cut up and mixed into his eggs, would usually suffice. He also loved a good chocolate muffin and a cup of coffee filled with creamer.

His late-night snacks would consist of a slice of four-cheese pizza and pieces of salami. Burgers, pizza, and fries, chicken: whatever was greasy, was good for him and he would indulge whenever he could.

A good lunch spot would be whatever fast-food restaurant he saw first. This was Bobby's daily life and he loved every moment of it. At some point, he began having neck pain. He figured this was normal due to the stress of is work. He had a pretty busy career with much responsibility. However, he began experiencing more muscle stiffness, fatigue, and soreness at the joints. His weight gain was increasing by the week as well. He decided he would go see his a doctor.

After getting a full checkup, Bobby's doctor informed him that he has some mild inflammatory disease. A combination of his diet and lifestyle were starting to weigh heavy on him. Lucky for him, it was still in the mild stages.

He was still a young man in his thirties, but if he did not change things fast, he would be lucky to make it into the next decade.

Bobby still had a lot of living to do, so he made some life-altering changes. The most important one was his diet. He would still eat eggs every morning, but he cut down heavily on the butter. After a little while, he used none at all.

He cut out the muffin and bacon and substituted some whole wheat toast. He drank his coffee black with half a teaspoon of sugar. He still liked his coffee a little sweet. For lunch, instead of getting a burger at a fast-food place, he would eat various fruits and salads, combined with various plant-based proteins for extra nutrition.

 Most of the time, he would make something healthy at home, like a sandwich made with whole wheat bread and take it with him. For a late-night snack, Bobby would eat an apple or avocado. He would indulge occasionally, but it was rare. This change in diet was not easy, but after a couple of weeks, when Bobby felt like a new person, he realized that it was totally worth it.

When Bobby went in for his checkup the following month, his doctor was very satisfied. He had lost 10 pounds; his mobility had increased tremendously and is lab results were impeccable. His energy levels throughout the day allowed him to be much more productive at work and in life. He still had a little way to do, but his progress so far had been remarkable.

Eating all of those fat filled foods may have brought some quick satisfaction, but the long-term effects were not worth it. In fact, the satisfaction of unhealthy foods was short-lived. The satisfaction of eating healthy, lasted all day. Especially since he was not feeling run down and exhausted. Most importantly, the timing was crucial. Lucky for him, he came in and got checked early, avoiding more serious health risks in the future. Bobby continues his new diet and is as happy as ever."

As you can see, Tommy and Bobby were heading down similar paths. Tommy ignored the warning signs, but Bobby didn't. Now they are on two completely different roads. These two stories illustrate just how serious inflammatory disease can be, and if caught early, can save you a world of trouble down the line. It can even save your life.

Don't wait until you need more aggressive treatment like medications or surgery. If you are concerned, follow up with a healthcare provider and make the necessary changes as soon as you can. The anti-inflammatory diet can be a miracle when dealing with early stages of inflammatory disease. It takes work, it takes commitment and it takes some sacrifice. But if you don't do it, you are sacrificing the worst thing you can; your health.

The Anti Inflammatory Diet is essentially an eating plan that is designed to prevent or reduce low-grade chronic inflammation. The key term is low-grade. That is why it is important to start early. The foods we ingest have a high level of influence on the amount of inflammation we experience, so sticking to an anti-inflammatory diet is essential to help avoid, resolve or reduce chronic inflammation. While more extreme and invasive measures are available and may need to be taken with more severe cases if something as simple as eating properly can avoid serious pain and health consequences, why not try it? Trading that greasy cheeseburger for a fresh salad may mean the difference between a healthy heart or a heart attack later on.

There is some controversy in the vegetarian world about exactly where the line is drawn. Veganism is considered the most extreme version of vegetarianism. However, some advocates will include poultry, fish and dairy products as part of the vegetarian diet. Others will say no living creatures period. Some very devout vegetarians, like vegans, will even say no animal products period. We are not here to resolve this debate.

However, we want to be respectful to those who embrace the vegetarian/vegan diet. Since there is a strong consensus that fish and dairy products are part of the diet or at least less extreme versions of it, we will include some fish and dairy products in our discussions. Especially since so many of these foods are a strong addition to the anti-inflammatory diet. This is definitely true of oily fishes. Of course, if you leave these foods out, you can still combat inflammatory disease and get the proper nutrients. So, don't worry if you are a vegetarian and you don't want to include these certain foods. We have your back.

In a nutshell, an anti-inflammatory diet consists of foods that help to reduce or resolve the inflammation process. In fact, they are foods that most nutrition experts would encourage you to eat anyways. Fruits, vegetables, plant-based proteins, whole grains, nuts, beans, and fresh herbs and spices are all good food groups to turn to when going down this avenue.

Most of these foods have compounds, like Omega-6 fatty acids, antioxidants, and polyphenols which have naturally occurring anti-inflammatory properties. Yes, this does limit the amount of food we can indulge, however, there is still a large variety of food we can choose from within these different food groups. There is a whole world of culinary goodness that will become open to you if you give it a chance and explore. Not only that, you will not feel awful after eating them. Eating should never make you feel worse than you already were.

We will discuss various foods in more detail later in this chapter. For now, remember that the anti-inflammatory diet is not a cure-all plan. However, it can help us make significant steps in the right direction.

Eat right and feel right: that is our motto for today.

Benefits of the Diet:

With the **anti-inflammatory diet**, there have shown to be multiple benefits for a score of different diseases. One of the biggest being heart disease. Several studies have shown that an anti-inflammatory diet has reduced the risk of atherosclerosis in the arteries. As well, reduction in blood pressure, blood sugar, cholesterol levels, and obesity have been a common result of the anti-inflammatory diet. It makes sense, as the anti-inflammatory diet steers us away from all of the foods that consist of dangerous fats, excess cholesterol, and high sugar contents.

As we mentioned earlier, the anti-inflammatory diet plays a significant role in reducing inflammation, which in turn, reduces the risks of more severe health risks. Many prescribed diets in the hospital, such as the cardiac (heart) diet, diabetic diet, and the renal (kidney) diet resemble the anti-inflammatory diet in many ways, while still having their own uniqueness.

For example, the kidney diet discourages eating too many beans due to their high phosphorus content and also foods like tomatoes or bananas due to their potassium levels. With the anti-inflammatory diet, all of these are still okay. Therefore, once again, it's important to check with a professional before starting a life-altering diet plan. We want to make sure the diet has its intended purpose without shortchanging us on the nutrients we need to function.

The cost of good health is nothing compared to the cost of poor health. Healthier ingredients may cost more at the beginning but can spare you big time in the long run.

Our sincere hope is that if you follow this diet, it will be a lifelong lifestyle change and not just a short-lived experiment. If it's just for that, don't even bother because the results could be even more exhausting. Following this diet is not a quick fix. It takes work, sacrifice, and commitment. If you don't make the proper lifestyle changes, you may need some quick fixes to save your life. In the end, when you wake up feeling energized and ready to take on the day, you will realize that the hard work was worth it. Nothing good ever comes easy.

Different types of food that are part of the Anti-Inflammatory Diet:

Now let's get into the specifics about the foods that are part of the anti-inflammatory diet. While eating the diet may limit certain ingredients, we hope that it won't limit enjoyment. In fact, if given some time, we are certain that it won't. The various food groups, as well as the herbs and spices, can be combined in all sorts of fashion to create delicious meals. Also, it certainly will not limit nutrients.

In this section, we will discuss various foods that are present inside of the different food groups that follow the "*anti inflammatory diet*" plan.

- Whole grains-Whole grains, such as whole-oats, whole-wheat bread, brown rice, oatmeal, and Quinoa. Do not confuse whole grains with refined grains as refined grains are more processed, and thus not as nutritious. Whole grains keep all portions of the grain intact, which provide all of its nutrition and health benefits. Stick to the whole grains and you will stick to the diet. Don't worry, you don't have to eat grass, hay or pure wheat. There are actually some delicious options here. Have you ever tried raw honey with fresh oatmeal? Maybe add a few berries on top? Yummy! Speaking of berries...

- Fruits-Some of the best **anti-inflammatory foods** include apples, cherries, berries (blueberries, raspberries, blackberries, and strawberries), oranges, grapes and avocados Many of the colorful compounds in the fruit have strong anti-inflammatory properties. Ever hear the term that an apple a day keeps the doctor away? This phrase is truer than we would like to admit. Of course, eating an apple a day may keep the doctor away, but if you don't go in for regular checkups, you're bananas. First the stories, now the jokes. We are on a role here. Include these high-quality fruits in your daily diet. Since there are so many different kinds, it is easy to change things up every day.

- Eat an apple one morning, a banana the next and then some blueberries the next. Trading in that chocolate candy bar for an apple or banana is a smart move in the long run. Wait, did we mention chocolates?

- Dark chocolate has been shown to exhibit some anti-inflammatory properties. Having it on occasion can still keep you on the anti-inflammatory diet route. Choose the chocolate that has a high percentage of cocoa. These will have flavanols, which are another compound that will help reduce inflammation.

- Vegetables-Leafy green vegetables like kale, spinach, and collards have great anti-inflammatory properties. In addition, vegetables like broccoli, brussels sprouts and cauliflower have anti-inflammatory effects due to their antioxidant properties. A good hearty salad can go a long way in making us feel good and satisfied. Be careful though, because many people will drown their salads with a lot of processed and unhealthy dressings. Don't worry though, there are healthier options if you just give them a chance. For example, squeezing pure lemon or lime can be beneficial and enhance the taste. If you are looking for a good dressing though, check out avocado dressing or cashew dressing. Both are great options that will satisfy the anti-inflammatory diet rules. Always double check salt content though. Salt can be hidden at times, and a silent killer. Vegetables, in general, are an important part of a wholesome diet. Fresh vegetables are very nutritive.

- Nuts-These include walnuts, almonds, pecans, and hazelnuts. Obviously, a handful of any of these is not going to satisfy anyone's cravings or make them full. However, various types of nuts can be added to foods, such as salads. Also, they can be used as a delicious snack, instead of a candy bar or chips. Various nuts, in general, have good types of fats that promote anti-inflammation.

- Make sure they are not processed kinds that are full of salt. Fresh nuts from your local grocery store or health food store will do. Roasting many of these different nuts can also enhance the taste. Keep some on hand with you and they will be a satisfying quick snack when you need it.

- Plant-based Proteins-These includes chia seeds, soy products, almonds, quinoa, Tofu, edamame, peanuts, beans, potatoes, kale, chickpeas, and lentils. People's biggest concern about not eating meat is where they will get their protein. However, there is a significant amount of protein in various vegetarian foods, and these proteins often create fewer chances of cardiovascular disease. Animal proteins will give you complete proteins with all amino acids but eating a variety of different plant-based proteins will do the same. Plus, things like quinoa and soybeans will also give you complete proteins. Think about some of the most powerful animals in the animal kingdom. Many of them have a vegetarian style diet. If it works for them, it can certainly work for us. "I feel as strong as a horse!" Some people will say. Well, horses are not chowing down on greasy hamburgers, that's for sure. Their eating some good old fashion way.

- Oily Fishes-Oily fishes like salmon, trout, mackerel, tuna, and sardines are oily fishes that are good for fighting inflammation. Many still consider this part of the vegetarian diet too, so we included them here. You can certainly leave these out if you choose to. However, they do have many health benefits and anti-inflammatory properties.

- Coffee-Several studies from top universities have shown that coffee and caffeine in general, have strong anti-inflammatory properties. Coffee contains an anti-inflammatory compound called polyphenols, which help to defend against chronic inflammation. A morning cup of coffee may do just more than help wakes you up. Remember not to go overboard. Watch that creamer and sweetener too. We are talking about black coffee here, not those crazy fancy drinks filled with sugar.

- In general, foods that are rich in antioxidants, like many of the ones mentioned above, have strong anti-inflammatory properties as well. Furthermore, foods rich in Omega-3 fatty acids, also mentioned above, are also a strong addition to the anti-inflammatory diet.

Much of the food we eat is rich in Omega-3 fatty acids as Omega-3 deficiency is very rare in the United States at least. Some examples of these foods include Oily fish (salmon, mackerel, sardine, and anchovies), flaxseeds, chia seeds, soybeans, plant oils, eggs, and milk. One of the most heralded anti-inflammatory diets is the Mediterranean diet. We will discuss this in more detail later in this Book when we get to the travel section. We have some delicious foods to talk about so don't go anywhere.

Other food options are tomatoes, green peppers, herbs and spices like garlic, cinnamon, rosemary, cloves, black pepper, ginger and turmeric, and sweet potatoes. It is advised to not use vegetable oils for cooking, but rather olive oil, soybean oil, or avocado oil. As you can see, the anti-inflammatory diet is largely vegan or vegetarian anyway. A big concern for many is that these types of diets lack many essential nutrients. This is a very legitimate concern. However, the anti-inflammatory diet is very well diverse and provides high levels of nutrition that our bodies need. We discussed proteins earlier, which is one of the more concerning nutrients we worry about lacking.

In further chapters, we will delve into more delicious meal plan options that will excite your palates. For now, many of these foods should satisfy your cravings and provide you the nutrition you need. While it is okay to indulge occasionally, it is important to remember that a healthy diet is good for your health and well-being as well as giving you a good quality of life. When you feel better, you live better. Imagine waking up in the morning and not feeling weak, not feeling bloated, not feeling pain and not feeling ill. A proper anti-inflammatory diet will help put you on the right track to a well-balanced life.

While we have promoted these foods as a way to reduce inflammation when you have it, it is far better to prevent an issue than fix it later. Imagine if you incorporated these foods into your diet, even if you do not have the anti-inflammatory disease. This can majorly reduce the chances of having it in the first place and avoid major health concerns later in the future. Don't pick poor lifestyle choices simply because they are not affecting you now. They may have negative effects in the future. They could be doing untold damage that you do not even realize. It is easier to prevent than to fix. Remember, many of these diseases are silent killers. Meaning they won't present themselves until it is too late.

Foods to avoid:

Food is an important part of our lives. It brings us happiness; it gives us memories; it gives us experiences. Food is essential and we should do our best to enjoy it to the fullest. Since we have discussed foods that you should incorporate into your diet to help reduce or prevent inflammation, we will also briefly touch on the foods to avoid. Diet obviously plays a huge role in our overall health.

Much of our diet consists of fatty, high cholesterol, high sugary foods, so they are very hard to avoid. Many foods that disguise themselves as healthy, are anything but that. Unfortunately, many companies have hijacked the health food market and it is very difficult to distinguish the good from the bad. In general, these types of food should be balanced with the healthier, anti-inflammatory options. The following is a list of some of the top foods and nutrients to avoid, especially if inflammation is already present.

- Foods rich in Omega-6 fatty acids are known to increase the body's production of inflammatory chemicals. These fatty acids do provide many other nutritional benefits that are necessary for us, so do not cut them out completely. Just balance them with the Omega-3 fatty acids we spoke about earlier and other foods associated with the anti-inflammatory diet. Some foods that are rich in Omega-6 fatty acids are red meats (burgers and steaks), French fries and other fried foods and margarine.

The jury is still out in a lot of ways on dairy products and whether they are good at fighting or increasing inflammation. It seems to vary based on the product itself. Dairy like yogurt seems to have positive anti-inflammatory effects, while things with more fat content like cheese and whole milk have a negative effect. The benefits of milk can also be determined by how it's made. Besides yogurt, not much is known about other dairy products and their relationship to inflammation. Even many nutritional experts have a hard understanding of it. As a short, if they don't make you feel good, don't use them.

- Sodas and other sugary drinks should be avoided at all costs. They bring little to no nutritional value. While many of the foods we eat and beverages we drink have both positive and negative results, there really is no benefit to soda. A cool sparkling drink may taste good on a hot day, but there are other options to quench your thirst. Not only that, sodas only quench your thirst for a short period of time. Plus, they can cause you to excrete more fluid too, resulting in further dehydration. Avoid sodas for a healthier option and be careful when choosing those healthier options.

- Sweets like cakes and cookies. It can be tempting to order that large piece of cake after a large meal but try to avoid it if you can. Food filled with high sugar content is one of the worst things for inflammation. Especially considering the portion sizes we have today. Eating refined carbohydrates can have similar results.

- Coffee creamers and anything else with trans-fat which raise LDL levels, leading to inflammation. Enjoy that cup of coffee, black, without the creamer. Other foods high in trans-fat include doughnut, snack foods like microwave popcorn, frozen foods, fast-food and ready to use frostings. It is better to stick with natural foods than processed foods as a rule of thumb.

- Refined carbs like white bread, white rice, pastries, white pasta, breakfast cereals, and refined grains can increase inflammation. Stick to the whole grains which are more nutrient rich at better at fighting inflammation. Have a bowl of oatmeal instead of that sugary cereal in the morning. If you're having toast, stick to whole wheat bread instead of white bread. Enjoy the pasta but make it whole wheat pasta.

- Avoid processed vegetable oils. Plant-based oils are recommended.

Most of these are probably foods that you have been told all your life to either avoid or limit. All the great stuff that we love, right? In actuality, many of the foods we mentioned in the previous section can be healthy and delicious, or even combined to create delicious foods.

While you don't have to cut out all the food, we discussed in this section completely, it is important to limit and balance with a healthy and nutritious diet.

As with any diet or major lifestyle change, it is important you do it in a safe and nondetrimental manner.

It is advised to consult a healthcare provider or nutrition expert when drastically changing diet plans.

While it's good to switch to more nutritious options, we also want to make sure we don't exclude necessary nutrients.

We will be driving this point home constantly like it's a broken record. Records? What are those? Look it up, please.

Chapter 3

History of Anti-Inflammatory Diet

To better understand the significance of the anti-inflammatory diet, it is important to research the history and fundamentals behind it. In doing this, we can shine a better light on the whole phenomenon.

As you will see, it is not a new fad that just gained popularity out of nowhere. A bunch of celebrities did not just start promoting it and now suddenly, it has taken over the world. Never do something just because it is popular. That being said, this particular diet has been popular for a long time.

The diet predates modern times and modern medicine. We will touch on the history here so we can better understand the fundamentals. Understanding our history makes it easier to understand our present.

The origins of the anti-inflammatory diet date back to some of the original healers in the world and throughout history. Many of these healers worked with natural herbs, foods, teas, and other holistic remedies to assist the body with its own healing process. Much of these practices are still performed by various people around the world.

Without having access to modern, manufactured medications, these natural healers had to make do with what they had. What they did have was an abundance of natural ingredients at their disposal to use for healing or preventing certain ailments. While there may not have been a lot of scientific research to back up many of their claims, much anecdotal evidence suggested that they were on to something. Much of what people discover of the past, helped people learn more during the present.

While the advent of modern medicines should be held up with pride, it is important to give credit to natural remedies that helped heal people for centuries. Much of it was related to the food people ate.

In more modern times, the anti-inflammatory diet really began getting more mainstream attention from the medical community in the 1970s. Around this time, researchers found that naturally occurring proteins found in our body were a major cause of tissue injury.

Before this time, it was believed to be pathogens from outside of the body. This new finding of substances in our own body damaging our own tissues was a big breakthrough for the researchers of this time. They began realizing that our own bodies' cells can do just as much, if not more damage than outside sources. Our body literally has the ability to destroy itself.

Remember earlier how we spoke of misguided inflammation? This is essentially substances in our own body attacking itself and its own internal tissues, like these proteins, were discovered to do. This was a huge breakthrough for the medical sciences and the makings of an anti-inflammatory diet.

Once they discovered this breakthrough, they could better understand how to fix it.

Then in the 1980s, further evidence suggested that various proteins in our bodies were either beneficial or injurious to our bodies' tissues. One of the newly named proteins of this time were called cytokines, which were produced by the immune system. The release of these proteins during the inflammatory process was seen to cause damaging results after the effects of chronic disease. Researchers also began using C-reactive protein, which is a marker of inflammation circulating the blood as a way to identify persons at risk of chronic disease.

More advanced research found that people with higher levels of C-reactive proteins also had higher levels of heart disease.

With much of the research indicating these results, a growing consensus to this day is that inflammation plays a very significant role in the pathogenesis of chronic illnesses like heart disease, lung disease, stroke, diabetes, kidney disease, and even some cancers. For this reason, many medical practitioners and nutrition experts are promoting certain anti-inflammatory diets with foods that will reduce the amount of inflammation in our bodies.

This reduced inflammation will result in decreasing or even preventing more chronic illnesses. The anti-inflammatory diet is becoming more prominent as the push to prevent illness rather than cure it is taking off. People are realizing once more that it is better to prevent a catastrophe than deal with its aftermath. The promotion of a proper anti inflammatory diet coupled with other major lifestyle changes can work wonders for aiding in chronic illnesses.

While we will never discredit the advances of modern medicine, we also want to pay homage to the healers and practitioners of the past. Without the work they did, we would not have made the modern-day strides to continue and advance health and medicine. We also cannot deny that techniques of the past were essential in improving health and we certainly should not avoid these practitioners' contributions for what we have today. Without there knowledge and discoveries, we could not have advanced as much as we have. If it worked for them in the past, then it can work for us today. Modern medicine is needed to deal with some of the advanced medical problems we have today.

However, with proper diet and lifestyle, we can prevent those problems from occurring in the first place. Both theories and practices can coexist.

Ancient Greek physician, Hippocrates, who is often considered the father of medicine, was one of the first to understand the impact of environment, diet, and lifestyle on human health. Before this, people just related it to external sources like Gods or demons. Hippocrates approach to medicine is far removed from today's medical practices. Modern-day medicine is believed to take a more curative and diagnostic approach, while with Hippocrates, it was focused more on patients care and a good prognosis. Basically, preventative care. Both schools of thought existed in Hippocrates' day, the other one sharing more similarities with the medical practices of today.

Even though much of Hippocrates principles are outdated in ways, his approach can still be heralded as well. With the advent of advanced techniques, we can cure illnesses that were death sentences in years past. It is amazing how far we have come with medical science and we will continue to do so as the years go by. However, our focus with the anti-inflammatory diet somewhat plays off of the teachings of Hippocrates and his beliefs of lifestyle, environment, and diet impacting our health. While at times, extreme measures and advanced medicine is needed, to deny something like diet and lifestyle not having an effect on health is irresponsible.

Let's consider this for a second: remember our two stories from earlier about Tommy and Bobby? Tommy did not use preventative approaches to fix his health. Now he needs to rely on more advanced medicine to fix his ailments. We applaud the fact that these advanced techniques are available to save Tommy's life. However, we also acknowledge that if Tommy made several lifestyle changes earlier, he may not have needed these more aggressive therapies. With Bobby, he made the changes in his diet early, and for that reason, his health is much better off. We contend that it is better to prevent a heart attack than cure one after the fact.

In Summary, the diet in some form has existed for centuries around the world. With further research and determination of the pathogenesis of several diseases, the benefits of the diet's effect on chronic illness are undeniable. We realize that we went more in-depth than we needed to in discussing the science behind the inflammatory disease. However, understanding the illness gives us a better understanding of the cure. The anti-inflammatory diet exists also in various forms around the world and we will discuss this further when getting into traveling with the **anti-inflammatory diet**. There is no one-size-fits-all plan when it comes to this diet and that is what makes it great. Anyone can find food that they love within the parameters of the diet.

Chapter 4

The Diet and You

Now that we have discussed the diet extensively, let's put it all together. We will bring it full circle and discuss how the diet can and will affect you.

It will impact you in a big way. Especially, if you are used to eating a lot of meat, high saturated fat, high sugar, and high cholesterol foods.

The anti-inflammatory diet pretty much eliminates all of that. Also, a common routine we have been taught is to have three large meals at breakfast, lunch, and dinner.

With the anti-inflammatory diet, it is suggested to have five or six smaller meals throughout the day.

Eating multiple times throughout the day keeps up your metabolism and decreases the major fluctuations in blood sugar that come from eating fewer and larger meals. This is easier on your internal organs, especially your pancreas.

The diet alone is not a cure-all. It should be coupled with a healthy lifestyle in general. There are much literature and information out there about living healthy in many ways. For this Book, we will still focus on the diet more than anything else.

The first thing you should do is identify the signs or symptoms that may be concerning to you. Whether you feel healthy or not, regular checkups are very important.

With the assistance of a professional, begin eliminating certain unhealthy foods from your diet and start incorporating more foods related to an anti-inflammatory diet. Do this whether you are dealing with inflammation or not.

For example, eat fewer red meats and poultry and start eating more oily fishes, beans, lentils, soy and tofu for protein. Furthermore, replace your unhealthy sugary snacks with healthier options like fruits.

Also, for meals, eat a vegetable, whole grains and various nuts for snacks. Having foods like this throughout various times of the day will increase energy, concentration and help you avoid more long-term illnesses. Prepare foods the night before so you have it with you for the next day. This limits the number of times you have to eat out. Diet and how it affects us is truly a science, so that is why it is important to consult a professional.

It is best to also eat around the same times every day. This can be quite difficult with the busy lives that we live, but with some extra effort, it can be done. Carry small, healthy snacks like almonds or apples with you. Allowing you to eat at a moment's notice.

Set aside a certain amount of time throughout the day to sit and eat. Eat a good meal before you start your day. Incorporate your eating habits into your everyday life and make them a priority. Making your dietary selections a priority is not really an option if you want a healthy and more fulfilling life. It is a necessity. Write things down, and you will remember them better. You will also start holding yourself accountable.

This chapter was written with the assumption that you are currently not following the anti-inflammatory diet whatsoever. For this reason, we gave you some of the most fundamental techniques to help integrate the diet into your lifestyle. We apologize if it may come off as judgmental, but we sincerely hope this will help you in your daily routine.

We will talk more about setting up a schedule further in this book. For now, think about ways you can replace certain unhealthy foods for more nutritious options. Replace that sugary coffee with black coffee or green tea. Replace that lunchtime burger for a fresh salad.

Replace that greasy pasta dinner for some whole wheat pasta. Finally, replace that late-night sugary snack for an avocado or banana. Enjoy the results of this new lifestyle.

Let's tell another short story. Oh, come on! Another one? Yes, they're not so bad, are they?

This will just be a short day in the life of someone starting an anti-inflammatory diet. Let's call it... A Day in the Life of Someone Starting an Anti-Inflammatory Diet. We'll call our person Amanda.

Amanda is planning to start a new life. After living with many health problems, she has decided to turn a new leaf and start a new diet that was directed by her doctor. It is Saturday night and she plans to start her new diet, the anti-inflammatory diet, the following morning. This is in relation to her chronic inflammation caused by some auto-immune disorder.

Her current diet and lifestyle are not compatible with the disease, so she has to make some changes. And she is willing to. After a fun night out with her friends, she goes back home and retires for the night. She is excited and ready to start her new lifestyle. She is also a little nervous too. This will definitely be a big change for her, and she will have to give up a lot of the foods she loves and is used to. She can do it though.

The next morning, it is Sunday and things are about to change. Amanda looks in her refrigerator and sees nothing but junk food. She has to fix this. She looks at her countertop and sees nothing but sugary foods. This is another thing that has to change. Amanda decides she has to go to the store and pick up a few things. But what will she eat for breakfast?

Normally, she would have some type of toaster pastry, or chocolate muffin and chase it down with orange juice or chocolate milk. She knew she could not do this today. She cannot start her new day by repeating the mistakes of the past. But she was not sure what choice she would have. She looked in her fridge a little bit more and saw that she has some eggs. She figures this is the best thing for her.

She starts breaking them apart and mixing them. As she is getting the pan ready, she realizes that she usually coats it with butter. She decides not to do that today. She continues to make the eggs. She also prepares a cup of coffee. Normally, she adds a lot of French vanilla creamer.

On this morning, she still adds a little bit, but just half the amount as before. She also adds just one spoon of sugar versus two. A few small steps in the right direction. She may not be able to make all of the drastic changes at once. It's ok though, it will be a slightly slow transition as long as she realizes she has to make the changes soon.

After Amanda is done eating her breakfast, she heads to the store. She has a list of various food products given to her by her doctor and dietician in order to stick to the anti-inflammatory diet. She walks down the various aisles and picks out a few things. She avoids buying and red meats for now. She picks up some tofu and salmon instead.

For snacks, she gets some almonds, peanuts, walnuts, and cashews. She also gets some carrot sticks and celery. While walking by the candy aisle, she looks but keeps moving. She moves to the dairy products and picks up some Greek yogurt, and some more eggs. She refuses to get more butter. The last thing she gets are some lentils, broth for her soups and various types of beans, including kidney beans and garbanzo beans. Her last stop before checking out is the fruits' section.

She picks up some apples, bananas, blueberries, raspberries, oranges, and avocados. As she is walking up to the register, she sees that she has foods from most of the major groups.

While standing at the register, she notices the candy bars at the checkout stand again. She tries to resist but then picks one up. It is one of her guilty pleasures. Well, she won't get rid of all of her bad habits in one day. After all, she has already made a lot of progress already. She is making a lot of the right decision.

After leaving the stores, she realizes that she has a lot of cooking to do. It will probably take her the rest of the day as she does not have many nutritious items at her home. As she is driving, she notices a Mediterranean restaurant, which she heard is some of the healthiest food around, so she stops in. She buys a falafel salad and pita bread with hummus. All pretty health food that will fill her up for most of the day. She takes her food and starts driving home, excited about trying something new.

When Amanda arrives home, she starts eating her food so that she can begin cooking. She really enjoys the falafel, which is a patty made from chickpeas. It is a very wholesome and delicious protein option. That mixed with the salad is really tasty for her. She cannot finish all of the pita bread and hummus, so she will save it for later. The food really filled her up and she was excited to try a variety of other foods after this. Especially, international foods which also follow the anti-inflammatory diet plan in many ways.

She slowly gets up from the table and starts putting things away. The first thing she realizes is that she has to clear her fridge of all of the junk she had in it before. This will take her a few minutes. She felt bad about getting rid of so much of her favorite food, but it was for her health. After getting rid of the old food, she stocked her fridge and cabinets with the newer items.

She was truly making a lifestyle change for the better. From now on, she would do her best to stick with a vegetarian anti-inflammatory diet. It would be tough, she knew this, but it would be worth it. The fact that she liked the falafel salad gave her inspiration to try new food.

After everything was put away, Amanda began cooking. With all of the ingredients she bought, she began cooking up some new meals that she never tried before. She was mixing the various beans that she bought with the various spices.

Not really knowing what she was doing but still willing to put in the effort. It would be interesting how this would all play into her new life. As Amanda stirred the pot, she was ready to begin the next phase. She was ready for life on the **anti inflammatory diet**.

This is Amanda's story. Maybe it will be similar to yours. Whatever the case, start incorporating the anti-inflammatory diet into your life. It will be worth it, but it won't be an easy task.

Later on, in this Book, we will look at a more in-depth schedule surrounding the anti-inflammatory diet and how it can play a role in your life. You will be able to interact more so and put yourself into that story.

And if you need a reminder: Whole grains, fruits, vegetables, nuts, beans, plant-based proteins and oily fishes (salmon, mackerel, tuna, etc.). Stick to these foods and you will stick to the anti-inflammatory diet.

Chapter 5

Tasty meals

We discussed previously the various foods and food groups that are part of the anti-inflammatory diet. Now, we will put it all together. We will discuss some specific recipes that are both nutritious and delicious. We mentioned before that you may have to sacrifice certain types of food, without sacrificing taste. Let's see if some of these recipes with tickle your fancy.

Now, this is not a cookbook, so we will not be getting into measurements or cooking methods in anyways. There are plenty of cookbooks out there available for that. We will simply name some dishes and discuss how they fit into the **anti-inflammatory diet**. Once again, we are sticking to **vegan** and **vegetarian foods**.

There is a lot of debate still whether or not things like fish and dairy products are part of a **vegetarian diet**. People who also eat fish and dairy products are considered a milder form of a vegetarian. Considering that certain fishes and dairy products are a major part of some **anti-inflammatory diets**, we have included them here. You can certainly leave those out and still have plenty of nutritious foods available to you.

Some people even include poultry like chicken in the vegetarian diet because it is not meat. We do not include it here, sorry. We are dedicated to making the world love vegetarian food. We want you to love it also.

- Freshly grilled salmon is a very tasty and popular dish. Many types of fish, like salmon, have a high omega-3 fatty acid content, which helps to reduce certain inflammatory proteins, like C-reactive proteins, in our bodies. There are many ways to grill salmon and adding extra vegetable can make it even better.

- Next up, we have red beans with brown rice. Here we have a combination of beans and whole grains. Two powerful food groups that play a huge part in the anti-inflammatory process. Beans and whole grains have several anti-inflammatory agents and antioxidants. If you don't like kidney beans, try pinto beans, black beans or garbanzo beans. There are several recipes out there to help you cook these various beans in a nutritious and tasty manner. It is interesting because you can get creative with your cooking. Make sure you are using brown rice. Avoid white rice.

- Sandwiches with whole grain wheat bread, and some onions combined with other vegetables, like leafy greens, tomatoes or avocados. Most of these vegetables and tomatoes have strong anti-inflammatory properties also. Sandwiches with a variety of different vegetables and whole grains are always a good option.

- Sweet potatoes without the salt, accompanied with black pepper, chives, and tomatoes. Avoid frying them in vegetable oil or you will lose the anti-inflammatory properties of sweet potatoes. In fact, bake it and don't fry it. And once again, cut out the salt. Salt is not our friend in this case.

- Arctic Char with Chinese Broccoli and Sweet Potato Puree. This dish is a combination of sweet potatoes, broccoli, balsamic vinegar, and Chinese mustard. You can substitute American mustard for Chinese mustard if needed. Once again, you can make these recipes your own.

- A nice regular baked potato without all of the fix-ins, especially without the sour cream. Remember that a baked potato is healthy, but when you start adding all of the sour cream, salt, and extra ingredients, not so much. It is better to just have French fries.

- A salad with spinach, kale, onions, garbanzo beans, and lettuce. A light salad that is healthy and will help fight inflammation. Can use a little olive oil dressing also. Perhaps even some lemon juice or a vinaigrette dressing.

- Smoked salmon salad with avocado dressing. This salad is loaded with salmon, which as we mentioned before, is filled with omega-3 fatty acid. Green lentils, spinach, red onions parsley and baby capers are also a part of this delicious salad. This is a filling meal that is rich in foods that help fight chronic inflammation. A full meal is rich with protein that would kick that red meat to the curb.

- Black Bean salad with cashew dressing. Black beans, various spices and herbs like garlic, cumin and turmeric, red onions, zucchini, fresh corn, red chili, and coriander leaves.

The cashew dressing is a combination of cashews, olive oil, lemon juice, and water. All of these foods are rich in antioxidants and anti-inflammatory agents. A combination of them together is the ultimate meal to fight chronic inflammation.

- Oat and berry acai bowl. A combination of a purple fruit called acai, a mixture of different berries, chia seeds, milk, and bananas. A rich breakfast meal that fights inflammation. Many of the compounds in colorful fruits like acai are great for fighting inflammation.

- Whole grain oatmeal is another strong breakfast food that fits the anti-inflammatory diet. Add some blueberries, bananas, strawberries, apples and many other fruits you desire. This is much more desirable than breakfast cereals.

- Roasted salmon with potatoes and romaine. A combination of fresh salmon, potatoes, romaine lettuce, lemon juice and paprika cooked in olive oil.

- Grilled Avocado, hummus, and sauerkraut. All great options and a great combination of fight inflammation. Again, give some of these foods a chance. They might surprise you.

- Buckwheat and chia seed porridge. Buckwheat is a great substitution for oats. Especially for those who have gluten sensitivities. A very good whole grain. Chia seeds are a great source of Omega-3 fatty acids.

- Buckwheat berry pancakes are a great breakfast food. It has everything you need to tackle the inflammatory disease. A great addition to the anti-inflammatory diet.

- Smoked salmon, avocado and poached eggs on whole wheat toast. Or, how about a whole wheat bagel. A great option either way.

- Quinoa and Citrus salad-some of these foods speak for themselves and just scream anti-inflammatory diet. We can practically hear this one yelling through the computer right now.

- Lentils, beetroot, and hazelnut salad. An exciting combination of anti-inflammatory foods. A great addition to any meal, night or day. Lentils seem to be taking over the world day by day.

- Roasted Root Vegetables-Maple syrup and fall spices added to a combination of vegetables. Sweet potatoes, beets, parsnips, turnips, and extra virgin olive oil. This is a delectable fall treat, especially with the addition of the maple syrup.

- Steak! Got you excited, didn't I? Yes, you can have a delicious steak!!! It is wholesome and delicious. Our next recipe will excite the heck out of you. It is time for some cauliflower steak with beans and tomatoes. Yes, a wonderful vegan steak option that is full of anti-inflammatory foods. Cauliflower mixed with various herbs and spices combines with beans of your choice and tomatoes. The New York strip or filet minion has nothing on this bad boy. No, we are not being sarcastic! Give it a try. We think you may be impressed.

- Lettuce wraps with smoked trout. Trout is another fatty fish rich in Omega-3 fatty acids used to fight inflammation.

- Zucchini pasta with pesto. Zucchini pasta is a great alternative to regular pasta. Especially for those with gluten sensitivities.

- Roasted cauliflower, fennel, and ginger soup are filled with anti-inflammatory compounds called polyphenols. Ginger adds some needed antioxidants.

- Lentil soup with sweet potatoes-Need we say more. This is a hearty soup and if you eat a bowl, it can be a meal too. But just in case, eat some more sweet potatoes on the side. A great source of fiber and proteins. Great for a cold day while staying inside.

- Salmon with green vegetables and cauliflower-There goes that cauliflower again. Maybe you can add that steak we spoke about earlier to this meal. Brussels sprouts are a good addition to this meal, along with many other green vegetables.

- Vegetable curry with carrots, red peppers and peas and two spoons of turmeric. Oops, maybe we should have put this in the international section instead. Oh well, curry is very popular around the world. Plus, we have already been getting a little international anyways. Don't worry though, there is more to come.

- Vegetarian Chili-Chili is a hearty meal to eat on a cold day. Or really, on any day for that matter. You can still enjoy a good bowl of chili while sticking to the anti-inflammatory diet. This can be a versatile dish filled with various types of beans and vegetables to your liking. Enjoy and make yourself a nice big bowl of vegetarian chili. Don't skimp on the beans and vegetables. A good combination would be kidney beans, red peppers, carrots, and onions.

- Whole wheat waffles with maple syrup, topped with blueberries and raspberries.

- Chickpea, cauliflower salad. Uses the cauliflower and chickpeas as the base, added on are lettuce, onions, and tomatoes. Very delightful salad to fight off inflammatory disease.

- A delicious salad mixed with red bell pepper, spinach, and goat cheese, topped with oregano dressing.

- Here is a good snack option: Chia seed pudding. A combination of chia seeds, coconut milk, maple syrup, pineapple, and raspberries. A great snack to indulge on for sure.

This is just the tip of the iceberg for anti-inflammatory recipes. We could write several types of cookbooks to include all of them. You can use the combination of various foods in so many ways in order to fit your palate.

We just want to emphasize that meal options are not so limited when sticking to an anti-inflammatory diet. Coming up with all these various recipes is quite joyful.

A great game you can make for yourself is to try and top what you make every day. See just how much of an anti-inflammatory meal you can make and judge which one of them would fight anti-inflammatory disease the most. Maybe, you can even hold a contest with your friends and give out prizes.

This will get your friends involved in your healthy lifestyle as well. We want you to and encourage you to be as creative as possible. It is easier to do things with a team anyway.

This is a lot to take in, we know. Just remember though: Whole grains, fruits, vegetable, nuts, beans, plant-based proteins, and oily fishes. Stay on this route with the foods and you will do well. I just want to thank you for making it this far.

It is amazing to be able to share these recipes with you and be an interactive part of your health and wellness. Keep reading for some great information.

Let's mention a few drinks, shall we:

- Green smoothies can be made in various ways. With much of the ingredients having anti-inflammatory effects. A popular recipe includes a combination of almond milk, bananas, mixed berries, flaxseed, and spinach.

- Green Tea has a rich source of a substance called polyphenol, which has been shown to reduce inflammation. Maybe, replace that coffee or Frappuccino in the morning for a nice cup of green tea.

- Coffee-A good cup of coffee is always nice. Coffee is known to have several anti-inflammatory properties. Brew some up today.

- Pineapple and ginger juice-Filled with celery stalks, cucumber, pineapple, apple, lemon, spinach, and ginger.

- Berry Beet Smoothie-Beets, oranges, strawberries, turmeric and ginger. Filled with a lot of fruits as well as herbs and spices that fight inflammation.

- Pure pineapple juice has been shown to reduce pain, inflammation, and swelling. Often times, given to people who are recovering from surgery.

- Apple Cider Vinegar Drink-Apple cider vinegar, lemon, honey, and cayenne pepper. This is really good for an inflamed stomach.

- Pickle juice-This has been a miracle for so many people and their ailments.

- Pineapple smoothie-Now this just sounds plain delicious.

- Fresh juice made from kale, celery, ginger, apples, and lemons. What a great combination of some powerful fruits and vegetable to fight inflammation. This is a great dichotomy of sweet and salty.

- Beets juice mixed with carrots, apples, lemons, and ginger. The powerful taste of beets will likely overtake this juice. Beets are a wonderful vegetable for our health and work well to prevent inflammation in our bodies.

- A vegetable juice with spinach, celery, cucumbers, carrots, and kale. Another great combination of vegetables.

- Infused water with cucumber and lemons. A great infused drink that is refreshing and also healthy.

- Drink a glass of lemon water every morning with some raw honey and apple cider vinegar. You can also infuse some other fruits into the water, like oranges or kiwi.

Just like with food, get creative with your drinks. Take all of the various fruits and vegetables and make your own drinks from them. One day, have a carrot, apple and pineapple juice. The next day, have a blueberry, strawberry and banana smoothie.

It is advised to avoid the premade processed juices that you find at the store. These options are often times no better than sodas.

Try to make your own or at least find a juice place that makes them fresh every day. From now on, make certain commitments to yourself. Instead of reaching for a candy bar, reach for some almonds. Instead of grabbing a processed cheeseburger from a fast-food place, make a salad or eat some fresh salmon.

Go to the Mediterranean restaurant and pick up some hummus. Go after fresh food and not quick food. Make more food at home instead of going out. If you are going out, go to a quality restaurant that serves fresh food. Make a commitment to yourself and to your health, because nobody else will.

There are many more recipes out there that are delicious and flavorful.

You can combine the various food groups in so many ways in order to make appetizing meals. Get creative and make it an art form. Challenge yourself and see just how extreme you can get in making an anti-inflammatory meal. Now, we understand that if you are a heavy meat eater, these meals may sound disappointing at first, but give them a chance.

Unfortunately, red meats do not fare well with this diet. Even so, we are sticking to vegan and vegetarian foods. A combination of these various foods and flavors will provide a rich, hearty meal that may even make you not miss any meat. They will also allow you to have the nutrients you will need that you think will be missing from a nonmeat diet.

We hope that these meal plans have tickled your fancy a little bit and you will give the anti-inflammatory diet a chance. If for nothing else, your own health and well-being. We will get into more delicious foods when we start talking about traveling the world and enjoying the various culinary treats from around the globe. Trust us, there is much more to come.

Chapter 6

Traveling with the Anti-Inflammatory Diet

Sticking to a strict diet should not negatively affect your lifestyle.

In fact, the whole purpose of discussing the anti-inflammatory diet is to help improve your overall lifestyle.

Why do something if it will just make you miserable. We are confident that eating the variety of foods in the anti-inflammatory diet playbook will satisfy your cravings and your palate. Maybe not at first, but it will grow on you. We are sure of this. One of the most fun things about traveling is being able to enjoy the various foods we come across.

These foods are delicious and offer so much variety. It is a great experience to walk around and partake in the various delicacies that exist. Unfortunately, many of these foods may not be the healthiest in their nature.

Most of them may not even come close to following the anti-inflammatory diet.

We would never want you to miss an opportunity to try some new food. Especially, if it is something you won't get a chance to try again. So, definitely indulge a little bit, especially when you are traveling and having the time of your life. Remember though, to not go overboard. Especially if you already have the inflammatory disease.

The level at which you have inflammation also greatly affects when and how much you can indulge. Definitely take this into account. No amount of fun is worth risking your health like that. You know yourself better than anyone else. We do not want you to become severely ill when you are traveling. Nothing could put a bigger damper on your world tour than this. We don't want you to end up in a hospital bed when you should be seeing the sites.

That being said, we want you to be able to travel, enjoy healthy meals and also get a taste of the distinct dishes without cheating on your diet. For this reason, we will discuss several culinary favorites from various regions around the world that will keep you devoted to the anti-inflammatory diet.

We will break this down place by place. We will continue with vegan and vegetarian options.

We hope that we have done a good job with that so far, so we will keep going with this. The world is ours for the taking, so let's get to traveling and see where we end up.

Mediterranean:

Ok, we will begin right here. This seems to be the Mecca of the anti-inflammatory diets. This makes a lot of sense as the majority if not all, foods and food groups that are considered part of the anti-inflammatory diet are also in the Mediterranean diet. Mediterranean food has a lot of influence from Europe, Eastern Europe and the Middle East based on its geographical location. Go to an authentic Mediterranean restaurant and you will see for yourself. A solid Mediterranean diet will give you energy and rarely ever make you feel bloated, ill or tired. The diet and region incorporate so much great food that is quite delicious. The vegetarian foods in this diet are flavorful to the point that you will not be missing that steak or cheeseburger. At least not for a while. And remember, there is always that cauliflower steak. Here are some popular meals included in the diet. Again, this is not a cookbook, so we will not be discussing specific measurements or food prepping processes.

- Classic Greek Salad-A strong stable that is part of Mediterranean cuisine. A combination of cucumbers, tomatoes, olives, red onions, feta, and Greek dressing make for a delicious treat. A Mediterranean salad is quite filling, but not overbearing. A nice whole wheat pita bread on the side is a great addition. You can eat this as an appetizer, but it will probably work as a full meal too.

- Spicy Escarole with Garlic-Escarole is a leafy green, somewhat bitter vegetable. By itself, it may not be that appetizing, but combined with other ingredients, it can become a tasty treat. This meal is a combination of the leafy green vegetable with garlic, olive oil, and red pepper flakes. It is light. Can be used as an appetizer or main course, depending on how hungry you are. Whatever the case, a great addition to the anti-inflammatory diet.

- Eggplant with yogurt and dill-This is a common side dish of the region. Roasted eggplant, garlic, shallots, and walnuts tossed with yogurt and fresh dill. A shallot is a type of onion and onions are a great addition to the diet. You will see a lot of dishes with eggplant in the Mediterranean diet. A very powerful food in fighting inflammation. Help kick inflammatory disease to the burb.

- Broccoli Rabe with Cherry Peppers-Not to be confused with regular broccoli, broccoli rabe is a green leafy vegetable that is part of the turnip family. The edible parts are the leaves, bulbs, and stem. In this particular dish, the bitter vegetable is mellowed out by adding spicy cherry peppers, garlic, and some rich parmesan cheese.

- Cauliflower Couscous-Couscous tossed with sautéed cauliflower and shallots. Cinnamon and dates are added for natural sweetness. Cauliflower is a vegetable that is a strong addition to the anti-inflammatory diet. It is also big in the Mediterranean diet. Cinnamon is also a great spice to add to the anti-inflammatory diet.

- Tabbouleh-An herb lover's dream come true. This is a salad that usually has a bulgur base, however, other things like quinoa and rice. Whatever the base, it is mixed with fresh tomatoes, onions, parsley, mint, and a tangy lemon vinaigrette. People are often generous with the mint and parsley to make it fresher and more flavorful. Bulgur is a cereal food made from several different wheat spices. Tabbouleh can be eaten by itself, or even with some pita bread.

- Pepper and Peanut Broccoli Stir-fry-Combination of red pepper, red chili flakes, Broccoli florets and chopped, roasted and unsalted peanuts.

- Bulgur Salad-Bulgur is a traditional whole grain. This salad is a combination of bulgur, cucumber olives, and dill.

- Falafel pita with lettuce, tomatoes, onions, and peppers. Falafel is a very popular protein in this type of diet, often replacing chicken or beef. It is a patty made from chickpeas. You can also have this as a delicious salad. What are you waiting for?

- Eggplant, lentils, and peppers cooked in olive oil. Yep, remember that olive oil, or avocado oil.

- Baba Ghanoush-Mixed eggplant, tahini made from sesame seeds, olive oil, and various seasonings. A very popular appetizer of the region.

- You can also just enjoy a good snack like some hummus and pita bread, or a nice yogurt topped with berries.

- Greek yogurt with strawberries and oats.

- A tuna salad dressed in olive oil.

- Mediterranean Pizza. A delicious pizza without all of the healthy fat. It is topped with cheese, vegetables, and olive. The crust is made of whole wheat.

- Egg white omelet with veggies and olives.

- Yogurt with sliced fruits and nuts.

- Broiled Salmon served with brown rice and vegetables.

- If you want to add cheese, choose feta cheese.

- The drink of choice for sticking to a Mediterranean diet is good old-fashioned water. Avoid all of those sugary juices.

There are so many recipes in the Mediterranean diet that would kick inflammatory disease to the curb. Unfortunately, we cannot mention all of them, because that would take a whole other book. Actually, maybe several since the recipes are so abundant. Just know that if you're following the Mediterranean diet, you are probably on the right track.

The best thing about the Mediterranean diet is that it is filling, but you will not feel heavy. You will probably never feel bloated. Great for the digestive tract. Your gut will be very happy with you. Mediterranean food consists of a strong combination of whole grains, fruits vegetables, beans, nuts, and various spices. It is indeed an anti-inflammatory diet eaters dream.

India:

If Mediterranean food is the ultimate anti-inflammatory diet, Indian food may just come in as a close second. Indian food often promotes a strongly vegetarian diet mixed with an abundance of herbs, spices, vegetables, beans, whole wheat, and lentils. The protein content is strong with Indian food. The food also promotes a high fiber diet, which has also been known to fight inflammation. Of course, Indian food is known for its spice level. Many people outside of the subcontinent can barely tolerate it. So, if you're asking someone to prepare you a dish, take this into account. While various spices can be very healthy for you, it does you no good if you can't eat it anyway. Take in the spices at your own risk and your own tolerance level. That being said, it will be difficult to find culinary options that are more flavorful than Indian food. Let's get our spice on.

- Before we start with specific meals, here are some herbs and spices that are powerful anti-inflammatories which are common in India: Bay leaves, black pepper, cardamom, and cloves. Along with some of their anti-inflammatory properties, these herbs and spices are used for a lot of ailments in general, like pain and the common cold on the Indian Subcontinent.

- Chole-This is a very popular dish made from chickpeas. It is combined with various herbs and spices like cumin, coriander, red pepper and bay leaves. Different regions of the country have different styles of cooking. Also, some people like to add various vegetables like tomatoes and onions. The chole, or chickpeas, are usually prepared ahead time in a slow cooker, or for a faster approach, pressure cooker.

- Rajma-A very popular Indian dish indeed. This is made with kidney beans combined with various spices to give it its taste, color, and texture. This is truly a hearty dish to indulge on. This is one of the most popular beans around.

- Various Dals-Dals are basically lentil-based dishes. There are many types of lentils that can be used and various different spices as well. For example, Chana dal is split chickpeas. These various lentils and spices can combine to make an abundance of different lentil soups that are fully capable of fighting inflammation. Here are some that can be found in most Indian stores and even international sections of many grocery stores: Udad dal, channa dal, masoor dal, moong dal. These are just a few. All of them are healthy options for an anti-inflammatory diet.

Are you hungry? Well, let's keep going.

- Curry-Curry seems to be one of the most well-known Indian dishes. Curry powder is a combination of various spices, including, coriander, cumin, and turmeric. It often comes in a premixed pouch, but you can certainly make your own. We have mentioned turmeric before because it is a spice that is very popular and effective in fighting chronic inflammation. Some healers have even used it on open wounds for quicker healing.

- Aloo-Mater-This dish is pretty much what is reads, Aloo=Peas, Mater=Peas. This combination of potatoes, peas and various spices is a strong antioxidant with anti-inflammatory properties.

- Goby-aloo-Another popular dish. This is a combination of Goby, which is cauliflower and aloo, which are potatoes. Also, mixed with various spices.

- Bhindi-This is one of the most popular dishes in India. It is loved by many for its taste, heralded at the same time for its extreme health benefits. It is a vegetable that is popular in many parts of the world. It is simply known as okra. Okra has a high number of antioxidants and has been known to have anti-inflammatory effects also. The uniqueness of Indian okra is how it is cooked. It is cut up and stir-fried with cumin powder, coriander powder, turmeric, red chili, and mango powder. The result is a tasty treat that is also very healthy. People can add salt as they please, but it must be limited for health reason. In addition to the okra itself, the combination of various spices adds to the health benefits.

- Chaat-Cooked potato patty with peas (called aloo tikkis), on the side, there is yogurt, chickpeas, the sauce made from cilantro, a sauce made from tamarind, and various spices added on. A delicious food often served as a portion of popular street food on street side carts called davas.

- Samosas-There particular dishes are fried, so you just have to be careful how you fry them. They can also be baked in some cases. An outer, tortilla-like covering is shaped in a triangular fashion and filled with potatoes, peas, and various spices like cumin, coriander, and red pepper. Often eaten with a sauce made from tamarind.

- Roti-This is a very common tortilla in India. It is made from whole wheat flour and served with almost any meal.

In this portion, we will talk about some common Indian dishes, known as raitas. She is a combination of milk, plain yogurt, and some spices. There are some different kinds of raitas and we will discuss those here.

- Cucumber Raita-This is the base mixture of the milk and plain yogurt. Added in are spices like cumin and coriander. To top it off, we add grated cucumber and voila. We have a delicious and nutritious dish.

- Boondi Raita-This is made in a similar fashion as the cucumber raita. However, instead of cucumber, we added boondi, which is basically fried and puffed chickpea balls.

See a pattern here? A lot of Indian foods are filled with various herbs and spices which are delicious and healthy all at the same time. Most of these meals are not eaten alone.

They are usually eaten with rice, preferably brown rice if you're sticking the diet or various types of tortillas. The most common types in India are called roti, paratha, and naan.

The best option of the three is definitely roti. Most Indian food has high fiber and high protein content. You may not even miss meat while you're indulging in some of these culinary delights.

Most of the essential herbs and spices that are included in the anti-inflammatory diet are also part of the Indian food diet. There is some confusion now. Is the Mediterranean diet or the Indian diet more anti-inflammatory friendly?

They both seem pretty neck and neck as far as the ingredients go. This may just become an argument for the ages. Maybe we can have a blind study done some day. Whatever route you go, you will have a tasty, healthy meal.

Before we go to the next region, we just want to mention Indian Chai. Indian chai is brewed with strong leaves and the addition of ginger, cardamom, cloves and various other spices based on preference make it a strong anti-inflammatory drink. Indian chai is drunken commonly with many meals, including breakfast and dinner. It is to India what coffee is to the rest of the worlds.

Mexican/Hispanic Food/Latin:

Since Latin America covers so many regions, we will discuss them in one section. Even though food is unique in a lot of areas. We will try to specify if a particular food is found in only a specific area. Take this into account though, a lot of restaurants will add a lot of unnecessary salt and fat to certain dishes.

Going to a local fast food Mexican place may not be the best option. These foods are good, assuming fresh and wholesome ingredients are being used.

- Guacamole and Veggies-Guacamole are made from avocados, which are packed with antioxidants and anti-inflammatory agents. Watch out for those salty chips that you may want to eat with it.

- Vegetarian Burrito-When getting a vegetarian burrito, just make sure to ask for the right ingredients. Ask for black beans and not refried beans. Choose brown rice over white rice. Ask for the salsa and not the sour cream. Finally, ask for some extra vegetables with your burrito. Doing all this will give you a healthy veggie burrito to help combat inflammatory disease.

- Soft tortilla tacos with black beans, lettuce, and tomatoes. Another great option to indulge on.

- Vegetarian Tortilla Soup-Tomato, garlic and onion broth mixed that submerged with some delicious tortillas. You can also add some black beans. Most people eat this with chicken, but we are leaving that out in order to stick to a vegetarian diet. Sorry, don't get mad at us.

- Red or black bean rice is also a healthy option. Make sure to stay away from refried beans.

- Here is a fun one. How about brown rice, with black beans, and guacamole.

- Chilled Red Bell Pepper and Habanero Soup-A combination of various spice, garlic, tomatoes, habanero, sweet onion bell peppers, and olive oil. Once again, a combination of so many foods that fight inflammation.

- This is something we want to mention here because it is much localized to a region. We have spoken extensively about nuts and their anti-inflammatory properties. There are many different types of nuts that fit in these parameters. One thing we have not mentioned yet are Brazil nuts. Since they are very local to Brazil, Bolivia, and Peru, we will mention them here. Brazil nuts have many health benefits, including reducing inflammation. These nuts are very energy dense and nutritious. Too bad they are not everywhere. That would probably kill their uniqueness though.

- One more thing we will mention here is a fruit called lucuma. It is a Latino superfood. It looks like an avocado from the outside has the texture of sweet potato and has a sweet caramel like taste. It originated in Peru. We are mentioning here due to its origin and just wanted to make you aware of it. This fruit is filled with antioxidants and has many health benefits, possibly even anti-inflammatory effects.

We just want to preclude the following with an explanation. The next few dishes we are about to describe are popular and even originated in Spain. Based on its Geography, Spain is part of the Mediterranean, so it may be more fitting to have it in that section. The food is also more familiar to that region. However, Spain is also a Spanish speaking country, so we have included it here in this section. Spain also has several distinct dishes. We may be splitting some hairs here, but just wanted to provide an explanation and the method to our madness. That being said, here are some popular Spanish dishes.

- Gazpacho-This is most commonly found in Spain and has many different variations. It is a tomato soup that is served cold, mixed with onions, garlic, olive oil and a number of local vegetables and spices. This is a popular treat on a hot summer day.

- Pisto Manchego-This is Spanish ratatouille which originates from La Mancha. It is a stew that is made from eggplants, tomatoes, onions, squash, and red peppers. Add some whole wheat bread and you've got a full meal for dinner time.

- Chickpea Salad-A very popular salad in Spain. Chickpeas are great for fighting anti-inflammatory disease and also a great source of protein for vegetarians.

- Spanish Rice-Tomatoes, olive oil, minced garlic, brown rice, with spices like chili powder, turmeric, and cumin. A very popular and healthy dish from the region.

- Spinach and Chickpeas-This dish is very popular in southern Spain. The spinach and chickpeas are accentuated by cumin, paprika, and garlic.

- Marinated Carrots-There is a Spanish word for these, but we can just call them marinated carrots. These are not your average carrots. They are marinated in garlic, oregano, apple cider vinegar, and various other spices. Also, very popular in Southern Spain. Truly, and anti-inflammatory diet lover's dream.

- Smoked Almond Romesco-A combination of tomatoes, peppers, almonds, bread, oil, vinegar, garlic, paprika, and honey.

Asian Food:

Here, we will talk about Asian food. Typically, we think of the greasy chow mein noodles and wonder how that can be healthy. Well, a lot of the food local to the region is not like this. Travel around and see for yourself. For this section, we will include all Asian countries as each separate one would create a lot of sections. Considering this Book, we have altered some of the recipes too to make them more anti-inflammatory diet friendly.

- Panang Curry with Vegetables-This is a rich, creamy, spicy, peanut coconut sauce mixed with various vegetables. You can get creative with the vegetables. Some options include red bell peppers and carrots. You can also add tofu for some extra protein. This is a popular Thai curry.

- Our next dish is roasted brussels sprouts and crispy bakes tofu with honey sesame glaze. This is a mouthful. Probably not something you're going to find on a take-out menu either. The brussels sprouts are roasted and put over brown rice with baked tofu added. The top is drizzled with a honey-sesame glaze.

- Spicy Kale and coconut fried rice-Great recipe with a lot of healthy Asian flavors.

- Vegetarian Lettuce Wrap-If you have gone to an Asian restaurant, you may have seen or had these. They are a pretty popular appetizer and maybe even a meal. This is a lettuce leaf topped with sesame-soy soba noodles and quick-pickled veggies. You can also add some edamame hummus. A great addition to any meal.

- Crunchy Thai Peanut Quinoa Salad-This is a combination of quinoa, carrots, cabbage, green onions, snow peas, and cilantro. This is all tossed together in a tasty peanut sauce. Quinoa is also a good source of protein.

- Peanut Slaw with Soba Noodles-This is a colorful slaw with soba noodles and tossed in sesame-ginger peanut sauce. Soba noodles are made from buckwheat. We'll talk some more about Soba noodle recipes.

- Soba Noodles with Miso-Roasted Tomatoes-The cherry tomatoes are roasted in miso, ginger, sesame, lime juice, and honey. All mixed together with the soba noodles.

- Soba with Miso-Glazed Eggplant-Japanese eggplant is good to use with this dish as it is a little sweeter. Mixed with green beans, sesame oil, miso paste, garlic, fresh ginger, spinach, and sliced green onions. All mixed together with the Soba noodles. Everything in this dish is a strong addition to the anti-inflammatory diet.

- Sesame Soba Noodles-Soba Noodles cooked with similar ingredients as before, but with the addition of a hard-boiled egg.

- Are you a fan of sushi? You can still have it. Just substitute white rice for brown rice. Try a salmon and avocado roll.

- Try some veggie sushi options too. They are plentiful.

- Miso soup, common in most Japanese restaurants. Great option as an anti-inflammatory food.

Italian:

Now things are going to start getting fun. Remember all of those pizza parties you had growing up. Remember that giant lasagna your grandmother made for you. Remember all of those greasy and thick breadsticks. Remember that oily garlic bread. All of that was healthy for you right. I mean, it is Italian food and real Italian food is light and healthy and very nutritious. So, go done to the pizza place and order that four-cheese pizza. The order that fully loaded meat pizza with all of the fixes in. And while you are at it, order that extra large garlic bread with extra marinara sauce. It is healthy for you after all. Of course, none of what we said here is true at all.

It is very true and authentic Italian food made in the region it is from is healthy. It actually follows the Mediterranean diet model, which is heralded as one of the healthiest diets in the world. Italian people know how to eat. They use fresh and flavorful ingredients. So, when you go to that pizza place down the road from you, know that you're not eating authentic, healthy Italian food. The food may be good, but it is anything but healthy. That being said, since authentic Italian does follow that Mediterranean model, it can definitely fit in the lines of an anti-inflammatory diet. People in Italy are some of the healthiest people in the world. Let's talk about some meal and have some tasty Italian food.

- Pasta-Yes, good old-fashioned pasta. Now, we have been heralding against pasta throughout much of this Book. However, cooking it in the methods used in Italy can create a healthy, fulfilling dish. First of all, cook your pasta al dente, meaning a little firm. This will reduce the glycemic index and reduce carbohydrate absorption. Also, though it is not typically Italian, you can substitute in Whole grain pasta instead. You can cook this pasta with olive oil, tomatoes, and garlic. This is a tasty pasta dish from the looks of it. And much healthier than the kind you find other places.

- Spaghetti with garlic sauce-Simple spaghetti or whole wheat spaghetti mixed with bits of fresh garlic. You won't be ashamed of having garlic breath when you're in Italy. It is a common staple in this part of the world. It also has a lot of health benefits.

- Garlic-Rosemary Mushrooms-Mushrooms are an amazing source of protein. Plus, garlic and rosemary are two wonderful herbs that will fight hard against inflammatory disease. We are getting quite far here in our Italian dishes. Let's keep going, shall we?

- Hasselback Tomato Caprese Salad-Whole tomatoes, cut, with layered in fresh Mozzarella cheese, basil and a drizzle of balsamic. This is a very tasty appetizer.

- Eggplant Parmesan-This dish is baked, and not fried. Rich eggplant provides some essential protein.

- Lemon Herb Salmon with Caponata and Farro-This is a fresh salmon piece, delicious in every way. Topped with herbs and served with brown rice and various vegetables.

- Spaghetti with Broccoli Pesto-A great vegetarian pasta recipe. Spaghetti al dente or whole grain spaghetti mixed with broccoli, pesto sauce, basil, and Parmigiano-Reggiano. The last one is a hard, granular cheese, which you can leave out if you'd like.

- Whole wheat pizza-It's important to use a base, or crust with whole wheat or whole grain. Most crusts made in Italy are thin, so they are not as heavy. Top this lightly with fresh mozzarella cheese, fresh tomatoes and basil. Delicious pizza that is also very light.

There may now be a three-way tie for healthiest food options with the Mediterranean, Indian and Italian food. What if you are able to have Mediterranean food for breakfast, Indian food for lunch and Italian food for dinner?

Sounds like a great day to me. We hope that we were able to introduce you to come delicious and healthy Italian dishes. See, Italian food does not have to be fattening and rich with refined carbohydrates.

If you use fresh ingredients that are light and healthy, you will get a nutritious meal that you will love. Food is definitely an important staple in Italian culture, and we are very glad to have introduced you to so many healthy meals from that region.

We hope this will satisfy your taste buds. Remember also, to get creative. Think about the various ingredients that you may have used over the years that are common in Italy. Some of these include oregano, parsley, basil, olive oil, and garlic.

Think of your own creative recipes and meal plans that will satisfy the anti-inflammatory diet. We have spoken in-depth about the various food groups involved in the specific diet. Use this information to help you create your own works of art. Good luck with creating delicious meal plans that are also healthy. I think there are enough meal plans in this book alone to last you a whole year. It is amazing how many dishes can be made from all of the various foods and we are just barely scratching the surface.

We are glad you were able to take this little trip around the world with us. Thank you so much for doing so. We had a blast discussing various meals from around the globe that will fit into the anti-inflammatory diet. We got a little hungry writing this chapter.

It was amazing learning about all of these amazing foods that exist in the world. The writers of a book often learn just as much as the readers. As you can see, the anti-inflammatory diet is a worldwide phenomenon, whether the world realizes it or not. Even if certain recipes do not go by the name of the anti-inflammatory diet, the food choices they use certainly do.

Once again, if you are a heavy meat eater, you may have been disappointed in this chapter a little bit. There is certainly a lot of great food in the world that includes meat.

We would love for you to learn about them. However, for this book, we are still sticking to vegan and vegetarian foods. No matter how tempting some meal plans may look.

There may be a lot of cross-over from one region to another, especially if those regions are in close proximity. Our hope is that in this chapter, we were able to cover most of the major areas in the world and give you a good understanding of the anti-inflammatory diet as it relates to culinary treats from around the globe.

We thank you for joining us on this journey.

Chapter 7

Setting Up A Schedule: Taking Action

Now we have the knowledge, time to put in the work. We have discussed the anti-inflammatory diet in great detail.

But, here's the deal, none of this information provided will mean anything if you do nothing with it. Period! Knowledge with action is ultimately meaningless.

We don't say that to be mean, just to be truthful. If you are ready to move forward with the diet plan, then let's take action and start incorporating it into your life. The best way to do so is by making your own personal schedule.

With this schedule, we will create lists of specific foods and meals you can eat to satisfy the diet. Of course, this does mean anything is unchangeable. This can simply be a guideline.

Let's get started by producing a weeklong schedule to give us an idea of how it can work. We will base this on a regular Sunday to Saturday schedule. Let's bring all of this full-circle and start incorporating it into your life. This is just a sample schedule. Obviously, you will make your own as you see fit. It is your schedule after all. Once again, this is just a guideline. Use it as inspiration, but you don't have to follow it to a T. We will move along with the assumption that you are just starting the anti-inflammatory diet. How about we call this a story? A week in the life of you.

Sunday:

The start of the week for most people. This is the day that sets up the rest of the week and how it will go.

You commonly hear people say that Sunday should set the tone for the rest of the six days.

This is very true and the diet you create will set up your cravings for the week to come. Start your Sunday off with some hearty meals. Start your week off the right way and kick off your anti-inflammatory diet in high fashion. What happened up to this point is history. Today, we start something new. Let's begin, shall we?

- Start the morning with a good morning. First things first, you probably have not drunken anything all night. Start off your day by getting hydrated. Drink a nice tall glass of lemon water. You can also add some apple cider vinegar if you please. A cup of green tea is a great thing to have for some energy and nutrients. A piece of fruit like a banana or apple and then a bowl of oatmeal with raw honey and some blueberries. Add some raisins to the top of that. A light, but hearty breakfast.

- For a mid-morning snack, indulge in some blueberries and almonds. A filling snack that will provide protein and antioxidants. Remember also, to keep hydrated with some water. Always keep some water with you. It is an important addition to any anti-inflammatory diet.

- For lunch, have a walnut salad with cranberries and some vinaigrette dressing. In the afternoon is where tiredness usually kicks in. People will often make this worse by eating a greasy meal at lunch. Lethargy will really start setting in at this point and there is still so much of the day left. Instead, have a meal that's filling and energizing all at the same time. A walnut salad will definitely fill you up, but not weigh you down. Compliment this with a glass of freshly squeezed orange juice. A piece of fruit like an apple can also be included.

- For a late afternoon snack, enjoy something like a banana or other favorite fruit. A late afternoon snack is important in order to keep up your energy levels and keep up your metabolism. Drink another glass of water while you are at it. This will keep you going until dinner time.

- For dinner, eat at least a couple of hours before bed. Perhaps a nice grilled salmon with some vegetables are a good option. Some carrots, celery, and potatoes will make it a filling and healthy meal. You will end your day feeling satiated, but not bloated. The main goal is to not feel awful after eating it. Plus, you definitely do not want to feel overly full right before bedtime.

- You may still be a little active after dinner, depending on your schedule. It is good to eat a light snack prior to bedtime. Maybe a nice cup of Greek yogurt will do you good. Having a light, healthy snack before bedtime will keep you from getting hungry overnight. It will also keep your blood sugars from fluctuating too much.

Sunday was a good day for our diets and our palates. We really stuck to the anti-inflammatory diet in this case. This was a great initial first step. It is just the first day and we have a long way to go. Remember though our week is just kicking off, so let's keep moving and let's stay focused.

Monday:

If you are like most people, Monday is the start of the work week for you. Of course, there are several non-regular schedules that are becoming more and more common. For this schedule, we will assume you have a 9-5, Monday-Friday work week. Our busy schedules during the week filled with work, family, hobbies and more can make it seem impossible to stick to a routine diet. It can be done though. It is time to get our Monday started and begin tackling the workweek.

- Rise up early for your day so you have time to make yourself a good breakfast before work. It is also advised that you prepare what you can the night before, to save you some time in the morning. For this morning, we will have a bowl of fruit, walnuts, Egg whites with some turmeric, and a glass of fresh apple juice. Start your workday off with some fresh food and be ready to attack whatever comes your way. Not attack in the literal sense. Of course, before you eat this, get hydrated with a nice glass of lemon water. Still, have that caffeine craving, make yourself another cup of green tea. Regular coffee works too, but green tea is usually a healthier option.

- You are having a busy Monday morning coming back from the weekend. You are feeling more energized than you usually do. The first couple of hours go by quickly. For a mid-morning snack, get a nice blueberry smoothie from the juice place in the lobby of your work. If you have one of course. If not, improvise with something else. Just have something light and refreshing. Avoid that vending machine though, it's evil.

- The afternoon rush is hitting at work. People are coming to you for all sorts of things that need to get done. Another couple of hours passes by without a breeze. For lunch, we can go to the Mediterranean. How about a large Greek salad? Greek salads usually come with a lot of fix-ins. It will be a satisfying lunch and you really won't need anything else, except maybe a glass of water. If you're craving a sweeter drink, consider some type of yogurt drink. Keep it Mediterranean for now.

- The workday is going along well after your healthy lunch. You still feel energized and ready to go. However, it is late afternoon again and you are probably hungry once more. It is time for the afternoon snack and luckily, you have something on you. It is a banana. After eating it, you are ready to finish out your day. Your Monday at work ends well. You were busy, but you stuck to your diet plan. Good for you.

- When you arrive home, it is time for dinner. What will you have though? There are so many options. Let's stick to the Mediterranean diet. It has been the theme for today. How about some hummus with pita bread, a bulgur salad and some type of fresh juice? Perhaps pineapple juice will compliment everything. This is a delicious meal and you feel great afterward. Time to relax and get some things prepared for tomorrow.

- For a late-night snack, let's grab a handful of walnuts. Those are always quite delicious and filled with Omega-3 fatty acids, which are needed to fight inflammation. Shortly after this, it is time for bed. Congratulations! That is day number two down and we are on a roll!

Our Monday has been successful. We had a full workday, but we stuck to our diet and were able to eat multiple types of food. Our week is going pretty well so far. We can lay in bed at night knowing that we ate well, we feel good and don't have excessing heartburn. Like we did so many times in the past. Feel proud of yourself. You deserve it.

Tuesday:

We are onto the third day of our week and we are feeling pretty good. So far, it has been easy sticking to our diet plan. We sleep really well at night. We feel good during the day. We are waking up in less pain and discomfort and we have accomplished so much already. It has been a blast.

- Now for breakfast, let's change things up a little bit. We will still start off our day with a nice tall glass of lemon water. We will drink a green smoothie, which is very filling. Plus, we will eat a banana. Let's also have something different from green tea. How about a nice cup of turmeric tea? We will try that this morning. Once again, you are feeling energized. You are ready to take on another workday. You arrive at work and all of your friends notice a kick in your step. You're boss notices this too.

- After completing all of your morning tasks, you are feeling hungry for a snack. Luckily, you have a container of strawberries in your lunch bag, so you indulge in some of those. The freshness of those strawberries gives you another kick in your step. You continue to feel good. The morning continues to pass by quickly and you remain busy and focused.

- For lunch, you kind of feel like going out. You want to stick to your diet plan though. Never worry though because down the street, is an excellent gourmet sandwich shop. When you arrive there, you notice that they have a veggie sandwich that uses a black bean patty. This is interesting, so let's get that. With the sandwich, we can add some lettuce, tomatoes, red onions, vinegar, red pepper, black pepper, and olives. We will leave out the salt, but the sandwich still tastes pretty good. It has been easy to stay on track with the food so far. This lunch was exceptional. Of course, let's wash it down with some water. Afterward, you go back to work.

- You get back to work after lunch and after a couple of hours, you get hungry again. You look in your bag to see what you have available and find some cut up oranges. A good healthy snack to help you finish out the workday. The rest of the afternoon foes off well. You did have some fires to put out, but because of the extra energy you have been having, it is easy for you to do so.

- After you go home, you are ready to have some dinner. You get a call though. It is a friend asking you to come to a party he is having. You have not seen this friend in weeks, so you really want to see him. But you don't want to mess up your diet. You decide to go through. It's important to see your friend. When you get there, there is nothing really for you to eat that satisfies the anti-inflammatory diet. It is not your friend's fault though because he doesn't know about your diet. You decide to suck it up and see what they have. Mostly, it is greasy food like chicken wings and pizza. There is a small veggie tray you can eat from, so that's something. You take a few bites, but it certainly does not fill you up. You look around for more food, but there is nothing else you see. You will still be at the party for another hour at least, so you really want to eat. You also don't want to seem rude to your friend. Well, there is no other choice at this point. You are at a party and want to enjoy time with your friend. I guess we can cheat on the diet a little bit. Have a slice of pizza and some chicken wings. The last few days have been good so celebrate a little bit. Instead of soda though, you just have plain water. You don't want to drink that sugary drink that will provide no nutritional value. You have a fun time for the rest of the party.

- When you get home, it's still a couple of hours until you go to bed. You decide a good snack to have are some carrot sticks. There taste pretty good with a little bit of lime squirted on them. You also decide to drink some lemon water with a touch of apple cider vinegar. This has always done wonders for your acid reflux, which just might occur because of the pizza. You had a couple of more slices than you wanted to. It's ok though. Tomorrow is another day.

You end the night feeling a little bad, but overall, it was a good day. Plus, you got to see your friend and spend some time with them. It is important to maintain a good lifestyle while eating well too. We are a total of three days into the week and things are going pretty well. It's time to call it a night and get ready for the next day. Good job getting through another day. Let's keep moving.

Wednesday:

You wake up on Wednesday morning and are feeling pretty good. A little bit tired because you did not sleep as well because of the greasy food you ate at night. It's ok though to indulge occasionally. Today is a new day. We shall see how it goes.

- At the start of the morning, you are feeling extra thirsty, so you make a taller glass of lemon water. It tastes pretty refreshing for the most part. For breakfast, you have another bowl of oatmeal topped with raisins, blueberries, raw honey and bananas. Also, you go back to drinking your green tea. The turmeric tea did not taste as good. It is okay though because not everything will satisfy your palate. You also have a cup of fresh yogurt with strawberries. A healthy and filling breakfast to start your Wednesday. It's time to make up from yesterday and get this day going right.

- After arriving at work, things are quite busy and hectic. It is okay because you have everything under control. You also have the energy to handle everything thrown at you. It's been so busy that you almost forgot your midmorning snack. Lucky for you though, there are some walnuts in your desk that you can have. They taste quite good and they give you the energy you need until lunch time. You are able to tackle the rest of the morning with ease. Your boss appreciates your hard work.

- Lunchtime comes around and you made yourself a sandwich with whole wheat bread, lettuce, tomatoes, red onions, and pickles. You are ready to indulge until your coworkers interrupt you. They want you to come to have lunch with them.

You really don't want to because you already cheated on your diet the night before. However, you realize they are going to have lunch at an Indian restaurant. It will be pretty easy to stick to your diet there and you remember that this particular place makes their food pretty fresh. You decide to go ahead and eat there. When you arrive, you scope out what they have. All of it looks pretty good, but you stick to the vegetarian portions. You fill up your plate with kidney beans, chickpeas, lentil soup, and potatoes. You also grab some whole wheat tortillas. This will be quite a satisfying meal indeed. For a drink, you just get some water. When you start eating the spicy food, you realize that water may not be sufficient enough to take away the burning sensation in your mouth. They have healthy yogurt drinks on the menu, so you decide to get one. It tastes sour, but pretty good overall with the meal. It was a nice lunch and you feel pretty good afterward. You stuck to your diet and spent time with your coworkers. After this lunch, everyone goes back to work to continue the day.

- When you get back to work, you immediately begin on your tasks that need to be completed for that day. There is much to do but you can handle it. When late afternoon hits, it is time for your snack. Since you have built it into your routine, your body almost knows by itself when this time comes. You are too full still for that sandwich you made, instead, there is a container of raspberries in your bag. You eat these and feel satisfied. You are able to finish out the rest of your day with ease. It is finally time to finally go home and rest.

- When you get home, you wonder about dinner. You had a fairly big lunch and are still pretty full. However, you decide to make some tabbouleh and eat some whole wheat pita bread. This is a light and refreshing meal. It is still pretty early, so you decide to go to the gym. There are some extra calories to burn off today. Indian and Mediterranean food. A pretty good combination to satisfy the anti-inflammatory diet.

- After the gym, you sit and watch some television for a while. Before retiring to bed, you eat a nice light snack. There is still some Greek yogurt left over.

This is your perfect late-night snack, especially when you add some blueberries. After eating this, you go to bed and end your day. There was a wide variety of food that you ate on this day and it all satisfied the anti-inflammatory diet plan.

We are officially past the halfway point of the week and things are going well. In fact, they are going pretty great. A lot of your eating habits are starting to fit into your routine by this point. It is important though, to not let temptation get to you. Also, it is important to do your research when determining what food is best for you. It can be tedious and exhausting, but it will be worth it because you will feel much better. You probably have already noticed the difference in your energy levels by sticking with the anti-inflammatory diet. Let's keep going and finish the rest of the week strong. You are doing great so far!

Thursday:

Okay, it is now the fifth day of the week. You get up early once more. You notice that by this day, getting up earlier is much easier than it was before. It is a combination of training your body and also having more energy from good food. Not only does a good diet help you function better during the day, but it also helps you have a more relaxing sleep at night. A proper diet works wonders for your ability to function, as you may have noticed already. It is Thursday already. This week is going by quite fast. Let's see how it goes.

- Once again, you start your day by drinking a fresh glass of lemon water. This drink always satisfies your thirst and gives you some energy first thing in the morning. You decide this morning that you want some extra protein. You make some egg white with tomatoes, green peppers, crushed black pepper, and turmeric. For a side, you eat a bowl of roasted almonds. You also drink a fresh green smoothie. You're not really craving the green tea today. Of course, the green smoothie is quite filling, so you are not able to finish it all at once. No worries though, because you can put it into a to-go cup. After this, you are ready to start your day. You head out your front and start heading to work.

- When you arrive at work, things are extra busy, so you immediately have to jump into action. There are many fires to put out today. Luckily, the extra protein is kicking in to help you keep moving. You are a little late due to the hecticness of the day. However, you still make time for your midmorning snack. You decide to go to the refrigerator and grab that green smoothie you made in the morning. It still tastes pretty good and gives you the strength to keep moving. The last couple of hours before lunch are brutal. You never really get a chance to sit down. Your mind and body are moving constantly. Good thing you had that extra protein in the morning.

- Come lunchtime, you are ready to eat again. Just so it didn't go to waste, you packed the sandwich for yourself that you did not eat the day before. It is still fresh and tastes pretty good. All of the vegetables with the whole wheat bread satisfies your diet plan well. For a beverage, you just wash it down with some water. There is a problem though. You are still quite hungry, and that sandwich did not fill you up. There is still some celery in your lunch bag, but you want to save that for later. You know that you are still going to have a busy afternoon, so you want to make sure you are full. Your only option right now is to get something from the vending machine. That evil vending machine. It is filled with nothing but salty snacks and candies. It has been a good week for you, so you decide a bag of chips won't hurt you. They taste pretty good and you definitely notice the extra salt. After lunch is finished, you get back to work promptly. Your body does not notice the unhealthy snack, so you keep moving and get things done. It is quite a busy afternoon, but you are able to handle everything well.

- It is late afternoon once more and you are ready for your late afternoon snack. You finish the celery sticks in your lunch bag, and they get you through the rest of the day. The busy Thursday workday is over. Finally, it is time to go home.

- When you arrive home you get ready for dinner. You want to get a little bit creative. For tonight, you make a burrito with black beans, tomatoes, lettuce, and onions. The first one tastes pretty good, so you make another one. You also decide to make some guacamole. It all tastes pretty good and fills you up.

At this time, you have been on the anti-inflammatory diet for about five days and have tried three different ethnic foods. You decide at this point that you will experiment more regularly with different foods to try many new things. Your old diet of hotdogs, burgers, and pizza is a thing of the past. This will also keep you from getting bored with the diet. You decide for dinner to drink some coconut water. First time trying it and it tastes good. You are excited to keep moving and keep getting better. There is nothing stopping you now.

- After working on the computer for a while, you have a late-night snack. You still have some cut up avocado left over from the guacamole. You decide to eat that. It is good, but also a little bland for you. You add some black peppers, and it helps a little bit. You are able to finish it and get some essential nutrients. The biggest thing you have noticed with your new diet plan is that with the variety of foods available, you do not feel like you are missing anything. Today was quite a good protein day overall.

So far, it has been five full days and you are sticking to your diet well. You don't miss your old way of life and are enjoying the direction you are going with your health. This is very important. Having a purpose and seeing results is a great motivator. We will continue on to Friday and see how we can finish off this week.

Friday:

- It is Friday morning and the weekend will be upon us soon enough. When you wake up in the morning, you have a craving for something sweet. First things first, you drink a glass of lemon water and get hydrated. This will be your staple from now on. A full glass of lemon water every morning. No matter what diet plan you follow, being hydrated is essential. After this, you grab a muffin, which you have been craving since you woke up. Luckily, it is a bran muffin, so not too bad. It has so much sugar. In addition, you have a banana and some yogurt with a cup of green tea. Overall, not too bad of a start for your day.

After eating, you head to work. It is Friday, so all of the tasks of the day are needing to be completed before the weekend starts. It is a busy morning indeed with nonstop meetings, emails, phone calls, and writing. When you finally get a chance to stop and eat, your boss calls you into his office. He compliments you on your work this past week and offers to give you more responsibility. This is an honor for you and could lead to bigger things in the near future. After the meeting, you quickly get back to work.

- After a few minutes, you remember about your morning snack. You quickly grab some coconut water and some pecans from your bag. They taste pretty good, but you are also pretty close to lunch, so you only have a few. At least with the busy schedule, you were still able to stick to your meal plan. The rest of the morning goes by quickly as you get back to doing the work you need. You really need to complete all of the pending tasks before the weekend starts or your Monday will be impossible to deal with.

- For lunch, you are craving a salad. There is a good place down the road that has pretty good fresh salads. When you arrive there, you order one with green beans, spinach, lettuce, red onions, cucumbers, and parsley. Your top it off with an avocado dressing that they have. All of it tastes wonderful. You are happy with lunch. You wash it down with a glass of beets juice that they make fresh there. The lunch was very filling and tasted quite good too. You feel energized once more after this lunch and ready to get back to work. It is still a little early, so you decide to take a quick walk. The fresh air feels good after you have been stuck in an office all day long.

- The afternoon is filled with more meetings, emails, writing and putting out many fires before the weekend. It has been a busy Friday and it was only halfway done. After a couple of hours, it is now time for a late afternoon snack. This time, you have a mixture of roasted cashews, almonds, and peanuts. You have learned by now to prepare a few things the night before to have on hand. The snacks fill you up for the rest of the day until you are ready to go home.

When your workday ends, your boss calls you into his office. He compliments you on a good week. He states that your work rate has improved tremendously all due to the new diet. Okay, well maybe we're taking things too far here. Whatever the case, your work week is completed, and you are ready to enjoy your weekend. You get a few final things closed out, say goodbye to a few people and then you are on your way.

- When you get home, you decide to order out. You go for Mediterranean food again and get a Greek salad, vegetarian pita sandwich with falafel made from chickpeas and some hummus with pita bread. The pita bread will probably last you through the weekend. All the food tasted exceptional and you still have the energy to do a few things. You decide to meet up with your friend at the movies. It has been a long week and you deserve a good night out. When you get there, you strongly resist there urge to get popcorn or candy. Your friend gorged on some junk food while you continued to resist. Honestly, you aren't even craving it at this point. The movie was nice and now you are ready to go back home. Before this, you and your friend have a chat about your new diet plan. He seems impressed and asks you more questions about it. You explain to him all of the various food groups and meals you can eat. You also explain to him about the increased energy levels and overall feelings of well-being. He seems interested in starting it someday as well. You both agree to follow a similar schedule starting Sunday. This should be a lot of fun.

- After arriving back home, you decide to have some carrots dipped in the hummus you have from before. It is a tasty little snack. After this, you end your night and are ready for another weekend. You fall asleep pretty quickly as it has been quite a busy day.

This has been a really good week for you so far. You have really been doing your part in fighting off inflammatory disease, simply by eating a healthy diet. I hope you are feeling good about yourself so far. You have done an impressive job sticking to your diet, even though you are extremely busy. You have also resisted a lot of temptations. There is just one day left in the week. Time to start day number seven of the anti-inflammatory diet. Good Luck!

Saturday:

The weekend is now upon you and you did a great job sticking to your diet during the week. Even with your busy work schedule, you made the time to always eat healthy meals. On Saturday morning, you sleep in a little bit. The movie ended somewhat late, so you also got to bed later than usual.

- When you wake up, as usual, you start your day with a fresh glass of lemon water. This has become almost a habit for you. You often crave this refreshing drink first thing in the morning now. For good reason too. It is a great drink to start off your day. After this, you start on your hearty breakfast. Just a week earlier, your Saturday morning breakfast consisted of greasy eggs, bacon, and sausage. This morning, all you are craving are egg whites with spinach, green peppers, and black pepper. Also, on the side, you have some fresh cut up strawberries, blueberries, and a whole banana. To drink, you have a cup of green tea. A far cry from what you used to have. An impressive change and a positive move towards fighting inflammatory disease. You indulge in your Saturday morning breakfast. Even though it is the weekend, you will not shy away from your commitment.

- After breakfast, you go to the gym, grocery shopping and run a few other errands. About midmorning, you remember to grab a snack. You get a fresh squeezed orange juice from one of your favorite juice places. Once again, the prior week you were getting your energy from coffee, sodas or energy drinks. Now, you are getting it naturally from the foods you eat.

- In the early afternoon, while still running errands, you stop to have lunch at an Indian Restaurant you have fallen in love with. For lunch, you have some whole wheat tortillas, potatoes with peas and various spices, curry, kidney beans, and some rice. They do not have brown rice, so you must settle for white rice. Overall, the meal is very tasty and quite healthy. All of the mixtures of the flavors are very satisfying to your palate. It really makes you not even miss eating meat.

At least for the time being. After lunch, you continue with your day. It is a busy Saturday, but you have the energy to handle it just fine.

- Around late afternoon time, you grab a snack, which is a small fresh protein shake you get from a local juice place. It is quite good. You opted for more than a snack because you will still be running errands for a while and need the energy. It still takes a couple more hours of running around in order to finish everything you need to do.

- Finally, you arrive back home and are ready for dinner. While you were out, you picked up a few things for the evening and the rest of the week. For dinner, you decide to make whole wheat pasta and some parsley salad. For a drink, you opt for some regular water. It is a great dinner for you that you really enjoyed. You look at all of the things you bought while you were out and are ready to get the week started and continue your newfound diet plan. The anti-inflammatory diet is definitely serving you well. After dinner, you relax and watch TV for a while. It has been a long day and you are tired.

- Well, it's late at night and its time to go to bed soon. Before that though, you call your friend and set up your schedule for the following week. You will be his support system and he will hopefully be yours too. You guys are able to plot out your whole week and are optimistic about how it will turn out. The first week went great, so no doubt the second week will be even better. For a late-night snack tonight, why don't you indulge a little bit? You have definitely earned it. How about some avocado ice cream? After that, time to go to bed. The week is completed. Well done!

Well, you made it through the first week on the new anti-inflammatory diet plan and you did great. Except for a few detours here and there, you stuck to your diet very well. Obviously, this was an exaggerated meal plan and just used as a guideline. We hope that it at least provides a good illustration of how it can fit into your schedule. We realize that your schedule is your own and you will have to incorporate the diet in your own way, based on your available times and your own taste buds. Our hope is that we have encouraged you to set up your own schedule and include this new plan into your life. Especially if you are already suffering from chronic inflammation or inflammatory disease. Once again, this is not a one-size fit all plan. We also advise you to seek out a professional when making life-altering changes, especially those that affect your body processes.

As was portrayed by this story, one can truly improve their overall health and livelihood by changing something as simple as the food they ingest. We hope that your own story has a similar result to the one we told. Bottom line is this: You have to take action in order to start making improvements.

Having knowledge does not mean anything unless you are ready to use it. Good luck and thank you for helping us bring all of this full circle.

Chapter 8

The Popular Diet:

So far in this Book, we have talked about inflammatory disease, how dangerous it can be and how to prevent and even resolve it with some lifestyle changes like the anti-inflammatory diet.

We went in-depth on the diet and included many different foods, both locally, and from around the world that follows the anti-inflammatory diet.

We still encourage you to get creative with your own meal plans as well. Cooking is an art form, so have fun with it.

We also helped you set up a schedule. Well, sort of. We made an example of a schedule for someone who may be changing over to an anti-inflammatory diet. You can follow that one or change it as you wish based on your own schedule and palate. We just hope that we helped illustrate how the diet can fit into your lives and how it can replace certain unhealthy foods you may have been eating.

We really enjoyed giving you all of this useful information and we sincerely hope that is able to help you get on the right track as far as healthy eating. Diet is crucial in fighting many chronic illnesses, and the anti-inflammatory diet has been found to reduce chronic inflammation, or inflammatory disease, which leads to a lot of chronic illnesses. We hope that you will not only read this Book once but use it as a reference over and over again. The information can be referenced on a regular basis.

As you can see, the concepts of the anti-inflammatory diet are quite simple. You eat the right foods and you will get the right results. What is important is that takes effort, patience, persistence, determination, and sacrifice. You have it in you, now make it happen.

Before we close out this Book, we want to share some stories about how the anti-inflammatory diet has helped so many people throughout history and modern times. We will also share stories of people who have lived a vegetarian or vegan dietary lifestyle.

We mentioned before how you should not follow something just because a bunch of famous people is doing it. We still believe this one hundred percent.

However, we feel that by showing examples of well-known people eating a proper anti-inflammatory diet can truly help shine a light on it. To be fair, many of these people were following an anti-inflammatory diet and may not have even realized it. Maybe you have followed it to a certain degree also. If so, we encourage you to continue.

The reason we used famous and more well-known people as an example is that it has more of an impact. A neighbor down the street who prevented himself from getting a heart attack may not be as useful or appealing to the masses. We do applaud that person though if this is the case for them. Let's get started.

Mike Tyson:

Well-known heavyweight boxer and media personality Mike Tyson was once the most famous athlete in the country. Maybe even the most famous person in the country period.

He captivated the world with his speed strength and style. The youngest heavyweight champion of all time. During his time as a boxer, he certainly was no vegetarian and was not following the anti-inflammatory diet.

During his reign, not much was known about the protein available in non-meat foods. At this time though, Tyson was working out constantly and could probably eat whatever he wanted.

Tyson admitted that he was not sure if he could have sustained a vegan lifestyle while boxing, but he says it might have been a possibility as many gladiators of the past were vegans or vegetarians.

After he stopped fighting and was not training either, Mike Tyson's weight ballooned up. At one point, he was weighing over 300 pounds. Eventually, he would change to a more plant-based diet and this would lead him to lose over 100 pounds and getting back down to his healthy weight. Mike is a great example of how the vegan/vegetarian, and in turn, the anti-inflammatory diet can have a positive impact on someone's life. Mike Tyson is still able to work out hard when he wants to. We applaud him for his accomplishments.

Kevin Smith:

Well-known comedian and film producer who has worked on many projects. He is famously known for the Jay and Silent Bob movies. Smith has had issues with his health off and on for decades. Especially in relation to his weight which has gone up and down constantly. At one time, he weighed over 400 pounds.

In 2018, Kevin Smith suffered a major heart attack after performing a stand-up comedy show. Luckily for Mr. Smith, he was rushed to the hospital and had emergency surgery, which saved his life. He had total blockage of one of his arteries, which would have been fatal if not treated.

After this frightening incident, Kevin Smith, with the guidance of his doctor, went on a plant-based diet, starting with potatoes and then slowly incorporating other foods week by week. This new diet plan served Smith well as he has lost well over 50 pounds and is a whole new person. He continues to maintain his healthy vegan diet until this day. Kevin Smith's story is a perfect example of how things were taken way too far with the ignoring of his health problems.

His story also perfectly illustrates how the combination of modern medicine and lifestyle changes can work together in congruency to save someone's life. Obviously, Kevin Smith needed extreme measures to save his life once he had a heart attack. However, afterward, he has worked hard on his diet to assure it won't happen again. We congratulate Mr. Kevin Smith for his great work on and off the screen.

Penn Jillette:

Penn Jillette is a famous magician, illusionist, and media personality. He appears on various news channels on a regular basis. He is part of the popular duo of Penn and Teller. Penn Jillette has a great act, or several great acts, that he does. He can make almost anything disappear, even parts of himself.

He did just that a few years back. Back in 2015, Penn Jillette ended up in the Emergency Room with extremely high blood pressure. He was also found to have 90% blockage in one of his arteries. He was a ticking time bomb for sure. He wanted to make a major change in his life for himself and his family. He knew that he could not be there for his kids and maintain the dietary habits that he had.

With the help of his doctor, Mr. Jillette went on an extreme diet. He ate nothing but potatoes with no salt or other additives. Just plain potatoes and that's all. After two weeks, he was already down several pounds. He slowly began incorporating other stews and vegetables into his diet in order to receive other nutrients.

This was similar to the diet plan that Kevin Smith had. In fact, Penn Jillette was the inspiration for Kevin Smith. After a few months, Mr. Jillette was down over a hundred pounds. It was an amazing transformation, to say the least. Mr. Jillette continues to maintain his weight and lives his busy lifestyle.

If the anti-inflammatory diet is good enough for them, it is certainly good enough for all of us. Just so we are clear, all of the people we have described so far lost a significant amount of weight by changing their diet plans.

This has worked out great for them, but they also had help. We want to make it clear that losing drastic amounts of weight quickly can be extremely dangerous if not monitored closely. For this reason, we always advise seeking the help of a professional when doing so. It will give you peace of mind also. The diet plans that the above people followed also follow the anti-inflammatory diet.

Let's talk now about some famous athletes. These high caliber performers earned their accolades while also maintaining a healthy vegan/vegetarian diet. We will share some examples below.

Hannah Teter:

Hannah Teter is an American snowboarder. She won the gold medal in the 2006 Winter Olympic Games and multiple other championships throughout the years. She has been following a plant-based diet for some time now and she states it has made her feel better than ever.

It has opened her mind to so many new things as an athlete. Hannah Teter has always appreciated protecting the environment, which led her to a vegan, plant-based diet. Since turning to a plant-based diet, she states that she feels stronger physically, mentally and emotionally. Hannah continues to compete as a professional snowboarder.

David Haye:

We spoke about professional boxer Mike Tyson. Now we will discuss a more recent champion in David Haye. David Haye was a very successful cruiserweight, winning multiple titles. After he researched the effects of a vegan diet on the healing process after suffering a serious shoulder injury. He realized that he did not need to eat meat to have the strength he needed to compete. He states that he has a full-time chef and nutritionist who help make sure he gets all of his nutrients while till following a plant-based diet. David Haye competed until 2018, then retired from the ring. If professional athletes can benefit from an anti-inflammatory style diet, then so can the rest of us.

Barney Du Plessis:

Who the heck is this? Well, if you are a bodybuilding fan, you probably know who it is. He is the world's first vegan bodybuilder and was Mr. Universe in 2014.

Du Plessis went vegan in 2013 after having a growing list of health concerns. He also retired from bodybuilding after this. When he changed his diet, it changed his fitness in a radical way. He feels that with a vegan diet, it allows him to train half as much, but still get better results. He feels that he gets more GMO-free and organic food by avoiding meat. After turning Vegan in 2013 and almost ending his career in 2013, he went on to win the prestigious Mr. Universe in 2014. That is a great story if we've ever heard one. Du Plessis and his partner are now doing their part to spread the positive message of a vegan diet. The way to a happy, healthy and prosperous life.

Nate Diaz:

Nate Diaz is a mixed martial artist who competes for the largest promotion for the sport in the world. He adopted a vegan lifestyle when he was 18. He was inspired by his older brother, who was already competing. He says that the vegan diet has made him a stronger and better fighter, plus it also makes him feel better the day after.

Meagan Duhamel:

Meagan Duhamel is an Olympic medalist pair skater and a four-time world champion. Meagan switched to eating whole grains, fruits, and vegetables when she read about a vegan diet in a book, she found in 2008. She read it cover to cover and was amazed by what she read. She stopped eating animal products after that and continued to compete at the highest level.

Gama Pehalvan:

We are really going into the annals of history for this particular person. Gama Pehalvan was born Ghulam Mohammad Baksh. Pehalvan was a world-class wrestler from India during the late 1800s and early 1900s who is often considered one of the greatest wrestlers in the history of time. He inspired many people down the line, including Bruce Lee.

On a regular day, Gama Pehalvan would wrestle about forty of his fellow wrestlers, perform five thousand squats, and three thousand pushups. This was his daily training session. One of the most unique things about Pehalvan was his diet. While it was not solidly a vegan or vegetarian diet, it mostly was and also followed the anti-inflammatory diet of today.

Here's a brief look at his diet. It would consist of 10 liters of milk, mixed with crushed almond paste. Three buckets of seasonal fruits and various fruit juices. He did eat chicken, so we can't say that he had a vegetarian diet. Of course, some people still call the chicken part of the vegetarian diet. A milder form of it. That is for other people to decide, not us. Nevertheless, his diet and lifestyle truly illustrate how fruits, vegetables, and dairy products promote health and energy.

Venus Williams:

Venus Williams is a famous tennis player. She is one of the great, if not the best, female tennis player of all time. After some health issues in 2011 related to an auto-immune disease, Venus Williams decided to adopt a vegan diet based on the advice from her doctors. This would continue her performance on the court, which is what she wanted. After trying it, she fell in love and has stuck to it ever since. Venus Williams continues to dominate on the court to this day. A great example of an anti-inflammatory/vegan diet helping someone with an auto-immune disorder. This has really been the basis for our Book today. Congratulations to Venus Williams for sticking to her diet plan.

Scott Jurek:

Scott Jurek is an ultramarathon runner and holds many personal records. While Jurek was in college, he saw multiple people suffering from health defects while he was attending physical therapy school. His mother also had multiple sclerosis. He saw veganism as a solution to many of the chronic diseases that were in his family's history. This was a long-term decision made by Jurek. One that he is very proud of. Being vegan still allows Jurek to perform at very high levels.

Jermain Defoe:

Jermain Defoe is a footballer/soccer player and one of the best goal scorers in the league. He believes that switching over to a vegan diet helped him in a big way during his comeback in the sport.

These are some amazing stories of some of the top-level athletes in the world and how they followed and even promoted a largely anti-inflammatory and vegan/vegetarian diet. If it allowed them to still compete at the highest level, there must be something great about it.

Since we discussed some high-level athletes, let's also discuss some celebrities, who often have to be in top form in order to do what they are best at.

Ellen DeGeneres:

Ellen is truly someone who is popular with the masses. She seems to be everywhere. In order to do this, she has to take good care of herself. She has to be in top form all of the time. She does it not so much for health reasons, but for animal rights. However, the proof is in the pudding and Ellen continues to live a high-level lifestyle on the vegan diet.

Usher:

Usher's father died of a heart attack in 2008. This inspired Usher to change his dietary habits to veganism. He wanted to adopt a healthier lifestyle and not have the same fate as his father.

These are just a couple of celebrities who have adopted a vegan lifestyle for various reasons. More often than not, it is due to a health concern, either imminent or probable. There is no denying that a vegan diet has so many health benefits, considering there is example after example of it helping somebody. There are even real-life examples of the anti-inflammatory diet helping someone with chronic inflammation.

Take Venus Williams as an example. According to her, she was able to get past her auto-immune disorder by changing her diet. A great story, indeed. There is also growing evidence that foods which fight inflammation work well to negate inflammatory disease and other chronic illnesses resulting from it. The growing evidence, coupled with the anecdotal stories, strongly support the positive benefits of the anti-inflammatory diet.

Are you experiencing mild inflammation? Do you just want to take positive steps toward improving your health? Then look into the anti-inflammatory diet and see if it will work for you.

The meat of this book has been the anti-inflammatory diet. We sincerely hope that the information provided will help you make the best decisions for yourself. There is a huge world out there full of vegan and vegetarian food. Go out there and enjoy it. Thank you for reading this Book.

Conclusion

Thank you for making it to the end of The Anti-Inflammatory Diet: Healthy Vegan and Vegetarian Meal Planning.

Let's hope it was informative and able to provide you with all of the tools you need to achieve your goals, whatever it is that they may be.

This book provided a lot of information about a nutritious diet that will provide many health benefits and may even save someone's life.

It is up to you if you would like to follow it in order to live a healthier lifestyle to prevent chronic illnesses and have a better quality of life.

Quality of life is what we are promoting the most with the anti-inflammatory diet. The next step is to start using the information presented in this book and begin incorporating it into your everyday life. We spoke extensively in this Book about the inflammatory disease and how to prevent or resolve it with a proper diet. The anti-inflammatory diet will provide you with nutritious and delicious meals. Include it in your own meal prep and create a daily, weekly or monthly meal schedule so you can stay ahead of the game. Avoiding serious health consequences is an important part of living a long and productive life. A proper diet is instrumental in creating that life for all of us. We know that we were often times blunt when going over information in this book. But we want to make sure people understand the risks of inflammatory disease and the importance of an *anti inflammatory diet*.

If you write it down, you are more likely to do it. You are more likely to do something if you get some type of enjoyment out of it. Enjoy it then. Try the recipes in this book, get creative with your own recipes, do even more research and just have fun eating great food. It may seem like a chore at first. Change is never easy, but often times, it is for the better. Especially with matters regarding our health.

Chronic **inflammatory** disease is no laughing matter. It is a disease that causes much suffering and can lead to many health problems down the line. Avoid these at all costs by sticking to an ***anti inflammatory diet***. The benefits will be tremendous.

Finally, if you found this book useful in any way, a five star review is always appreciated!

DISCLAIMER

ANTI ANXIETY DIET

Put An End On Anxiety, Reduce Depression And Stop Panic Attacks With This Plant Based Diet. Anti Anxiety Food Solutions And Natural Remedies That Help The Body Heal And Stay Calm.

ANTI ANXIETY *Diet*

PUT AN END ON ANXIETY, REDUCE DEPRESSION AND STOP PANIC ATTACKS
WITH THIS PLANT BASED DIET - FOOD SOLUTIONS AND NATURAL REMEDIES
THAT HELP THE BODY HEAL AND STAY CALM

OLIVIA JOHNSON SMITH

Description ("Anti Anxiety Diet")

Anxiety is a common disorder that affects many people. Treatments vary from medication and coping mechanisms to **diet** and exercise, but what actually works best? Which foods and dietary habits cause <u>anxiety</u>? Which foods treat and ***reduce anxiety***?

This book provides an in-depth look at how the brain and body function under *stress*, how events and *stress* impact anxiety and why eating well balanced, whole foods full of nutrients is key to the prevention and treatment of **Anxiety**:

- What foods help treat anxiety while reducing stress?
- How simple is it to change food options and the significant improvements these changes make in your brain's health, cognitive processes, and functions?
- The basic science behind anxiety, stress, the basics of neurotransmitters and how diet can improve chemical balance in the brain.
- How gut health and balancing your body's natural microbiome is essential to your brain's health and the connection.

This book includes practical guides for creating shopping lists, including nutrients, avoiding deficiencies, and creating weekly meal plans to keep you on track to a better way of eating and living. The complex systems of the brain and body are explained, with their various connections to different vitamins, minerals, and naturally occurring chemicals that we can obtain through our everyday meals as a form of medicine. Healing the body with proper nutrition also provides other benefits and goals:

- Stronger cognitive ability and improved brain function
- Prevention of brain-related diseases
- Improvement of digestion, weight loss and increasing your metabolism
- Reduced stress, elevation of mood and warding off depression

Foods that heal are more than healthy: they are delicious, and the options for recipes, including breakfast, soups, bowls, desserts, and smoothies are limitless! Eating well and keeping healthy doesn't have to be a lifetime of restrictions and limitations.

Focusing on nutrients and the numerous foods that contain them opens a new world of opportunity into many new decadent and delicious options for a better way of eating and living.

The **Anti Anxiety Diet** is for everyone and can benefit everyone, whether they experience the symptoms of anxiety, or wish to prevent them through diet. Reading this book, you'll be able to accomplish the following goals for easier living and decision making:

Recognizing the benefits of all foods, and why some are more important than others for nutritional value.

Exploring the world of fermented foods and their numerous benefits.
Grocery shopping for the world's most nutrient-rich foods economically and successfully.

Connecting the various functions of your body and mind with nutrition and exercise: how they work together to improve overall health and well-being.

Short-term and long-term goals and how to make them work for a lifetime of *anxiety-free living*.

Whether you are currently looking to improve your brain's health or searching for a better way to eat, this book will give you the tools and guides you need to plan, prepare and begin a new diet and path to a better, healthier future.

Fourth Book : Anti Anxiety Diet

TABLE OF CONTENTS

CHAPTER 1

CHAPTER 2

CHAPTER 3

Adapting to an Anti-Anxiety Diet.

Reduce the Carbohydrates and Sugar in Your Diet.

Eliminating Processed and Packaged Foods.

Choosing Whole Food Options That Fit into Your Diet and Lifestyle.

Yogurt, Kimchi, and Other Fermented Food Options.

High Alkaline Foods, and Avoiding Overly Acidic Options.

Replacing Foods that Trigger Anxiety, Inflammation and Gut Health Issues with Healthier Options.

CHAPTER 4

Your Gut Health: What You Need to Know.

The Importance of a Healthy Stomach Lining.

Dysbiosis: What Are the Causes and How it Can Be Prevented and Treated.

What Foods Treat and Prevent Dysbiosis?

Leaky Gut Syndrome: What are the Causes and Treatments?

Avoiding a leaky gut: How can diet help?

CHAPTER 5

Reducing Inflammation and Boosting Your Immunity.

Reducing inflammation and promoting healing in your body: top foods for reducing inflammation.

The Importance of Microbiome and your Immunity: What is a Microbiome and How Does it Protect and Maintain Good Health?

Selecting Foods and Supplements that Boost the Immune System for Optimal Performance and Function.

CHAPTER 6

Moods and Food: How to Achieve and Maintain Balance.

How What We Eat Impacts Our Mood and Reduces Anxiety.

Ketogenic and Low Carb Foods: How They Improve Cognitive Ability, Mental function and reduce stress.

Genetic Predispositions for Anxiety.

Deficiencies and Their Link to Anxiety and Unbalanced Mood and Health.

Reducing Stress and Strengthening Your Adrenal System.

CHAPTER 7

Neurotransmitters: Understanding Your Brain's Signal System and How it Works.

What Are Neurotransmitters and How Do They Work Together to Affect Your Brain's Health.

The Different Types of Transmitters and How They Function.

Chemical Balance Is Vital for Good Brain Health.

How Diet Impacts the Function of Neurotransmitters.

Foods for Overall Support of Neurotransmitters.

Brain Food: The Top Choices for Optimal Health.

CHAPTER 8

Meal Preparation and Planning for the Anti-Anxiety Diet.

Clearing the Space in Your Pantry, Refrigerator, and Freezer for Better Options Ahead.

Recipes and ideas for easy meal preparation.

Smoothies.

Breakfast Bowls.

Salads and Platters.

Healthy Snacks and Sides.

Easy Lunch and Dinner Meals.

Curried Butternut Squash Soup.

4-Week Meal Plan for the Anti-Anxiety Diet.

CHAPTER 9

Exercise and Diet: Why Keeping Active Combats Anxiety.

How to Approach Exercise: From Inactive to Low or Moderate Activity and Beyond: How Increasing Your Efforts Makes a Big Difference in Your Mind and Body's Health 141.

CHAPTER 10

Long-term Benefits of Implementing the Anti-Anxiety Diet into your Lifestyle.

CHAPTER 1

Food as Medicine: How it Works to Heal and Support your Mind and Body

A busy lifestyle, hectic work schedule, family, and many commitments create a challenging, juggling act for many people. For most of us, it's a daily struggle to keep up with ever-growing demands, deadlines, and continual multi-tasking that seems to never end. As a result, stress is a major factor in our daily lives and it impacts every aspect of it, from our health, relationships and family to coping mechanisms and handling too much at once. Anxiety is often the result of the cumulative effects of constant stress, coupled with a lack of sleep, support and good nutrition.

While anxiety and related conditions, such as depression have many causes and triggers, scientific research indicates a healthy, balanced diet and lifestyle, can help support and significantly reduce their impact.

This is an introductory chapter that explores how food is more than three meals a day, but rather, a sustainable, realistic way to keep our body and mind healthy. Food plays a central role in how we function and feel; it nourishes us, but also heals and strengthens us mentally and psychologically. What we eat is important, as well as how we eat: the foods we choose when we use food as a source of comfort or as a habit; our relationship with food has a direct connection to our well-being.

How Food is Like Medicine and Why it is Beneficial for our Overall Health

Food is like medicine because of the many nutrients and potential for prevention and treatment of many medical conditions. What we eat impacts our mood and how we function. There is a direct link between our diet and chronic illnesses and diseases. Not only does food affect our physical well-being, but it also impacts our emotional and psychological health. In combination with stress management, a good night's sleep and exercise, good food choices go a long way to prevent and treat a lot of conditions.

The way we eat now varies considerably from our ancestors, who hunted and foraged for food from its natural habitat: wild game, seeds, nuts, leaves, and berries. Food gathered and hunted was eaten in its natural state, with little or no preparation or cooking.

Over time, certain foods were combined for taste and enjoyment, though as we became more domesticated and living busy lives, canned foods, "TV dinners" and other convenience foods became popular, replacing their natural sources. Over the past century, food products have become more processed and packaged than ever, and while some packaged supplements and vitamins are a good way to support a balanced diet, enjoying food in its most natural form is ideal for gaining the most out of its nutritional value.

When you think of medicine, you may immediately consider a doctor's prescription, new drugs on the market advertised online or television, or holistic treatments with herbs and vitamins. Food is also a medicine that gives us a lot of vital nutrients and benefits when we choose from whole, natural sources.

Natural, raw foods are high in enzymes that help our bodies absorb nutrients contained in them. For example, apples and citrus fruits are high in antioxidants, while spinach is high in iron. Our bodies absorb these nutrients best when food is raw, as the enzymes contained in them are active and preserve nutrients while the food remains uncooked. Enzymes also aid in digestion and gut health, which is discussed in another chapter. Choosing fruits, vegetables, and other foods in their most natural state is the best way to obtain the optimal level of vitamins, minerals, protein, healthy fats, and fiber needed for a healthy lifestyle.

What is Anxiety and How Does It Impact Your Health?

Anxiety is a common condition that affects many people from all around the world, from different social and economic backgrounds. While some people experience anxiety only at certain times in their life, when triggered by a stressful event or tragedy, while other people are regularly and continually impacted by anxiety.

In cases where anxiety is long-term and regularly experienced, it is called generalized anxiety disorder. The symptoms of this disorder vary from one individual to another and include sensations of fear and tension, increased heart rate and in some cases, palpitations, physical tightness, such as clenching jaws or muscles and challenges with focusing and concentration, among others.

When diagnosed with an anxiety disorder, treatments often include therapy, dietary changes, and/or medication. While all of these treatments can vary in their success, depending on the severity of the condition and how regularly they are used, this book focuses on the science-based benefits of nutrients and how each foods we eat and include in our daily meals have a significant impact on anxiety and related conditions, such as depression and mood imbalance. In focusing on what we eat, as part of a healthy lifestyle, including regular exercise and activity, we can learn to heal our bodies inside and out, while treating anxiety and related disorders.

A Dietary Approach to Healing and Prevention: How What We Eat Makes a Difference in How we Feel

How we eat makes a major impact on our bodies and how we function. Choosing natural, well-balanced foods with lots of nutrients is key to preventing a lot of illnesses. The root of many conditions stems from stress and our gut health, which are both strongly linked to anxiety. In order for our brains to function effectively, we need a steady, healthy stream of nutrients to maintain a stable mood and mental function.

We reach our optimal level when we choose good quality foods that contain all the daily nutrients we need, including vitamins, fatty acids, proteins, and antioxidants. These are the "building blocks" or foundation of healthy mental function, and in turn, this impacts how we feel and react. When we consume too many foods high in processed sugars, artificial additive and preservatives, this has a negative impact on our blood sugar levels, which causes inflammation and can impair the brain's ability to function well.

Bacterial imbalance in the gut can also trigger other health problems, including mood changes and chronic indigestion. Anxiety is caused by an imbalance on diet and lack of nutrients, which is also connected to gut health. While many people are prescribed medications to treat anxiety, digestive issues, and related ailments, they often overlook diet as a powerful way to achieve better health for their mind and body. Maintaining a healthy, natural diet is the best way to fine-tune your body and mind's balance for optimal health.

Whole Foods and Why They are the Foundation of a Good Diet and Health

Choosing foods that are fresh (or frozen), such as fruits and vegetables, nuts, seeds, grains, and proteins (meat and alternatives) is vital for maintaining overall good health. Many popular diets may promote natural eating, though the convenience of packaged "natural" foods and supplements often take the place of whole foods. Although there are good quality supplements that can positively enhance our health, research brands, ingredients, and nutrients. There are two main categories of nutrients to track for a balanced diet: macronutrients and micronutrients.

Macronutrients refer to broad categories of nutrients that we require certain amounts to maintain a healthy diet. Whole foods are the best source to find a balance for a good diet, and this includes factoring in the daily macronutrient and micronutrient requirements. While these can vary depending on our goals, it's important to consider the nutrient "count" and value for everything we eat. For example, on a ketogenic diet, healthy fats are increased to approximately three-quarters of your total macronutrient intake, followed by proteins at twenty percent and carbohydrates making up the remainder:

Macronutrients

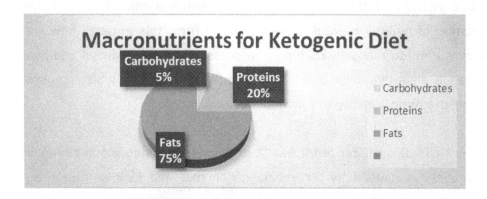

While this chart focuses on the three main macronutrients, which are vital for building a healthy diet, they can also include fiber and water as part of the requirements. Drinking lots of water and including as much fiber as possible is ideal for any way of eating. If you are following a diet that is more moderate in carbohydrates, proteins, and fats, with less focus on weight loss and more on maintenance, your macronutrient balance may resemble the following:

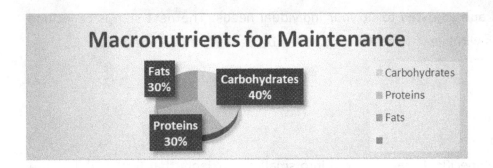

For weight training and building muscle, increasing protein, while maintaining a significant amount of healthy fats and limiting carbohydrates are key.

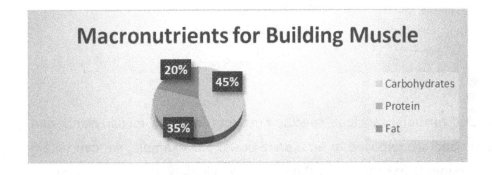

Which macronutrient portions are the best for an anti-anxiety diet? There are a few factors to consider: not all proteins, fats and carbohydrates are the same. They are a high-level category of nutrients that can be further divided into smaller categories called micronutrients. The main focus should be first on choosing the right macronutrient categories for your lifestyle; the more active you are, increasing carbohydrates are a good source of fuel, while weight loss and reducing carbohydrate intake as a goal is best suited to the ketogenic diet. A moderate, daily way of eating doesn't have an exact percentage set for each macro category, as this can be tweaked and adjusted to fit your individual needs. The next step is to include as many healthy options within each section as possible by tracking micronutrients.

Micronutrients

Micronutrients are more specific, breaking down into smaller, nutrients that further define the types of foods we should choose for our diet. Examples of some of the main categories of micronutrients are as follows:

- Phytochemicals
- Antioxidants
- Vitamins
- Minerals

Each of these can be divided further to include specific nutrients found in foods, plants and substance that we consume and are exposed to on a daily basis. For example, we can obtain our daily requirement for vitamin D from the sun, though the availability varies depending on your region and time of year. To avoid deficiency, milk and non-dairy options are often fortified with vitamin D to ensure it is a part of our diet.

Phytochemicals

Phytochemicals are compounds commonly found in and produced by plants. They contain a lot of properties that guard the body against cancer and promote healthy cell growth. Eating a plant-based diet or a way of eating rich in raw vegetables is an excellent means to gain the benefits of phytochemicals. They also play a role in protecting plants against viruses, bacteria, and other materials that hinder their growth, including fungus. Phytochemicals also intercept carcinogens, preventing them from attacking healthy cells, which also helps prevent cancerous cell growth.

What are the Different Types of Phytochemicals and Where Can They be Found?

Beta carotene and Carotenoids

Beta carotene is an example of an important phytochemical found in vegetables and some fruits. Carotenoids and beta carotene are often found in orange-colored vegetables and fruits, such as carrots, yams, squash and apricots. They are good for eye health and vision, and often found in foods with vitamin A.

Isothiocyanates

Isothiocyanates are found in vegetables such as cabbage, broccoli, and cauliflower. This family of vegetables also includes bok choy, brussels sprouts, kale and various greens.

Resveratrol and Polyphenols

Two other phytochemicals that may be less known are resveratrol, which is found in red wine, and polyphenols, which is in some teas.

Since there are plenty of phytochemicals found in many common whole foods, they are fairly easy to include in your diet without too much effort. Some foods contain more phytochemicals than others, and the best sources are raw, whole fruits and vegetables. Other ways of including phytochemicals include supplements, though since they are very accessible in many foods, it's almost unnecessary.

Antioxidants

Antioxidants are known for many benefits, including preventing heart disease, cancer, and fighting and/or preventing certain types of infections. The best way to include antioxidants in your diet is by consuming raw fruits, vegetables, nuts and seeds. One of the most important functions of antioxidants: their ability to stop free radicals (unstable molecules) from invading and damaging healthy cells. Free radicals are produced when your body is exposed to pollution, and other unhealthy environments, such as smoking and ingesting high amounts of chemically (unnaturally) processed junk foods. When free radicals are present, they are dangerous, as they have the ability to cause genetic damage to your body's cells. This can trigger many other diseases, including cancer and chronic conditions. Antioxidants are a powerful means to thwart free radicals from damage.

Examples of Antioxidants

Lycopene, lutein, beta carotene, selenium, including certain vitamins (C and E) are examples of antioxidants. They are found in many foods, making their inclusion in your diet a simple task. Foods that contain antioxidants include dark and leafy green vegetables, such as broccoli, cabbage, cauliflower, kale, various sprouts, and a variety of different fruits: mango, cantaloupe, berries, and many others. Green and black tea, as well as certain herbal teas, contain antioxidants. Certain strains of green tea have a very high concentration of antioxidants, making them an excellent way to strengthen your immune system and cellular function. Healthy cellular growth is essential to a healthy brain and helps improve anxiety and cognitive ability.

Lycopene

Lycopene is a carotenoid that is found in certain foods that are usually red in color, such as tomatoes. Other vegetables and fruits that contain this nutrient include watermelon, cherries, strawberries, and red carrots.

Lutein

Lutein is known for its beneficial impact on eye health, as it helps prevent macular degeneration and other common eye diseases. The positive effects on healthy cell growth also benefit by preventing type 2 diabetes, heart conditions, and certain forms of cancer.

Selenium

Selenium is a very strong antioxidant that boosts the body's immune system, reduces stress and inflammation. People with life-long chronic conditions, such as hepatitis or HIV, may also benefit significantly from selenium, due to its positive effects on immunity. This nutrient is also good for helping the thyroid function and improves other conditions, such as chronic fatigue and improving mental function. Nuts, fish and other types of meat are good sources of selenium. While it's an important nutrient to include in your diet, high doses may cause some irritation, ingestion and nausea, especially if you take too much in supplement form while consuming food with high amounts. A little will go a long way: including even a small portion of fish or nuts in your daily diet, for example, is sufficient for gaining the benefits of selenium.

Vitamins C and E

Vitamins C and E, also categorized as antioxidants, are included in more detail under the next section for vitamins. When consumed in raw foods, the body can absorb them better with enzymes and use them well. They are both found in many common fruits and vegetables, and beneficial in supplement form as well.

Vitamins

Vitamins are found in many different foods: eggs, dark leafy greens, fermented foods, and virtually all fruits and vegetables. Some vitamins, such as C and E, are also considered antioxidants. Good quality supplements and tablets can be an important way to boost your daily requirements or meet them, especially in regions where certain fresh foods are not as available or limited. There are many different vitamins and researching their properties, categories can be a lot of work and take time, though worthwhile to become familiar with all sources of nutrients.

The Main Types of Vitamins and What They can do for Your Health

There are many types of vitamins that provide numerous benefits for your health. Vitamins can be divided into two main groups: water-soluble and fat-soluble. Water-soluble simply describes vitamins that can dissolve in water, which includes vitamins B and C. When consumed, they are absorbed into the body and carried through the bloodstream into the different tissues and organs. They are not stored by the body and it is impossible to overeat or overconsume them: excessive consumption of water-soluble vitamins is easily flushed out of the body with no ill effects. In addition to vitamins B and C, beta carotene is also water-soluble. Fat-soluble vitamins, on the other hand, cannot dissolve in water and can be stored in the body. They are absorbed and move through the small intestines, delivering nutrients through the blood. Any excess fat-soluble vitamins can be stored in the body, until they are needed, in liver and fat tissues. Ensuring there is enough fat-soluble vitamins in your diet is invaluable for preventing deficiencies. Examples of fat-soluble vitamins include A, D, E, and K.

Vitamin A

The benefits of vitamin A include vision and eye health, improving immunity, good cellular growth, and bone development. This vitamin can be in either water-soluble or fat-soluble form and found in many natural food sources.

Vitamin B

There are many different forms of vitamin B, each of them with their own unique benefits for the mind and body. B1, thiamine, helps the body process food, breaking it down further to absorb nutrients and use as energy. B2 is also known as riboflavin and works to strengthen muscles, the nervous system, and promote heart health. This vitamin's ability to support and strengthen nerves also prevents and reduces anxiety associated with stress. B3 or niacin, like B1, also aids the body in using food as fuel and energy and helps improve skin, hair, and eyes.

B5 or pantothenic acid improves metabolism and adrenals. B6 or pyridoxine strengthens brain and heart health, while B7, known as biotin, works similarly to B3 to improve skin and nails. One very important benefit of biotin is how it supports breaking down carbohydrates for fuel and helps the body use protein. This supports healthy metabolism and contributes to weight loss and management in the long-term.

Folic acid, otherwise known as B9, is popular as an essential nutrient for prenatal health and often included as a supplement during pregnancy. Folic acid is a key component in developing the nervous system and helps fetal growth. Foods that contain folic acid include dark green vegetables and citrus fruits. B12 is not produced by the body, though it is vital to include in your diet. Usually only found in meats, many vegetarians and vegans may be at risk of deficiency, if it wasn't for fermented soy, such as miso and tempeh, which contain this vitamin. Some dairy and vegan substitutes are also fortified with B12.

Vitamin C

Also known as an antioxidant, vitamin C is famous for the prevention and treatment of the common seasonal cold. It is also powerful in fighting diseases, viruses, and infections, and may have anti-aging benefits.

Vitamin D

We can absorb vitamin D from the sun, though it is often considered one of the most common deficiencies in our diet. For this reason, many foods are fortified with vitamin D, including milk, other dairy products, and non-dairy options (nut-based milk, for example). The benefits of vitamin D include anti-aging properties, bone density and strength, and helping the body absorb calcium, which can have a positive effect on arthritis.

Vitamin K

This vitamin is fat-soluble and can be found in eggs, dark green vegetables, and soy. It helps blood clot and contributes to bone and muscle strength.

Minerals

Minerals are found in meat, certain dairy foods, vegetables, and some fruits. The most important fact about minerals: your body cannot produce them, and they are vital for good health and function. Minerals contribute to healthy brain development, muscle, and bone health.

Examples of Minerals

Calcium

Calcium is an important mineral for building and maintaining healthy bones and muscle. Milk, yogurt and cheese contain calcium, as well as other dairy and meat products. It is also found in many vegetables, specifically leafy greens, such as spinach, kale, and broccoli. Some foods are fortified with calcium to ensure we get our daily requirements, such as packaged snacks, cereals and juices, though it's better to get our daily calcium from sources that naturally contain this mineral.

Potassium

Found in watermelon, potatoes, and bananas, potassium is a natural way to reduce water retention. It's also an electrolyte that helps fluids and nutrients flow in the body while helping to eliminate waste. It regulates metabolism and can prevent high blood pressure, which is associated with potassium deficiency. This also has an overall positive impact on the brain and mental health.

Phosphorus

It's available in many foods, which means you're likely not deficient in this mineral. Seafood, meat, cheese, nuts and seeds all contain phosphorus. It helps energize cells and support bone growth and development.

Magnesium

Sometimes used in supplement form, on its own or combined with calcium, magnesium is often deficient in many diets. It is vital for many important functions, such as treatment and prevention of type 2 diabetes, chronic headaches, heart disease, and anxiety. Due to the importance of this nutrient, always choose foods that contain magnesium. If you feel that deficiency is a risk, a supplement or tablet containing magnesium can be a good alternative.

Sulfur

Like magnesium, Sulphur is beneficial to the nervous system and mental health. We absorb this mineral from naturally healthy fats and proteins. It helps with skin and bone development, and also supports the nervous system.

Chloride

Found in common table salt, chloride promotes pH balance and aids in our digestive system, which in turn, improves the nervous system. Other sources of chloride include tomatoes, olives and celery. Becoming with the different kinds of micronutrients, their benefits and the foods that contain them is a great resource for managing your diet and ensuring that all nutrients are included. While managing macronutrients is important for maintaining a healthy weight and body, keeping all micronutrients in your diet, or as many as possible will guard against many diseases, chronic stress and conditions.

CHAPTER 2

Anxiety and Diet: The Connection That Matters

How Food Choice Impacts Your Mood and Mind: The Basic Science Behind It

The science of how food and diet impact our mood and how our brain works is connected to the overall function of our body.

Modern medicine tends to treat the specific section of your body experiencing a problem: a pill for indigestion or a remedy for a headache, without much consideration for the underlying cause and reason for it.

The source of anxiety and mood changes are directly affected by what we eat. While there is no specific food or substance that causes mood changes, there are findings that link certain types and groups of foods with a higher prevalence of depression, such as consuming too much red meat, and the radical change of mood as a result of refined sugar and processed foods.

How Do Micronutrients Impact Brain Health

As noted in the list of specific minerals and vitamins, maintaining a properly balanced diet with the daily requirement of micronutrients is essential to supporting our nervous system, promoting digestion and healthy growth and strength of our bones, muscles, tissues and brain. A lack of even one or two nutrients, resulting in a deficiency, can shift your state of health significantly. Our brain's cognitive process and the emotions and moods we experience are directly impacted by the nutrients in our diet or lack thereof.

Gut health plays a key role in our brain's health due to the hormones released, some of which enter the brain or are produced there. This is the reason why maintaining balanced bacteria, and a healthy stomach lining is vital to your brain's health. The body is connected in many more ways than it may seem and nourishing your body and mind as a whole will reap many more benefits than separately, as Western medicine tends to practice.

Healthy, whole food is an important way to increase energy, building healthy cells and tissues, and maintaining a fit body. It is also just as important for mental fitness and how our neural activity works. Even on a molecular level, omega 3 fatty acids have shown positive effects on cognitive abilities, as well as regular exercise and a balanced diet. Seafood and foods with similar protein and healthy fats tend to support the brain's health and improve conditions already present, such as mood disorders, anxiety, and depression.

Top foods for an anti-anxiety diet

The food we choose to eat has an impact on our emotional and mental health. The reason for those food choices is often driven by an emotional response, such as a craving for a specific flavor or snack, a comfort in times of stress or difficulty. When we decide what to eat in this state of mind, we often make an uninformed decision, which leads to unhealthy habits. Chocolate, chips, deep-fried foods, and sugary drinks are among the worst and most addictive options. Once we begin a cycle of "treating" our cravings and stress with poor choices, the impact on our mood and anxiety only worsens. The best option requires planning in advance, and making healthier meal and snack options readily available, to avoid the pitfalls of cravings:

- Design a shopping list with healthy, balanced foods in mind and when you're not hungry. Create the list after a satisfying meal, even one day in advance, and give yourself time to reflect on those choices. This is where the foundation of a solid diet begins.

- Shop along the outside aisles of the grocery store, where all the fresh produce and foods are usually located. You'll find most packaged foods are inside the central aisles and choosing products from here should be limited. Check the ingredients to ensure there...

- Buy from local farmer's markets, where foods are fresh and within a short traveling distance, making them both environmentally friendly and natural.

- Take note of your cravings when you shop, and make sure they do not become the sole decision-making factor in your food choices. This often leads to emotional eating, especially in situations where stress is present, or a significant, possibly traumatic event has occurred in life. It is easy to become side-tracked with less healthy choices that appear tasty and satisfying at the moment, though will become regrettable in the long run. If it is beneficial to have a friend or family member present during your grocery shopping, as a means of support to choose the right foods, this can make a positive difference and lead to shaping better habits in the long-term.

- If you eat a food item, or several, that are not healthy and you feel the effects, don't feel guilty! This will happen from time to time. The best approach is to step back and take note of any reason(s) for the decision. Sometimes we "cave in" to cravings, or emotional responses to foods that we know are not healthy, simply because they taste good. In some cases, it's an occasion or special event that will trigger a craving now and again. This is only temporary and can be overcome with better decisions the next time.

Which foods should you choose when shopping? Think natural, whole foods with little or no additives. Some foods are specifically good for preventing and treating anxiety, due to their nutritious value, and they make a perfect addition to your grocery list:

Seafood

Fish is called brain food for a good reason: it is rich in protein, calcium, omega-3 fatty acids that provide an abundance of nutrients for your brain. A deficiency in fatty acids has been linked to mental disorders and conditions. Seafood is also excellent for building muscle and increasing healthy fats without carbohydrates. The low carb factor is good for weight loss, and a good way to build strength during exercise.

Tuna and salmon are both excellent choices for seafood, though depending on where the fish is bought or caught, some varieties of tuna can contain high amounts of mercury. If this is a concern in your region, limit your intake to smaller portions, and supplement with other forms of nutrients in fish that can be found in vegetables, fruits, and other whole foods.

Avocado

If you are vegan or vegetarian, enjoying avocado regularly will give you a good dose of healthy fats very similar to fish. Avocados are an excellent source of vitamins and fiber for keeping your body's metabolism regular, and they are easy to digest, which contributes to good gut health. This fruit is an excellent source of fuel for energy before a workout, and just one avocado can be a filling snack or small meal on its own. Avocados provide a lot of health benefits, from weight loss and improved brain function to reducing the risk of heart disease, type 2 diabetes and cancer.

They also combat depression and anxiety, which are connected to nutrient deficiencies.

Avocados contain vitamins K, E, C and B6, as well as various minerals, including potassium and magnesium. Avocadoes contain omega 3 fatty acids, which are one of the best ways to nourish your brain's health and prevent anxiety. They are a staple in low carb, high-fat diets and considered a "super" food by nutritionists, due to the sheer amount of nutrients in just one serving. In terms of sugar content, avocados are a low glycemic fruit, which is good for providing regular insulin levels in the body. Regular consumption of avocado keeps many deficiencies from developing.

Coconut Oil

There are numerous benefits to coconut oil, as well as MCT oil (the extracted fat from coconut). Good oils and fats are best consumed in their natural, raw state, in order to gain the most for your brain's health and cognitive function. A consistent supply of coconut oil, as well as other healthy fat sources, keeps your brain well-nourished, which helps guard against anxiety and depression, both of which are linked to nutrient deficiencies.

Coconut oil is also great on the outside of our bodies, as well as inside. It makes an ideal hair conditioner (or moisturizer), skin cream and lotion.

On the inside, coconut oil and MCT oil, like avocado, is high in healthy fats. It can be consumed as it is, or used in cooking, baking, and raw food recipes. MCT oil, the fat of coconut oil, is similarly beneficial for weight loss and brain function. With the popularity of the ketogenic and similar low carb diets that promote high consumption of healthy fats, MCT oil has become more common and available as a supplement for smoothies, coffee, tea or used in recipes. Unlike coconut oil, it is flavorless and can mix well into many foods and drinks.

Berries

One of the best fruits to choose for healthy eating is berries. They are high in phytochemicals, antioxidants, fiber and vitamins. These include strawberries, blueberries, blackberry and raspberries. Fresh or frozen, they make a great addition to breakfast, dessert, or as a snack. They are considered one of the healthiest foods on the planet, and for a good reason, due to their high nutrient content and numerous health benefits. Even in small portions, berries are potent and rich enough to make a positive impact.

Berries help regulate insulin and keep blood sugar levels down, which means they effectively prevent the onset of type 2 diabetes. For people who already have diabetes, berries have shown improvement in their insulin levels within a short period of time. When blood sugar levels are low and consistent, this has a positive effect on our brain and mood as well, maintaining balance and preventing reactive situations brought on by stress and anxiety.

The high fiber in berries helps the body absorb nutrients, aid digestion and keep the metabolic process regular. The anti-inflammatory properties in berries also prevent and treat inflammation and relieve stress. This is most beneficial when combined with regular exercise and activity.

Blueberries specifically contain a high amount of vitamin C and other antioxidants, making them a powerful tool in reducing the stress associated with anxiety. They support the production of healthy cells and may also contribute on preventing cancer. They are naturally sweet and can often be added to desserts or smoothies with no added sweeteners.

One of the best advantages of berries is how inclusive they are in every diet: low carb, high protein, vegan, vegetarian or any diet. Fruits that may be restricted due to high sugar or starch do not include berries, which are suitable for even the strictest diets and meal plans. They do not require much preparation and can be enjoyed as a delicious snack on their own, or with some dairy or coconut milk as a dessert.

Bone Broth

Gaining popularity in paleo and ketogenic diets, bone broth has become a staple in a healthy, low carb, high protein diet. It is more nutrient-rich and satisfying than regular broth, as it is prepared over a longer time period, approximately 20-24 hours of steeping bones to get most out of the minerals they contain. There are many advantages to including bone broth in your diet, even if it's a small amount once daily or several times per week.

Aging takes a toll on the bones, joints and body in general. The collagen in bone broth, along with other nutrients, provides relief from conditions that develop as we age, such as osteoarthritis, skin conditions and aging, bone density loss and joint pain. The hormonal balancing effect of bone broth also promotes better sleep while increasing energy and better mood stability.

Collagen is a protein produced in the body. It is vital for protecting organs, muscles, bones and keeping the gut lining healthy and strong. Due to its elasticity, it also has an anti-aging effect on the skin and body, which also relieves a lot of symptoms and conditions related to a middle or older age. Collagen is also the main ingredient in bone broth, and consuming it regularly will provide an abundance of benefit regularly.

Preparing bone broth is time-consuming, especially when made from scratch. While this is a great way to get the most out of leftover poultry or beef bones, bone broth is often available in convenient powder form, that can be prepared with boiling water. Essentially, it can be made within several minutes as a hot drink for a quick source of fuel and nutrients, which makes it an excellent choice for getting the most out of healthy eating when you live a busy life.

Green leafy vegetables

Dark, leafy and green vegetables are the best option for an anti-anxiety diet. This is due to the low glycemic level and high nutrient factor. Dark green vegetables contain high amounts of iron, magnesium, and calcium, all of which are important minerals required for overall good health and strength. They also contain a wealth of other nutrients, including fiber, folate, vitamins C, K and carotenoids. While dark green vegetables are not always a favorite choice of food, considering their bitter taste and sometimes difficult texture, an acquired taste can develop and there are many recipes and options that make eating dark greens enjoyable.

While all vegetables are healthy, dark greens tend to be more nutrient-rich and a good choice when you want to avoid deficiencies as much as possible. Regularly including dark greens into your meals will help ensure you maximize their potential. To include them as much as possible, they are included in recipes and meal plans in the following chapters. The following dark greens listed below are easy to find and make an excellent addition to any meal.

Spinach

Spinach helps transport oxygen throughout the body and contains vitamins K, A and C. It also contains iron and magnesium, which helps with energy and maintaining a healthy level of iron, which is subject to a deficiency in many diets, specifically vegan. Spinach is versatile in meals, accompanying eggs for breakfast, as a base for a salad, in curries, soups and as a simple side dish. This vegetable works well with many spices and compliments many flavors.

Kale

Known as a bitter-tasting vegetable, kale has grown in popularity due to its health benefits. It's considered one of the most nutrient-rich foods in the world, due to the sheer number of vitamins and minerals it contains: copper, magnesium, vitamins B6, C, A and K, among many others. Kale is low in fat and high in fiber. There are different varieties of kale (green, red and black), each with a slight change in texture. Kale belongs to the cabbage "family" of vegetables, which also includes brussels sprouts, broccoli, cauliflower and collard greens. Some of the most significant health benefits of kale include anti-aging and cancer prevention. It's also an anti-depressant, which can also help treat anxiety. Kale is often added to salads, as a side or main dish and is popular to include in freshly squeezed juices and smoothies.

Broccoli

Similar to kale in its relation to cabbage, broccoli has long been considered one of the most anti-cancerous foods, due to the antioxidants it contains. It's an anti-inflammatory food, which helps with digestion and brain function. Broccoli contains most of the same nutrients found in kale and supports bone health. It's a delicious vegetable, either raw or cooked, and makes a great addition to soups stir fry meals, salads and casseroles.

Arugula

Potassium, calcium, vitamins C, B and K, are among the nutrients found in arugula. Arugula helps with blood clotting and improving the function of the immune system. Supporting the heart and nerves, arugula is beneficial for anxiety. It's often added to salads and as a topping on burgers, sandwiches and wraps.

Lettuce

One of the most often uses vegetables in salads and sandwiches, lettuce provides iron, calcium, potassium and vitamin C. Certain types of lettuce, such as iceberg lettuce, contains a lot of water, which is important for hydration, especially during hot and humid weather. Lettuce is often combined with other greens in salads, and as a raw garnish or side with skillet meals.

Nuts and Seeds

In general, nuts and seeds make excellent choices for snacking and as a part of a regular diet, due to their high fat and nutrient content. In addition to having a supportive effect on your brain's health and supporting a balanced mood, they help protect cells and prevent cancer. Selenium is one of the main nutrients in nuts that promotes cellular health. Even a small handful of nuts each day can make a significant difference in the way you feel and function.

Almonds

One of the most popular tree nuts in the world, almonds, is also among the healthiest and tastiest. Added to virtually any type of meal, from desserts, stir-fries and smoothies to nut butter and salads, almonds provide many benefits. They are rich in antioxidants, vitamins, healthy fats and minerals, all of which are vital for your brain and bodily functions. They can be enjoyed either raw, with or without salt or roasted. In low carb baking recipes, ground almond flour makes an excellent alternative to high carb wheat flour and is also naturally gluten-free, a benefit for people who have a gluten intolerance. Almond is also available as an oil, butter and often extracted and added as a flavor to desserts and pastries.

Vitamin E is a fat-soluble vitamin found in almonds, which guards against damage to cells and protecting their membranes. This vitamin has been reported as having a preventative effect and reduces the possibility of cancer, Alzheimer's disease and heart ailments.

Blood sugar and insulin levels are regulated due to almonds' low sugar and high fat, protein and fiber levels. Magnesium also plays a role in maintaining healthy blood pressure levels and almonds can provide the daily requirement of this mineral on their own. Other benefits from almonds include lowering LDL or "bad" cholesterol while increasing HDL or "good" cholesterol levels. Almonds also promote weight loss due to their high fiber content and can provide an abundance of nutrition in just one handful.

Cashews

With high levels of magnesium, phosphorus, zinc and iron, cashews are another healthy snack to include in your diet. They can be combined with other nuts, such as almonds, or enjoyed on their own. Cashews are commonly added as a topping to Asian dishes or in snack mixes (combined with various nuts and/or dried fruits). Cashews are becoming more popular as a non-dairy beverage (cashew milk) and can be added to cookies and other baked desserts. They tend to cost more than other nuts, though can be added to your diet in small amounts.

The health benefit of cashews includes promoting healthy levels of good cholesterol, regulating insulin and sugar levels in the body, preventing type 2 diabetes and strengthening bones, joints while increasing energy. Cashews, like other nuts, contain high levels of healthy fats, which have a positive impact on brain health and cognitive function.

Peanuts

Often avoided due to rising peanut allergies, which prohibit many foods containing peanut and peanut-derived products from being included in meals at schools and some places of work, peanuts can be easily substituted with other nuts and/or seeds. For many people, peanuts and products containing peanuts are a staple in the diet. Peanut butter is a common and easy way to satisfy a peanut craving while receiving a significant dose of protein and healthy fats.

Peanuts are healthy for many reasons: they contain a lot of fiber which promotes weight loss, protein for building muscles, numerous vitamins (B6, and E) and minerals (magnesium, iron, phosphorus, and zinc, among others). All these ingredients in peanuts help prevent diseases by lowering high blood pressure, slowing the aging process, regulating blood sugar and improving skin conditions. There are promising results for women experiencing the onset of postmenopausal symptoms, where the healthy fats in peanuts maintained healthy levels of cholesterol.

Brazil Nuts

Brazil nuts are high in selenium and have a positive effect on improving mood and reducing anxiety. It's also considered an anti-carcinogenic, which means it helps prevent the formation of cancerous cells. Brazil nuts have shown good results for thyroid function. They are a good source of iron and selenium, both of which promote a healthy thyroid. Brazil nuts are a great snack and usually enjoyed in combination with other nuts and/or seeds. They are also high in fiber, which helps maintain a healthy weight.

Macadamia Nuts

Macadamia nuts are added to bread, cookies or enjoyed as a snack on their own. They are high in healthy fats and can be ground and added to make baked goods, sometimes replacing less healthy options as a better alternative. Macadamia nuts are filling and even in small portions, they can satisfy hunger quickly. Despite being more expensive than other varieties of nuts, macadamia nuts can be bought in bulk and enjoyed in small amounts, even as little as three or four each day, to enjoy the benefits of their nutrients.

There are many other benefits to your health from eating macadamia nuts regularly, including the prevention of cancer, promoting a healthy brain and neurotransmitter function, regulating hunger signals (to avoid overeating), preventing heart disease and improving metabolism. Weight loss is another benefit of including macadamia nuts in your diet. Some studies indicate that the type of fat in macadamia nuts is of a higher quality than other nuts, which makes them a preferred choice for this reason.

They can also curb cravings for other foods, and once incorporated into your diet; you may cultivate a craving specifically for macadamia nuts, which makes them a good snack to have on hand to avoid eating other foods with less nutrient value.

Other benefits include improving liver health and function and decreasing cravings for and reliance on alcohol. Macadamia nuts have a buttery flavor and are a good source of healthy fats, protein, vitamins and minerals.

Hazelnuts

Hazelnuts are often found as a snack combined with other nuts and added to various chocolate desserts and spread for its pleasant flavor. This variety of nut contains a high amount of dietary fiber, which aids in weight loss and improving bowel function. The healthy fats, vitamin and minerals contained in hazelnuts support and improve insulin levels and production, improve cell function and protection, heart health and lowering cholesterol. Other benefits include reducing inflammation, improving virility in men, and fertility in women and better reproductive health in general. Hazelnuts contain vitamin E and protein, in addition to healthy fats, which improve brain function.

In general, nuts are high in monounsaturated fats, which are building blocks for a healthy brain and mental function. Protein, vitamins and minerals contained in nuts also provide a substantial amount of support for the whole body and all of its functions, including the regulation of mood and emotional balance. For this reason, including nuts into your daily diet is an essential way to meet all or most of your nutrient requirements and avoid deficiencies.

In addition to the benefits of various nuts, seeds also contain many similar nutrients and provide similar properties to improve health. Seeds are often added with nuts or eaten on their own as a snack, either raw, roasted or flavored. Like nuts, they are available as a packaged snack, though they are best enjoyed in raw or lightly roasted form. Many packaged nuts and seeds may contain flavoring that may enhance the taste to a more sweet, salty or spicy option, though additives and hidden artificial ingredients may be included and should be avoided as much as possible. Seeds are easy to add to a meal or recipe as an ingredient or topping.

Chia Seeds

Chia seeds contain a good amount of omega 3 fatty acids, as well as calcium and protein. Chia seeds have the effect of helping the body produce more fatty acids, which helps reduce inflammation. This is accomplished by increasing ALA in the blood, which the body converts into other different types of omega 3 fats. These include eicosatetraenoic acid, known as EPA, and docosahexaenoic acid, otherwise known as DHA. A staple in low carb and ketogenic diets, chia seeds are used in salads, energy drinks and bars, puddings and cereals (both hot and cold).

They provide a good dose of energy while filling you fast and reducing hunger, thus avoiding overeating and promoting weight loss. Chia seeds may be able to reduce appetite and blood sugar levels. In one study, people with type 2 diabetes noticed a significant reduction in blood pressure over a period of approximately three months, and a reduction in inflammation, due to eating chia seeds regularly.

Pumpkin seeds

Pumpkin seeds contain a good amount of potassium, which provides electrolytes to the body, reduces stress and keeps blood pressure manageable. They also contain zinc, which is a key component for the development of the brain and nerves and can help balance emotions and mood. They are tasty on their own as a snack and can be added to cereal and/or as a topping for desserts or a yogurt parfait.

Sesame Seeds

These seeds are excellent for promoting healthy gut bacteria, which supports brain health and improves digestion. Sesame seeds contain lignans, which helps with hormonal balance in the body. This has the effect of preventing certain types of cancers, including breast cancer. Sesame seeds also prevent heart disease and lower blood pressure and cholesterol. Some research indicates that women in the postmenopausal stage have been able to improve their hormone levels, while decreasing blood pressure, after consuming sesame seeds for several weeks regularly.

Other benefits and studies indicate lower inflammation results from eating a regular amount of sesame seeds, which provides relief to people who suffer from osteoarthritis and joint pain. Some studies show improvement in muscle damage and other injuries associated with sports and athletic activity.

Sesame seeds are common in many Asian dishes and used to make tahini (sesame butter), which is a common ingredient in many dips and dishes, including hummus. Sesame seeds are a great topping for desserts and pastries, either raw or roasted.

Sunflower seeds

Sunflower seeds are high in protein, monounsaturated fats (healthy fats) and vitamin E. Like many other nuts and seeds, sunflower seeds decrease inflammation and promote healthier bones and joints, by relieving pain and stress. This has a positive impact on well-being and mood. Healthy cholesterol and hormonal levels were reported in women during and after menopause. While sunflower seeds have the effect of reducing both "good" and "bad" cholesterol, their benefits are plenty and they make an excellent addition to the diet. Sunflower seeds are often enjoyed salted with other nuts as a snack.

Hemp seeds

Hemp seeds are very high in protein, making them an ideal source of this nutrient for vegans and vegetarians who rely on getting their nutrients from plant-based sources. In fact, hemp seeds are considered one of the few plants that contain a complete source of protein to meet any the daily dietary needs of this nutrient. When a food contains a complete source of protein, it means that it includes more than your body can make, including essential amino acids, which need to be consumed to reap the benefits.

Seeds are one form that hemp can be added to your diet. Hemp hearts are another more readily available product that can be found in grocery stores and natural food markets. Flaxseed oil and oil products that combine flaxseed oil with other oils is another option for consumption. Oils are usually added in the same way that seeds are, only they are easier to mix with salad dressings, such as balsamic and drinks. The health benefits of including flaxseeds into your diet regularly include treating symptoms of eczema, increasing healthy fats for improved brain function, moisturizing skin and reducing dryness and supporting a healthy heart.

Flaxseeds

These seeds are an excellent source of omega 3 fatty acids, fiber and protein. Flaxseeds contain polyphenols which are antioxidants. They protect the body against cancer and infection. In their full form, with the shell, they are difficult to digest and break down.

For this reason, flaxseeds are usually ground or crushed and added to smoothies, energy bars, cereals and as a topping on a yogurt parfait. Flaxseeds can also be pressed into oil and usually stored in a dark-colored bottle, to preserve freshness. Other health benefits include reducing tumor growth, particularly in breast cancer, weight loss and maintenance, lower cholesterol and improved blood circulation. There are also promising results on hormonal regulation in women of all ages, due to lignans contained in flaxseeds. Lignans are also known as phytoestrogens, which are like the same type of estrogen produced in the body.

Cocoa and Dark Chocolate

Cocoa and dark chocolate contain nutrients that elevate the mood. It's a win-win situation if you happen to crave the flavor of chocolate, as long as a dark, unsweetened variety is chosen. There are many desserts and recipes that combine unsweetened cocoa and/or chocolate in combination with low carb sweeteners, in the form of cakes, puddings, energy bars and smoothies. The benefits of dark chocolate originate from the flavonoids it contains, which have a positive effect on the brain and mood regulation. It can also reduce inflammation in the brain, which promotes healthier cell growth while increasing serotonin and improving neurotransmitters that regulate mood.

Turmeric

This spice, even in small amounts, can be very effective in treating anxiety and depression. Turmeric is commonly used in a variety of Asian dishes, and becoming more popular in drinks, including kombucha. The active ingredient responsible for improving mood and anxiety is curcumin, by reducing oxidative stress and lowering inflammation. This ingredient also has a positive effect on reducing anxiety. Due to its mild flavor, turmeric can be added to virtually anything from desserts to smoothies, curries, soups and skillet meals.

Green Tea

There are many different strains of green tea, with sencha and matcha the most common and popular. Once only available in Asian supermarkets and restaurants, green tea drinks, powders (as a supplement or addition to recipes) have become increasingly popular in recent years, due to the number of benefits provided. The high level of antioxidants, which rival many fruits and vegetables, promote mood stability and have a calming effect while providing the body with energy.

Green tea also helps the body produce serotonin and increase dopamine, both of which enhance and improve mood. Any variety of green tea is suitable, depending on your preference. Sencha green tea is often used to make tea, while matcha is used to flavor cakes, pastries, cold drinks and puddings. When choosing a green tea beverage or product, avoid drinks and products that contain added sugars and additives, which are common. The best option for green tea, as with any tea, is to purchase in its natural, whole form, like leaves or crushed into a powder. As a tea, served cold or hot, it is a suitable replacement for coffee, juice and energy drinks.

Chamomile Tea

This tea is created from chamomile flowers and has a calming effect on the nerves and brain. Chamomile can help promote a good night's rest while fighting inflammation and promoting relaxation. These benefits are due to the flavonoids contained in flower, which also reduces the effects of anxiety and may also fight bacterial infections. It can be consumed regularly, even daily, with no ill effects. Chamomile tea has a mild and pleasant flavor.

Cinnamon

A common topping for desserts with a distinctive flavor, cinnamon has excellent benefits for balancing mood and improving health. Among the benefits of cinnamon include reducing blood pressure and reducing inflammation in the body. Cinnamon can be used as a replacement for a sweetener, or in combination with a low carb sweetener as a dessert or cereal topping or added to a smoothie to boost flavor.

Asparagus

Dark green leafy vegetables often get noticed for their high nutrient content, including iron and fiber, though there are other greens that are very beneficial to reducing anxiety, and asparagus is one of them.

This vegetable is associated with elevating mood levels and decreasing depression, due to containing folic acid, which also helps support nerve and brain health.

The benefits of eating asparagus include its delicious flavor and texture, which is a good addition to many different types of meals during the day.

It can be prepared in a casserole or grilled as part of a side dish. Asparagus is also a great addition to an eggs benedict plate or stir fry.

How Gut Health Is Important for Your Mood: Balancing Bacteria with Fermented Foods

For many, the mere thought of fermented foods conjures imagines of strong, pungent tasting sauerkraut or a mild, yet distinctive flavor of yogurt.

The following chapter provides more details on the most common types of fermented foods, all of which support and promote a healthy gut.

While these types of foods may seem off-putting to some, there are different varieties and options to consider including their significant benefits.

In addition to the fermentation process, which increases the nutrient value, there are a lot of other benefits to these foods, including calcium, fiber and protein, and in some cases, antioxidants.

CHAPTER 3

Adapting to an Anti-Anxiety Diet

Reduce the Carbohydrates and Sugar in Your Diet

One of the most important factors in adapting to an anti-anxiety diet is to reduce the level of carbohydrates in your food. This doesn't have to be a drastic change; a gradual reduction in carbohydrates makes a significant difference in a couple of weeks. The first place to eliminate or reduce carbs is in foods with added sugars and trans fats. This includes packaged baked goods, pastries, cakes, candies and in some cases, dried fruits and snacks, as these are not always naturally dried:

- Does your food item come in a package? If so, can you choose a natural, whole food instead? For example, choosing fresh apples instead of sugary apple sauce or dried apple snacks.

- Trans fats are one of the worst ingredients in food and are found in cookies, chips and deep-fried foods. It's best to avoid these completely and find a healthier alternative, such as a handful of mixed nuts instead of potato chips. Monounsaturated and polyunsaturated fats refer to the natural, healthy fats found in whole foods, and should be included in place of trans fats as much as possible.

- Does the food item contain added sugars and/or more than one type of sugar? If so, it's going to impact the blood sugar level and glycemic balance in your body, which impacts your mood and overall sense of stability. Regular consumption of sugary foods, if products that indicate "natural sugar" can be deceiving and are usually high in carbohydrates, which the body converts to glucose. If consumed frequently, they can have a negative impact on your health.

- If you choose to buy supplements as part of your diet, are the ingredients synthetic and/or do they adequately cover the daily requirement you need for the nutrients they provide? Ask a professional nutritionist, doctor or dietician if in doubt about a particular supplement or tablet, as they are not all created equal. Some have far more quality and value than others and may be worth spending more money on if this is the case. If the world of supplements and vitamins is new to you, research, ask questions and take note of your experiences with the different products you try.

Some natural sweeteners can replace refined sugars and natural sugar and sweeteners in order to reduce and maintain normal blood sugar levels in your body. This has a significant impact on your brain's health as well. A spike in sugar can be momentary, though it can severely impact your brain, mood and stress levels within minutes. By replacing sugars (both refined and natural) in your diet, you will also reduce the carbohydrates, which can also trigger sugar spikes and changes in your body:

Stevia

This natural sweetener is extracted from the stevia plant, which is found in South America. It's become more common in many keto-friendly snack, drinks and desserts, and it's usually mixed with other low carb sweeteners. On its own, stevia is sweet in flavor, though not as similar to sugar as other low carb options. Some research indicates stevia may lower blood sugar levels and help regulate insulin in both human and animal studies. For this reason, it's combined with other flavors to enhance a more "sugar" taste. Stevia is available in most stores as a liquid or as a powder.

Monk Fruit

Known for its very similar taste to sugar, monk fruit grows in some southeast regions of Asia. Due to its sweetness and low glycemic level, it makes an excellent substitute for sugar and other artificial sweeteners. Monk fruit can work well on its own, or mixed with other low carb sweeteners for coffee, tea, and baked goods. It's available in granules and resembles sugar both in taste and appearance.

Erythritol

Another common low carb sweetener is erythritol, which is often combined with stevia to improve the taste. It is used similarly to monk fruit, as a coffee or tea sweetener and in recipes for baking...

Xylitol

Xylitol is becoming more available as other low carb sweeteners, though it is often avoided for one major reason: the risk it presents to household pets, such as cats and dogs. A warning or cautionary label is often attached to this product, so that pet owners are aware and can take necessary precautions. For humans, there is no risk associated with this sweetener, and it can be used in place of sugar and other high-calorie syrups and sweeteners. Xylitol is available in granules, similar to monk fruit and erythritol.

Sucralose

Although this sweetener is often used as a condiment for hot and cold drinks, it's not recommended for use in baking or cooking, where the elevated temperature will alter the chemical compound, making this sweetener unhealthy. If used at all, it's not the best option, though should only be added to foods and drinks that will not be heated. If you wish to keep sugar in your diet and restrict the amount to small portions, it's best to stick with natural sugars found in fruits, as they are absorbed more effectively and quickly by the body than their refined counterparts. Examples of natural sugars that can be enjoyed in moderation include maple syrup, honey, agave, prunes and dates.

Eliminating Processed and Packaged Foods

Make whole foods the centerpiece of your diet and eliminate as many processed and artificial foods as possible. For every snack that is unhealthy, there is always a better option available, whether it is in the bulk store, grocer or local farmers' market. Eliminating all packaged foods from your diet completely, while ideal, is often not a realistic goal, due to the rising costs of whole foods, such as fruits and vegetables and organic options, such as meat and dairy, that are free of hormones and chemicals.

Choosing Whole Food Options That Fit into Your Diet and Lifestyle

Low Carb Foods

In reviewing the many whole foods and their benefits to your brain's health, there are several common factors found in many of the foods covered in this book, which indicate a preference for low carb, high-fat foods.

The nutrients that support brain health promote gut, and digestive health and overall reduction and prevention in many stress-related diseases are just some of the common denominators that all these foods share. Reducing the number of carbohydrates in your diet and food intake means there is less opportunity for high blood sugar.

When you consume foods high in carbs, your body will convert the carbohydrates and glucose contained in these foods into fuel, storing the remainder in the body. Even if you are active, and tend to burn fuel quickly, continually eating high amounts of carbs will eventually increase the amount of glucose in the body that will not be used, and fat stores, a better source of fuel, will not be used until the carbs and glucose stored in the body are used up, as they are considered primary fuel.

Low carb foods are beneficial because they keep the carb content down while increasing the fat in our diet. In keeping the carb and sugar levels down, your body will search for the next source of fuel, which is fat. When your body switches from burning carbs to fat stores, this process is called ketosis. During this stage, your liver will produce ketones for energy and your body will actively burn fat for fuel, which has a significant impact on weight loss and energy levels. Reducing the amount of sugar in your diet does not have to mean switching to ketosis in order to benefit from low carb foods. Simply reducing high sugar foods and replacing them with moderate to low carb options can make a major difference in how well you feel.

There are studies that suggest low carb diets and the reduction of sugar can provide a healthy mental balance, therefore reducing stress, anxiety and depression, all of which are rooted in nutrient-deficient diets. By simply changing a lot of what we eat, a significant improvement in our mood, well-being and overall health can be achieved.

Plant-based options

Increasing the amount of plant-based food options in your diet is another beneficial way of reducing processed and refined sugars, which have an ill effect on moods and emotional response. While meat, dairy and eggs can be healthy in moderate amounts, there is a general shift towards reducing meat and including more plant-based options as part of a regular, balanced diet. When considering plant-based foods, choose whole, raw fruits, vegetables, legumes, nuts, seeds and soy.

Soy products are a good source of plant protein and nutrients, providing many, if not all, daily requirements for most nutrients we require for good health. When choosing soy foods, take caution with the ingredients, as some soymilk, butter, tofu and other products can contain additives that hinder the benefits of soy. If you have an allergy to soy or experience some side effects, such as bloating, which can affect some people, a better alternative is fermented soy products, such as miso and tofu, both of which are covered in the next section under fermented foods.

Yogurt, Kimchi, and Other Fermented Food Options

Fermented Foods: A Foundation for Balanced Gut

Bacteria

Fermented foods promote good bacteria to flourish in the stomach, while helping the overall balance of microbial levels in the gut, resulting in better digestion, stronger immunity and maintaining a healthy weight.

Sauerkraut

Known as traditional German food, sauerkraut usually accompanies European dishes as a side, though it can be added more regularly. It's a type of fermented cabbage, which originally became popular in Asia several thousand years ago, due to how the fermentation process can preserve food.

Sauerkraut is excellent food with many health benefits on its own too, including improving digestion, relieving stress and anxiety, weight loss and supporting heart health.

It can also improve mental function and strengthen bones. Sauerkraut is high in iron, fiber and vitamins K and C. The fermentation process involves the digestion of natural sugars in the cabbage by microorganisms and forming them into organic acids and carbon dioxide. The results of fermentation include the growth of probiotics, which are found in other fermented foods and are one of the primary methods for supporting gut health. Probiotics directly benefit the gut lining by supporting good bacterial growth and balance.

Kimchi

A Korean dish, kimchi is popular in several variations: fermented cabbage, which is like sauerkraut, radishes and other vegetables. It's also spicy and accompanies milder flavored foods well for this reason. Kimchi is delicious in many varieties; it often accompanies stewed beef, pork or seafood in Asian dishes. Aside from supporting gut health with probiotics, kimchi prevents stomach cancer and has anti-aging properties. The high level of nutrients and antioxidants contribute to healthy skin, hair and support vision health. It may also help cholesterol.

Yogurt

In its natural, unsweetened and unflavored state, yogurt is full of probiotics that protect and "coat" the stomach, and aid in digestion. Yogurt is high in protein, calcium and live bacterial cultures, all of which benefit the stomach lining and overall health, including supporting healthy teeth and bones. While most people choose low-fat yogurt on a diet, it's best to select a natural, unsweetened, unflavored full-fat yogurt (such as Greek or Icelandic), as there are more nutrients and less sugar. Yogurt is versatile, in that it can be added to many dishes, dips, sauces, smoothies and desserts. On its own, yogurt can be a refreshing snack.

Kefir

Like yogurt, kefir is fermented, and best in its unsweetened and unflavored form. It tends to be thinner in consistency than yogurt, making it ideal as a drink and an ingredient in smoothies. Kefir offers a high level of probiotics than yogurt, which makes it a more powerful support system for gut health and stomach lining. It helps prevent osteoporosis, improves bone health, and contains antibacterial properties that fight infection while strengthening the immune system. Drinking just one glass of kefir daily can improve your overall amount of daily nutrients and meet some of the requirements in just one serving. Due to the high amount of bacterial cultures and sensitivities to lactose, kefir can cause some initial irritation. For this reason, it's best to enjoy with natural fruit or with a light meal, like salad or cereal. Drinking ginger tea or adding ginger to kefir can further aid with the benefits of digestion. There are non-dairy alternatives for both kefir and yogurt made from cultured coconut milk.

Tempeh

Prepared similarly to tofu, tempeh is the fermented, soy-based version with a stronger, "rougher" texture, ideal as a meat replacement. While tempeh can be consumed raw, most people enjoy adding it to a cooked meal, usually as a meat replacement in stir-fries, pasta or casserole dishes. The fermentation process in tempeh effectively "consumes" the actual soybeans, forming them into various amino acids, which are beneficial for supporting neurotransmitters and brain health. Some people are concerned about the effects of soy on estrogen and other hormones in the body. While tempeh contains plant-based hormones known as phytoestrogens, they are "tamed" during the fermentation process, allowing for better digestion. People who experience intolerance towards soy-based foods may find the tempeh and miso, both fermented versions of soy, are easier to digest without any side effects.

Miso

Often served as a side in many sushi restaurants, miso is usually prepared as a pleasant tasting soup that contains a mild, distinctive and pleasant flavor, miso is an easy addition to any diet. Like tempeh, miso is fermented soy, with the added benefit of B12, which is a rare find in plant-based foods and usually deficient in vegan diets. Due to fermentation, miso provides support to gut health and is linked to improving calmness and a reduction in anxiety. Miso is high in protein, calcium, probiotics, vitamin K and fiber. There are several varieties of miso, which are usually in a thick paste form, making them easy to add to soups, sauces and other dishes:

- White miso is made with fermented soybeans and rice. It is called "white" or "shiro" miso due to its pale color, which is very mild in flavor. It's fermented for one or two months at the most.

- Red or "aka" miso is fermented for up to three years, which significantly strengthens the flavor.

- Yellow or "shinsu" miso is fermented longer than white miso, though not as long as the red variety, making it a moderate version for taste.

Kombucha

A fermented tea drink, usually prepared as a cold tea beverage, kombucha has grown immensely in popularity, due to the variety of flavors and enjoyable taste. Slightly alcoholic due to the fermentation process, kombucha can be enjoyed by anyone to support and improve stomach lining and gut health. Kombucha drinks are currently offered in many different flavors and varieties, which are available in most grocery and natural food stores. Kombucha strengthens the immune system and digestion.

It is usually fermented from green tea, and flavored with various natural options, such as fruit, ginger and honey. Fermented foods, in general, are excellent for your health and can be easily added to your diet to increase the nutritional value and maximize overall health. If you have extra time, many fermented foods can be prepared at home, which includes yogurt, sauerkraut and even kombucha. With the growing popularity of these foods, fermentation kits and supplies are becoming more readily available in stores, making the process easier and convenient.

High Alkaline Foods, and Avoiding Overly Acidic Options

Choosing foods high in alkaline have a significant benefit on how our brain functions. This is due to our body's natural alkaline or basic balance, which is just above 7 (around 7.35 to 7.4) on the pH scale:

0	1	2	3	4	5	6	7	8	9	10	11	12	13	14

Acidic   pH neutral   Alkaline

Maintaining a healthy pH balance is an important component in overall brain and body health and this includes choosing foods less acidic and more alkaline in nature, as this has a neutralizing effect on high acidic levels in the body.

Meat, dairy and grains tend to be higher in acidic properties, while fruits and vegetables tend to be more alkaline.

Even citrus fruits, which contain citric acid, convert into alkaline when consumed. Generally, plant-based foods tend to be more alkaline based on the pH scale, with a rating over seven. The following foods contain the highest amounts of alkaline:

- Cucumbers: lowers blood pressure, supports connective tissue in muscles.

- Watermelon: high in fiber and easy to digest; also high in potassium which reduces water retention in the body.

- Avocado: high in antioxidants, fiber, and essential fats.

- Spinach: contains a lot of vitamins (C, A and K), as well as iron and calcium.

- Kale is another option that can be combined with spinach or as a replacement: high in many vitamins and antioxidants.

Other high alkaline foods include bananas, peppers, nuts, seeds and various spices. Including these foods in your diet will guard against indigestion, acid reflux and other conditions associated with an acidic diet. While eating foods that are more acidic, like meat and dairy, is acceptable, it's important to balance the portion of acid-producing foods with higher amounts of alkaline choices.

Replacing Foods that Trigger Anxiety, Inflammation and Gut Health Issues with Healthier Options

Many healthy food options play an important role in our mental and physical health, including combatting depression and anxiety. There are also specific foods that are best to limit or avoid altogether, as they do not adequately satisfy hunger and thirst, and cause hunger pains too soon after. These are known as empty or "filler" foods that have little or no nutritional value. Fortunately, there is an appropriate and healthier replacement for each of these.

Fruit juice

The label may read 100% pure juice, not from concentrate and/or "freshly squeezed," though it's far from that of its natural source. When packaged juices are prepared, a lot of nutrients are leeched out or removed as a part of the process. This results in a product that is mostly comprised of water and sugar. The folic acid, vitamin C, and fiber in orange are far more effective and available than orange juice. If you enjoy a particular fruit juice, choose the actual fruit in its natural form to enjoy. Squeezing your own lemonade or simply adding lemon or lime to water can increase the electrolytes in your body while giving you the full benefits of the fruit.

Pop or Soda

Carbonated beverages are popular, from sparkling water to juice and pop. These are very high in sugar, nearly 30 grams of sugar in each can of soda, which contributes to an increased chance of developing type 2 diabetes and obesity, among other conditions as a result. Diet soda is not any better, because the refined sugars are simply replaced with artificial sweeteners that contain harmful ingredients. These sweeteners may contribute to unhealthy cell growth and increase the likelihood of tumor growth.

High amounts of sugar wreak havoc on mood stability and can impact the way we react emotionally. Anxiety attacks may increase as a result of sugar, as it can increase blood sugar, blood pressure, which applies more stress on our heart, liver and brain.

Bread and Toast

Bread is not always a bad choice, depending on how nutrient-rich it is. While there are some low carb, highly nutritious bread options available, white bread without any nutritional value is loaded with carbs and hidden sugars. For this reason, it is best to avoid, whether it is eaten fresh or toasted. If this type of bread is a regular part of your diet, it can be a challenge to reduce and eliminate it altogether. For this reason, reduce gradually, and replace it with a more nutrient-dense and lower-carb version of bread, or simply trade a slice of bread for a lettuce wrap, salad or other food option.

Low-Fat Foods

Avoid low-fat foods at all costs. Not only are they full of additives, sugars and other artificial ingredients, but they also provide little to no benefit in the long-term. Fats, both healthy and unhealthy fats, add natural flavor to many foods we enjoy. When they are removed, they are often replaced with an unnatural flavor or additive to mimic the missing taste. Low-fat salad dressings, yogurts, margarine and similar products are all examples of chemically enhanced foods due to low-fat content. It's best to skip the low-fat foods and look for natural, full-fat options instead.

CHAPTER 4

Your Gut Health: What You Need to Know

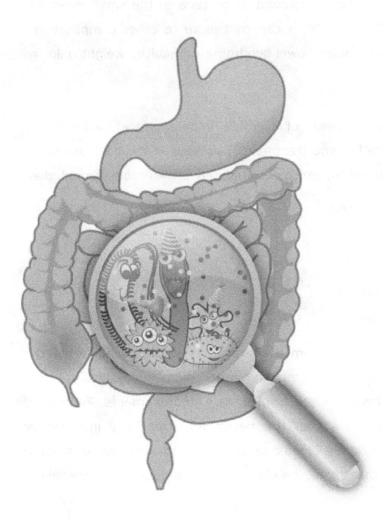

The Importance of a Healthy Stomach Lining

Maintaining good gut health is key to the prevention and treatment of many diseases and conditions that stem from a healthy digestive system. The gut microbiome, or bacteria, is one of the most important factors in maintaining a healthy stomach lining.

Dysbiosis: What Are the Causes and How it Can Be Prevented and Treated

Dysbiosis is a condition that occurs when the microbial (microorganisms, bacterial growth) is imbalanced, causing different issues with the overgrowth of bacteria in the small intestines and disturbances in the body's flora. This condition can contribute to other complications, such as chronic fatigue syndrome, inflammatory bowel syndrome, unhealthy weight gain, as well as certain types of cancers. C.

Difficile is an illness that occurs as a direct result of microbial imbalance and bacterial. It's contagious and often leads to hospitalization and treatment. Dysbiosis is the basis for many conditions that stem from bacterial overgrowth, which is completely preventable through diet. We are as healthy as what we eat.

What Foods Treat and Prevent Dysbiosis?

When a gut infection or similar result occurs from dysbiosis, physicians usually treat the condition with medication. Irritable bowel syndrome and other digestive issues are also treated with medications, though can benefit more from dietary improvements. Fermented foods are one of the best ways to improve your gut health and treat any infection or imbalance in bacteria. Before adding healthier foods to your diet to improve or prevent dysbiosis, there are a number of items that should be eliminated from your diet, especially if you experience symptoms of this disease.

These offending foods include, but are not limited to, the following:

- Processed meats. Avoid any meat products in packaging, as they contain nitrates, carcinogens, and other unhealthy preservatives and additives that will negatively impact your health.

- Foods high in carbohydrates, such as corn, baked goods and grains.

- Foods high in sugar and syrup, even natural sweeteners, such as agave, maple syrup and honey.

- Dairy products, such as milk and cheese, though small amounts of yogurt and kefir may be helpful, in conjunction with medication.

Some foods which are normally beneficial for gut lining and health may be difficult to consume during an infection, and therefore, extra care should be taken to gently introduce healthier foods once symptoms begin to lessen. Ginger is a great way to improve digestion and can be enjoyed in a milk tea, with lemon. Alkaline-based foods are another good way to improve an infection, in that it neutralizes the acidic impact on the gut lining.

Leaky Gut Syndrome: What are the Causes and Treatments?

A leaky gut is a condition or state in which the bacteria and toxins from the stomach "leak" into the bloodstream, causing inflammation throughout the body. While there is no official medical term for this condition called "leaky gut syndrome", and some professionals in the field do not recognize it as a disease specifically, it does contribute to many other syndromes, such as bloating (due to inflammation), fatigue, digestive problems, reactions to foods (sensitivities and allergies), among other conditions.

Diet can help prevent a leaky gut, and promote better bacterial growth and balance, which keeps a lot of other illnesses and conditions from developing.

There are certain common foods and drinks that should be avoided, or at least significantly reduced until they can be eliminated:

- Sugar. Natural sugars in fruit (fructose) is acceptable in small to moderate servings, though most foods we eat are loaded with processed sugars and sweeteners (both natural and unnatural). For this reason, it's best to avoid sugar wherever possible, even in its natural form. Sugar is simply abundant in most foods, and excessive intake contributes to conditions such as type 2 diabetes, obesity, and volatile changes in mood and emotional responses. High amounts of refined sugars, which are usually paired with other additives and artificial ingredients in products, can contribute to depression and contribute to poor choices since these foods can become habit-forming when regularly consumed.

- Excessive alcohol. An occasional indulgence isn't going to cause any problems, though drinking too much at once and/or frequently can severely damage your liver, kidneys and impact digestion. Many alcoholic beverages contain sugar and chemicals that interfere with our body's natural balance. Some beer and wine, in moderation, is acceptable, though should be avoided in excess.

- Foods that lack nutrients (packaged, processed foods). Avoid processed food wherever possible. They contain more artificial ingredients than nutrients and often contain labels touting "all-natural" or "no preservatives," though this is often inaccurate and misleading, as many preservatives are not regulated, and manufacturers can easily "hide" them under natural ingredients.

Avoiding a leaky gut: How can diet help?

To avoid or treat a leaky gut, avoid as many acidic foods as possible, and choose more plant-based options. Choose fermented foods, fresh fruits and vegetables, and obtain as much protein and nutrients as possible from plant-based foods.

During an infection or leaky gut, avoid or restrict meat and dairy, until there is an improvement in your gut health.

Diet considerations during a stomach infection or other gut issues should include gentle foods that are easy to digest.

Even probiotics, which are present in fermented foods, and aid in the prevention of many gut health issues and related diseases, may need to be temporarily avoided, due to the gut's reaction to probiotics, even though they are beneficial.

Ginger tea, chamomile tea, foods without caffeine and sugar are strongly recommended until your stomach shows signs of healing.

CHAPTER 5

Reducing Inflammation and Boosting Your Immunity

Reducing inflammation and promoting healing in your body: top foods for reducing inflammation

Inflammation is painful, uncomfortable and is your body's response to other conditions that need to be treated. It's important to keep your body's daily nutrients in check to reduce and avoid inflammation. These are known as anti-inflammatory foods or having properties or ingredients that prevent and treat inflammation:

- Coconut oil
- Walnuts (other nuts and seeds are beneficial as well)
- Turmeric
- Ginger (this also helps with digestion, and "calms" the body)
- Blueberries (all berries are advantageous, though blueberries contain the highest amounts of antioxidants)
- Salmon and fatty fish in general

Other tips for avoiding inflammation include reducing sugar and glucose-producing foods, such as bread, pastries and grains.

The Importance of Microbiome and your Immunity: What is a Microbiome and How Does it Protect and Maintain Good Health?

The microbiome refers to the total genetic environment in our body that includes bacteria, viruses, protozoa and fungi, among other microbes. It serves as a means to protect the immune system and plays a role in maintaining bacterial balance in the gut. When it is imbalanced, due to an infection or disease, there are various effects, such as weight gain, bloating, high blood sugar and related conditions. An unhealthy diet will not only contribute to an imbalanced microbiome, but it will also have a long-term effect of producing chronic pain, inflammation, and other disorders.

Selecting Foods and Supplements that Boost the Immune System for Optimal Performance and Function

The way we eat and the amount of nutrients we include in our diet has a significant impact on every part of our body and mind, from the way we think, respond and feel to how our body fends off viruses, fights infections and builds immunity.

All these mechanics will not function well or at all without nutrients, which is why including as many varieties of foods from the lists of macronutrients and micronutrients in chapter one is vital to maintaining a well-functioning body and mind.

Foods and supplements should be chosen carefully: for their nutrient content first and for the quality. Foods that are not fresh or subjected to numerous pesticides and additives, even fruits and vegetables, should be avoided. Wherever possible, choose organic and local foods to minimize the number of potential chemicals that are added. The longer foods travel for the purposes of importing, the more likely they are to be sprayed or chemically treated to prolong their shelf life. When choosing imported goods, there are organic options available. Foods with a hard shell or skin tend to be the best option, where selection is limited, as sprays and other additives may not seep into the fruit as much (or fewer chemicals may be used).

Supplements, such as vitamin tablets, protein powders and similar products provide a boost to our diet and can fill in many nutrient gaps to ensure we avoid deficiencies. In regions where certain fresh foods are unavailable or scarce, supplements can improve your nutrient level and can be stored for long-term use, unlike fresh sources. Fresh fish, for example, may be highly contaminated in some places, despite all of the fats, oils and protein they provide. In this case, adding an omega 3 supplement and/or fish oil extract is a valuable resource and a reasonably healthy replacement with less risk of toxins.

CHAPTER 6

Moods and Food: How to Achieve and Maintain Balance

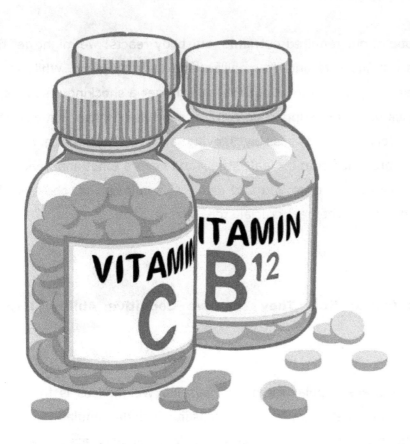

How What We Eat Impacts Our Mood and Reduces Anxiety

Anti-stress foods and supplements

Minerals, vitamins, antioxidants, phytochemicals and many other nutrients play a role in how our body manages stress.

When we experience a stressful event or occurrence, we cope by using up a lot of energy, in the form of stored nutrients already in our body. Certain vitamins are used up quickly, such as vitamin B and when we are stressed, we can become deficient in specific nutrients very quickly. Increasing the number of nutrients in our diet, particularly the ones we use the most, is effective in meeting our daily requirements and avoiding deficiency.

When we lose all or most of one of our required nutrients, our body reacts: we might get the "jitters" or shaky. Our moods will fluctuate and de-stabilize, and we may panic. While these are rational experiences in reaction to a serious event that can trigger a shocking response, it is also vital to get our body back to a more supportive state as soon as possible. Initially, this may include deep breathing, focusing and possibly moving away from a dangerous or frightening situation. Anxiety is brought about by fear, stress and severe emotional reactions. Once in a position where it is possible to cope and find peace in a calm place, boosting the nutrients in our body and mind become the next crucial step.

Ketogenic and Low Carb Foods: How They Improve Cognitive Ability, Mental function and reduce stress

The ketogenic and low carb diets are popular for many reasons. Weight loss is the major reason for adapting to a low carb diet, though other reasons include regulating insulin, prevention of type 2 diabetes, reducing (and eliminating) seizure activity associated with epilepsy, as well as the prevention and treatment of many other diseases. The ketogenic diet was initially developed to treat specific diseases over one hundred years ago and was found to be very successful as a treatment for long-term weight loss and maintenance, which is the reason for its renewed popularity. Choosing whole foods that are low on the glycemic scale and low to moderate in carbohydrates will benefit stabilizing mood and anxiety. Without the constant fluctuations in glucose, our response level and feelings will remain consistent and focused, rather than impulsive and erratic. Following a diet high in fats, proteins and nutrients is imperative for reducing stress, while improving cognitive function and response, by feeding our brain with the proper fuel to perform well.

Genetic Predispositions for Anxiety

Scientific studies on the prevalence of anxiety and related disorders indicate that while there is a genetic predisposition for this disorder, there are many other factors that play a role in contributing to the condition, such as environment, diet and life experience. If at least one family member experienced a form of anxiety, your chances might increase when certain factors occur or are present, which makes you "predisposed" to the condition. This doesn't necessarily automatically suggest that having a relative with anxiety, depression or another condition will increase your chances automatically, and there are many ways to reduce the likelihood of its development, whether genetic or not, through regular exercise, calming techniques, developing coping mechanisms and a healthy diet.

Deficiencies and Their Link to Anxiety and Unbalanced Mood and Health

How does a nutrient deficiency contribute to the onset of anxiety and/or mood disorders? It may not be the cause of the disorder, though it will contribute to its manifestation and further impact the toll that anxiety and stress will take on your body and mind. Nutrients build, support, and help as function at our best so that we can fight and prevent disease. When we experience stress or injury, our body will use any tools and nutrients necessary to "fix" and heal as quickly and efficiently as possible. It is at this moment when maintaining and consuming as many nutrients as needed becomes the most important. Without the building blocks for our body and mind, we break down other cells and experience a number of symptoms related to nutritional deficiency.

These include skin disorders, loss of bone density and stunted growth, and loss of memory. In severe cases, where long-term deficiencies continue, the very same disorders and diseases that a good diet prevents can begin to develop. It is during a state of deficiency, where the naturally occurring chemicals and receptors in our brain become affected and mood changes, including anxiety, can develop.

Reducing Stress and Strengthening Your Adrenal System

Identifying stressors and triggers for anxiety are important tools for understanding what causes panic attacks and related responses, and how we can strengthen our mind and body, including the adrenal system. A stressor is defined as an occurrence, item, or event that triggers an emotional response and increases stress. This could be a naturally occurring agent or chemical that is present in our environment, that we have little or no immediate control over.

A stressor can also be a certain individual or situation that presents a threat or challenge, which results in stress. A difficult memory, experience or traumatic event can cause common items, words or thoughts to trigger an anxious response. This can manifest in the form of an odor, word or gesture.

When we face a stressful, frightening experience or event, we exhibit a "flight" or "fight" response. In some cases, we might simply freeze, in a state of shock, as a delayed response. When we respond with a flight-or-fight response, it is our adrenal glands that initiate this process. The adrenal glands are located just above the kidneys and produce hormones in response to stressful events. The two glands that make up the adrenals include the adrenal cortex and the adrenal medulla. The adrenal cortex gland is responsible for producing hormones that regulate metabolism and assist your body in responding to stressful situations.

The type of hormones this gland produces is cortisol aldosterone. The other gland, adrenal medulla, is located towards the inside of the glands (the adrenal cortex is located towards the outer section of the glands). The adrenal medulla produces a set of less essential hormones that respond to stress.

There are several known disorders that can occur within the adrenal glands, either due to poor development or other reasons. These occur when either one or both glands fail to produce enough hormones or create an overproduction.

Addison's disease, Cushing's syndrome, and adrenal cancer are among some of the disorders. Fortunately, there are foods that can boost the performance of the adrenal glands, making them produce a more balanced level of hormones, and therefore providing a better response to stressful situations. These foods include lean meats (poultry, fish), eggs, legumes, dark and leafy green vegetables, whole grains, nuts, and seeds. Some dairy foods are also beneficial for the adrenal gland system, especially yogurt, which protects the stomach lining and reduces stress.

CHAPTER 7

Neurotransmitters: Understanding Your Brain's Signal System and How it Works

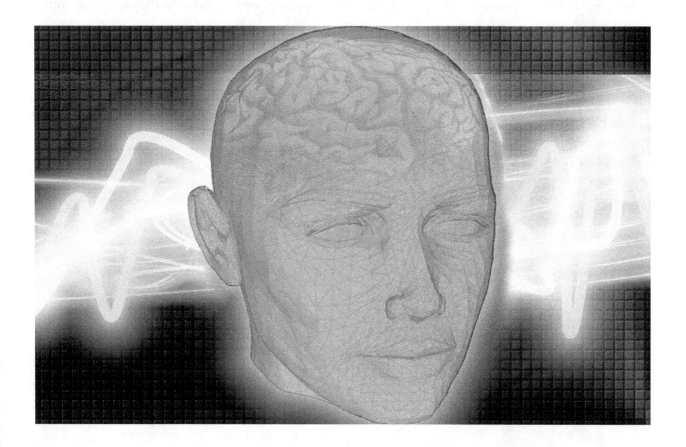

What Are Neurotransmitters and How Do They Work Together to Affect Your Brain's Health

The brain's signal system is comprised of neurotransmitters, which effectively "communicate" in order to function. Without proper transmission and the nutrients to support their functions, the brain suffers in different ways.

Neurotransmitters function by releasing a chemical substance at the end of a nerve fiber. This travels across a synapse, which triggers a transfer to another nerve fiber or muscle fiber or similar structure. In basic terms, this is the process by which the brain communicates with the rest of your body. In order to keep neurotransmitters performing well and quickly, good nutrition is vital. Consuming the right foods and nutrients is important for maintaining good brain function and avoiding imbalance, which leads to many conditions and disorders. It's helpful to become familiar with the different types of neurotransmitters, as they all have various roles and functions.

The Different Types of Transmitters and How They Function

There are different types of transmitters that function in the brain, with their specific tasks. In simple terms, they can be thought of as chemical messengers that transmit information from one area to another. This is done by communicating between neurons by crossing a "bridge" or synapse. Electrical signals must be converted or altered into chemical signals in order to be successfully transmitted. This is done when the signal is received by a neuron through a synapse, which absorbs the signal, changing it back into an electrical signal from a chemical one. The process is complex, though, in simple terms, neurotransmitters require amino acids to form and function. Amino acids are obtained through your diet, which makes what you eat extremely important in how your brain functions.

Glutamate and aspartate

Glutamate and aspartate are amino acids that are considered non-essential. Glutamate is released by nerve cells and sends signals between nerve cells. One of the most important roles in these neurotransmitters is the maintenance of memory and learning processes. Aspartate works together with glutamate as neurotransmitters, both of which are considered excitatory neurotransmitters, due to their effects on neurons. The impact they have is "excitatory," which means they increase the chances that a neuron will send or "fire" a signal. This sequence is known as an action potential and increases the chances of another neuron receiving the signal. Overall, these amino acids work together to improve the strength and chances of a transmission's success.

Gamma-aminobutyric acid

Gamma-aminobutyric acid is a type of amino acid that occurs naturally and works as a neurotransmitter. This specific transmitter works in the brain, functioning as a chemical messenger. Also known as GABA, this neurotransmitter is known as inhibitory, due to how it affects certain brain signals by blocking or interfering with them. It can have the effect of decreasing neuro activity in the nervous system.

How does GABA work? It attaches itself to a protein in your brain, known as a receptor. The effects of this process can have a positive impact by reducing sensations of stress, fear and producing a calming effect overall. Due to the positive results of this natural-occurring amino acid, it has been synthesized into supplements, and can also be found in certain types of foods, such as fermented soy and vegetables, including kefir and fermented milk. Maintaining GABA amino acids in your diet can have many related benefits, in addition to a calming, stress-reduction effect, including a reduction in seizures, lowering anxiety and incidents of panic attacks, improving symptoms of ADHD (attention deficit hyperactivity disorder) and stabilizing mood.

Other benefits of GABA include lowering blood pressure, improving sleeping patterns, and reducing insomnia and fatigue. Implementing this amino acid into your diet through whole foods is the best option to avoid having too much, though there is little to no risk associated with supplements. Some of the side effects, while minor, may include headaches, muscle pains and stomach irritability.

Serotonin

Serotonin is another neurotransmitter that is directly responsible for regulating mood, emotional and social responses, digestion, sleep, sexual behavior and function. Low levels of this transmitter have been linked to depression, which is often treated by increasing serotonin levels and elevating mood. Serotonin is built out of proteins, which are the basic components that form this neurotransmitter, which is done through a natural chemical conversion process. Ensuring that your brain has enough protein is vital to maintaining and producing adequate levels of serotonin.

How is serotonin linked to depression and anxiety? Scientific studies on the effects of serotonin indicate that a low amount or imbalance can contribute to an increase in both depression and anxiety. Low production of serotonin has a direct effect on mood as well as other related conditions such as obsessive-compulsive disorder, sudden shifts in mood (to sadness and/or anger) and panic. Some research indicates that depression may develop as a result of suppressing new cellular growth and regeneration, which is where serotonin plays an important role. Synthetic versions of serotonin, also known as SSRIs in the form of anti-depressant medications are often prescribed for treatment. SSRIs work by increasing the brain's production of new cells, which increases serotonin and improves mood.

Unfortunately, there are a lot of side effects associated with anti-depressant medications, some of which can be severe, depending on the individual. For this reason, many people choose to alter their diet to improve and increase the production of serotonin naturally.

Acetylcholine

Acetylcholine is a neurotransmitter that has an impact on how muscles contract and function, regulating sleep and REM function and pain responses in the brain. When there is a deficiency in this specific chemical, which is released by a nerve cell, symptoms include muscle weakness. It's a vital neurotransmitter that maintains healthy muscle development and function. This process includes transmitting signals between skeletal muscles and motor nerves.

Certain medications may have a negative effect on these neurotransmitters, and since acetylcholine is essential in activating muscles, any impairment can lead to paralysis or spasms, from mild to severe. To ensure your body avoids deficiency, adequate amounts of calcium, sodium and potassium should be included in your diet.

Dopamine

Like the effects of a drug that produces a "high," this occurs when dopamine is released, signaling a "reward" effect in the brain. This sensation can be characterized as "euphoria." In addition to this sensation, which is produced by the release of dopamine, this neurotransmitter is also responsible for focusing and memory, which makes it an important chemical to maintain.

Emotional control is also affected by the amount of dopamine in the brain; it also helps with the regulation of movement and experience motivation, which in turn, encourages us to take action in order to experience the reward associated with motivation, in order to achieve the pleasant effects of the brain's release of dopamine.

Dopamine and serotonin work together to regulate mood and emotions. An imbalance or deficiency in one or both can increase the chances of depression and anxiety. Together, they regulate sleeping patterns and REM. When dopamine levels drop, there is an increased risk of certain conditions and diseases, such as Parkinson's, as well as muscle pain, cramps and sensations of stiffness. Low dopamine is also associated with a higher prevalence of anxiety, which can be reduced by ensuring you have balanced levels of both dopamine and serotonin. Eating a low carb or ketogenic diet can have a positive effect on maintaining adequate levels of amino acids, including dopamine.

Norepinephrine

Norepinephrine is a chemical that is released in the brain in response to stress. When a stressful situation occurs, your body responds by transmitting this amino acid, which sends signals between nerve cells. This neurotransmitter is comparable to adrenaline, in that is has a similar effect when released. The effects include elevating blood pressure and glucose levels. For people with very low blood pressure, norepinephrine is used as a treatment for hypotension. Due to the negative effects of this transmitter, due to causing an increase in heart rate and blood pressure, regulation of norepinephrine by stress management is important.

Similar to dopamine, norepinephrine can provide a sensation of "euphoria" in high doses, similar to a high. This can be brought on by using stimulants, in the form of drugs, foods or drinks. Coffee and beverages high in caffeine can have this effect. For this reason, it's best to avoid or limit these in your diet.

Chemical Balance Is Vital for Good Brain Health

Chemical imbalance is a term used often to describe certain ailments or conditions of the mind, including depression, anxiety and other conditions that affect how we think, perceive, and feel. When there is too much or too little of certain chemicals in the brain, it has the effect of an imbalance, which can manifest itself in many symptoms from physical pain and weakness to mood and emotional changes.

Certain medications, while they are beneficial for treating many ailments and conditions, may alter the chemical balance as a side effect. Most changes in brain chemicals are temporary and usually, reset or balance on their own. Where chemical imbalances become serious is when they are severe and long-term, causing panic attacks, depression and anxiety.

Improving your brain's health is as simple as eating healthy and keeping active. While many of the brain's processes are complex in nature, our ability to control what we eat and how we live is vital to our overall good health and well-being. The general strategy for improving brain health and chemical balance include the following:

- Avoid stressful situations as much as possible. It's not as easy for everyone, as work, family and everyday issues in life can produce stress. Despite all the scenarios that we cannot avoid, stress can be reduced by limiting our exposure to certain situations, taking measured breaths when we are faced with a challenging situation, and eating healthy foods on a regular basis. Drinking plenty of water is often overlooked, though just as important as maintaining a balanced diet.

- Exercise and keeping active. All forms of exercise are beneficial, as they release dopamine and increase serotonin levels. High impact workouts, such as running, cycling and swimming help maintain weight and keeping your hormones regulated, while yoga and stretching can calm and heal tension and stress in the physical body while soothing your mind. Meditation and deep breathing are also very beneficial for your body following a workout. Not only does regular exercise raise serotonin levels in the brain, but it also maintains their level consistently.

- Exposure to sunshine. Something as simple as spending time outside on a sunny day will make a major impact and improvement on our mood and balancing the chemicals in our brain. During the winter and colder months, even more so in regions with reduced sunlight, there are reports of increased depression due to lower levels of serotonin. Only a minimal amount of time spent outside is needed in order to gain the benefits of sunlight, which also provides vitamin D, an essential nutrient that our body requires.

- Getting a massage. This may be overlooked as a luxury or pampering, though massage therapy has tangible benefits that help elevate mood and calm the mind. Massages reduce stress by decreasing cortisol and increasing serotonin. The techniques used in specific massage therapies can help work through tight, stressed "knots" in muscle tissue, that when released, give a sense of relief.

How Diet Impacts the Function of Neurotransmitters

The strength of neurotransmitters and their ability to communicate lies with good health from diet and lifestyle. There are specific foods and nutrients that contribute to the production and regulation of the brain's chemicals, as well as their balance. For each of the main neurotransmitters covered in this book, there are certain foods that can support their function and production. Acetylcholine, the neurotransmitter responsible for working with the central nervous system, can be enhanced by eating certain plant-based foods, such as squash, eggplant and spinach.

These vegetables contain a certain amount of this amino acid and can help regulate acetylcholine in the body. Other foods that support this function are peas, mung beans (and beans in general), radishes, as well as some fruits, including oranges and certain strains of strawberries. Certain herbs and other natural sources contain Ach, or acetylcholine, such as nettle and mistletoe. While these are more difficult to find in local and common grocery stores, specific herbs in dried leaf or powder form can be found at many natural food and supplement stores.

Another amino acid that can be found in foods is dietary glutamine acid, which helps with the production of glutamate. Many foods contain this amino acid, making it simple to maintain a good balance of this chemical in the brain. Glutamic acid is naturally found in many varieties of meat, including poultry, pork, beef and seafood, as well as some dairy products, such as cheese. Certain foods have a high level of this amino acid, which specifically include certain meat and other foods, like coffee, salami and caviar.

Seaweed is an example of a plant-based source of glutamic acid. A lot of packaged and dried foods also include this chemical, though it's best to avoid the processed foods altogether in favor of natural food sources for the best quality in amino acids.

GABA, or gamma-aminobutyric acid, is found in salt, certain types of beans and peas. Soybeans are one of the most common food sources that contain GABA, which also support its production in the brain. Raw beans are often better for a higher source of this amino acid, as opposed to cooked. Raw soybeans, such as edamame beans, are an excellent way to increase GABA production.

Many grains have the effect of increasing GABA as well, such as rice (all varieties), barley and wheat. If your way of eating limits carbohydrates, then choosing raw soybeans or other soy foods are the best option. Other low carb options that support GABA production include spinach, which can contain a high level of this amino acid, especially when consumed raw. Kale, broccoli, certain teas and mushrooms also provide a good source of support for GABA neurotransmitter.

Dopamine, the chemical that releases a sense of happiness or "bliss" is an important way of keeping your mood elevated. Foods that improve the production of dopamine include bananas and plantain, as well as avocado. Avocado is an excellent choice for the nutrients it contains, in addition to supporting dopamine production. Avocado is also low in carbs, high in fiber and healthy fats, which are also beneficial for your brain's function. Foods high in antioxidants, including green tea, berries and dark green vegetables, are also recommended. Foods high in alkaline are also good for maintaining levels of dopamine and have the benefit of improving memory, mood and cognitive function. Eggplant, tomatoes, spinach and peas are among the foods that provide support for this amino acid.

A vital chemical that keeps mood stable and anxiety in check is serotonin. Maintaining high levels of serotonin is easier than choosing specific foods, as they are found in nearly all fruits and vegetables, in varying amounts. The seeds in some fruits are also strong support for dopamine production and maintenance.

Foods that contain an exceptionally high amount of dopamine include paprika, tomatoes, pineapple, passionfruit, lettuce, green onions and hazelnuts. Spinach, as with other amino acids, is almost always an excellent way to support all neurotransmitters in the brain. If in doubt, choose spinach and dark greens for overall amino acid support and production.

Foods for Overall Support of Neurotransmitters

Instead of focusing on specific amino acids and neurotransmitters, it's easier and most beneficial to include foods and supplements that generally support all neurotransmitters in their production and regulation. These foods are common and can be found without much effort. Including all or most of these options in your diet is essential to balance the brain and body for optimal performance and balance.

Eggs

One of the most popular breakfast foods, eggs, supports the production of dopamine and serotonin. Eggs also contain a good amount of fatty acids and protein, both of which are important for your brain's health.

Seafood

Like eggs, fish contains a lot of omega 3 fatty acids and promotes the production of both dopamine and serotonin. The protein and calcium in fish such as tuna and salmon are exceptionally healthy for your brain's function and in general, good for the regulation of all neurotransmitters.

Spinach

One of the "super" foods that can support all neurotransmitters is spinach. If you need an easy and short list of foods that provide the most benefit, add this dark leafy green vegetable every time. Spinach is also high in antioxidants, iron and other minerals that support the body and brain well. It's an easy food to digest, which is beneficial for gut health.

Nuts, Seeds, and Berries

These foods are grouped together due to their combined benefit for all amino acids or neurotransmitters, with dopamine and serotonin being of most benefit. As with other plant-based foods, nuts, seeds and berries are at their best when consumed raw as a snack or as part of a meal.

Brain Food: The Top Choices for Optimal Health

When we think of "brain" food, the usual foods that spring to mind are fish and oils that provide the building blocks of a healthy brain. Based on the foods featured in this book, avocados, seeds, nuts, berries and green vegetables are among the frequently mentioned options for general health, disease prevention and overall mental well-being. More specifically, these foods are labeled "brain" friendly not because of a certain function for neurotransmitter support, but for overall brain health, which supports the body's functions as well.

Seafood, and more specifically, "fatty" fish:

Fish is always a good option for health. Fish with elevated levels of healthy fats is the best choice for your brain. Examples of fatty fish options include salmon, sardines and trout. Our brains are significantly made up of healthy fats, which is why they are such an integral part of maintaining optimal brain function overall. Without sufficient fats in our diet, we risk impairing our cognitive abilities, as well as other parts of the brain, which include memory, mood and emotional responses. Omega 3 fatty acids slow the aging process and prevent the onset of Alzheimer's disease.

Eggs are always a good option, as an alternative to or in addition to fish. For vegan diets, flaxseeds and hemp seeds are a great source of healthy fats and amino acids.

Coffee: More than Caffeine

While caffeine may be the first ingredient that comes to mind when you think of coffee, it also contains a substantial dose of antioxidants that help support good mental function and alertness. In fact, those antioxidants in the coffee are likely more responsible for your sense of alertness and "waking up" than the caffeine it contains. While some people may avoid coffee for its stimulant effect, which may irritate the stomach and cause "jitters," it can improve overall mood and increase focus and concentration. Over a longer period of time, regular consumption of coffee can guard against certain neurological conditions, such as Parkinson's and memory loss.

Oranges

Citrus fruits are a good source of vitamins and fiber and make a great addition to any diet. Oranges contain a high dose of vitamin C, which is a powerful antioxidant that supports the brain's health and prevents damage to mental function as we age. Other foods rich in vitamin C include peppers (cayenne and bell peppers), tomatoes, strawberries and kiwi.

Overall, any foods rich in omega 3 and 6 fatty acids, antioxidants and nutrients are good for your brain's development, cognitive function and longevity. The more of these foods we include in our diet, the better chances we have of keeping balance and avoiding chemical imbalances associated with anxiety, depression and other mood disorders. The following chapter provides a step-by-step guide to implementing a diet for your brain's health.

CHAPTER 8

Meal Preparation and Planning for the Anti-Anxiety Diet

Preparing Your Shopping List with Anti-Anxiety, Gut Health and Whole Foods in Mind: Making the List Work for You and Your Budget.

The best rule of thumb to get started on your new way of eating: keep your food choices simple, natural and easy to access. Healthy foods do not need to be costly or complicated but focused on the primary macronutrients and micronutrients that focus on supporting your neurological health and overall well-being. The first step to creating your shopping list is to focus on the primary categories of macronutrients.

The chart below focuses on simple choices for each macronutrient category, as covered in chapter 2. While some food options may contain more than one group of macronutrients, such as eggs (protein and healthy fats), this will make choosing these foods easier, as they provide more than one type of nutrient.

To maximize food for your brain's health, choose more options from the fats and protein categories and fewer from carbohydrates. In choosing which foods to include as carbs, consider their source: are they packaged or fresh, and do they contain additives? Rice, for example, can be an appropriate option in small to moderate amounts, though bread, pasta and high carb foods may provide the body with too much glucose.

Simple carbohydrates such as those found in potatoes, bananas and other fruits or vegetables containing starch, are a better option due to high levels of other nutrients, such as fiber and potassium.

Macronutrient	Food options
Protein	Salmon or tuna
	Eggs
	Beef or pork
	Chicken or turkey
	Tofu, miso and/or tempeh
Healthy fats	Avocado
	Coconut oil
	Peanut butter
	Nuts (almonds, cashews,
	Seeds (chia seeds, pumpkin seeds)
Carbohydrates	Rice
	Dark chocolate
	Bananas
	Potatoes
Others (fiber, water)	Spinach, lettuce, arugula, kale, other leafy greens
	Berries
	Citrus fruits
	Turmeric, salt, pepper, other spices
	Green tea, black tea, coffee
	Low carb sweeteners (and/or natural sweeteners in small doses)

The macronutrient list above can be expanded to include many more options for grocery shopping or minimized to focus on one or two items per list each week. For variety, switch up the different options to rotate between vegetables, nuts, meats and other foods. Try a new food once or twice each month, and research its nutrients to learn about its value and benefits.

Clearing the Space in Your Pantry, Refrigerator, and Freezer for Better Options Ahead

Before you begin your next shopping trip, take an inventory of all the items currently in your kitchen and food storage areas. When you begin a new way of eating or diet, some people get an impulse to remove everything and start fresh with a new set of rules for eating. While this may seem like an exciting way to get started, it can be expensive and could result in wasting a lot of foods that may actually be appropriate.

In the Refrigerator

Check the crispers for fresh fruits and vegetables, and make sure to consume them within a few days, or at the very latest, within one week, to ensure they are fresh. Take note of how long foods last: citrus fruits may last longer than apples, for example, while fresh leafy greens should be consumed within one or two days of purchasing, especially if they are purchased from a local, organic market or store.

Dairy, eggs and meat items usually last a week in the refrigerator, depending on how fresh they are when purchased. Take note of expiry dates and only buy what you can consume within one week. Meat can be stored in a freezer for several months, and once dethawed, should be used within a couple of days. Keep eggs stored near the top of the fridge, or in one of the side compartments, to keep them separate from other foods and avoid breakage.

Non-dairy alternatives and soy foods such as tofu, soymilk (and other non-dairy milk), and tempeh should be stored similarly to meat and dairy, as they are perishable. Tofu, once opened from the package, can keep up to one week, and should be stored in an airtight container, submerged in water. Change the water daily to maintain freshness. Some marinated tofu products may not require the added water, though should be stored in a sealable container, and used within several days (up to one week). If you choose to purchase flavored and/or marinated tofu, read the ingredients carefully to ensure there are no added sugars or artificial items.

Store bread, bananas and other similar perishables on top of the refrigerator or on the kitchen counter, for easy access. Certain bread that contains sprouts and raw ingredients should be refrigerated. Avocados can be stored in the fridge until they are ready to ripen or soften.

In the Pantry

This is where all the dry foods are stored: pasta, rice, grains, cereals and spices. If you plan to greatly reduce the number of carbohydrates in your diet, your pantry will no longer contain many of these foods once you begin to implement new foods. What can be done about the high carb foods already stored in the cupboard? Use them up until they are done or donate the foods to a local charity. Since they are non-perishable, they will last for some time and do not have to be used at once.

When space is cleared in your pantry, consider the following options for your shopping list:

- Turmeric
- Pink Himalayan or sea salt
- Black pepper
- Cayenne and/or chili pepper flakes
- Dried basil, dill, oregano, sage, paprika, and other spice and herbs
- Green tea leaves and/or powder
- Coffee beans (or an alternative, such as black tea or dandelion coffee)
- Seeds: pumpkin, chia, sesame, sunflower, hemp hearts, and other seeds
- Nuts: almonds, cashews, peanuts, brazil nuts, and pistachios
- Dried berries and coconut flakes
- Dark cocoa powder
- Low carb sweeteners in powder or granules: stevia, monk fruit, and others. If you prefer to keep them fresh and plan on long storage, they may be kept in a resealable container in the pantry or refrigerator
- Cinnamon, cardamom, curry powder, and other spices for flavoring dishes

Customize your choices to fit the menu items and meals you wish to prepare and include in your weekly plan. This may vary from week to week or monthly. If there is additional space in your pantry, consider adding pickled and/or sealed jar foods, as a back up to fresh options in the fridge:

- Dill pickles
- Olives (green or black)
- Coconut oil (this can also be refrigerated, to prolong shelf life)
- MCT oil (this can be refrigerated once opened)
- Pickled foods (beets, eggs, etc.)
- Jam and other preservatives (natural jams and low carb options are best)
- Peanut butter, tahini (sesame butter), almond butter and other nut-based spreads

In the Freezer

There are many options, depending on the amount of space you have. A small freezer combined with a fridge may be a small space, though, with some creative organization, it can hold enough for a month or more. A large, stand-alone freezer can hold a lot of meat, frozen berries and prepared meals for the long-term. If you prepare meals ahead, such as a week in advance, a large freezer provides a great way to divide and store for a week or longer. This is also a good space to store a large meat order from a local butcher or a large batch of homemade stew or broth.

Recipes and ideas for easy meal preparation

One of the most satisfying and enjoying aspects of starting a new diet is experimenting with new recipes. You can start with one or two new recipes each week, or begin an entire plan from scratch as an overhaul from your previous diet. Either way, implementing your new and improved way of eating is an adventure with the benefits of reducing anxiety and improving your brain and body's health. This section's recipes are divided into groups for easier navigation and implement most of the foods listed in this book for consistency.

Smoothies

Smoothies are a quick and easy way to get your nutrients in a snap, with very little preparation and work. They are ideal for breakfast, or before a workout. These are a good option for a busy, hectic schedule and with the right ingredients, they can replace an entire meal and quickly satisfy hunger. Before preparing a smoothie, consider the nutrient options and combinations. Most milkshakes and/or smoothies begin with a "base" such as juice or milk.

If you choose juice, avoid packaged juices, and instead squeeze or add the desired fruits and/or vegetables to a juicer for fresh results, before adding to your smoothie. For simplicity, and to save time, freshly squeeze the juice the night before, so that your ingredients are ready the next morning. The smoothie recipes in this section are good options as a meal (replacement meal) or snack.

Avocado and Coconut Smoothie

This smoothie is an ideal way to start the morning and contains a wealth of fiber, fats and vitamins to kick start your brain before you begin your day. To prepare for this recipe, ensure avocados are ripe by setting outside of the fridge (on the kitchen countertop, for example) to allow them to ripen overnight. If already soft, keep the avocados in the fridge, so that they do not become overripe: this is especially important in hot weather, where foods tend to perish faster.

Coconut milk is used as a base in this recipe. It is thick like dairy milk, which may be preferred or thinned a bit with water and/or almond milk, which is thinner. Some grocery stores offer combinations of non-dairy milk products, such as cashew and coconut milk, or coconut mixed with almond milk. For simplicity, coconut milk is used in this recipe, though can be substituted or supplemented, as desired.

Adding a low carb sweetener is an option, though not required. Other ways to boost the nutrient value of this smoothie include adding soaked (softened) chia seeds, hemp and/or coconut or MCT oil, and protein powder (plant-based, such as pumpkin or soy). The basic ingredients of this smoothie are as follows (for one to two servings):

- 1 ½ cups coconut milk
- 1 large or medium ripe avocado
- 2 tablespoons natural and/or low carb sweetener

Pour the coconut milk into a blender, followed by the large avocado (peeled, pitted), then add the sweetener and any other desired ingredients or supplements. Mix for approximately 30 seconds and taste test the result. Add more sweetener and/or milk as needed. Once the taste is adjusted to your preference, this smoothie is a great breakfast or pre- or post-workout treat.

There are other options and variations for this smoothie:

- Add one ripe banana with another ½ cup of coconut or almond milk. This will yield at least two servings
- Add one or two tablespoons of sesame butter for a protein boost, in place of a supplement. Almond butter is another good option.

Berries and Banana Smoothie

This smoothie can be altered in several ways, beginning with the base: juice or milk. If you choose a juice as the base, select a naturally squeezed juice, such as ripe berries (one cup of berries blended into 1/3 cup of water), or fresh orange juice. Avoid sugary, cartons or jugs of juice, which hinder the nutritional value of the recipe. Bananas contain a good amount of potassium, fiber and natural sugar, as well as berries. For this reason, no sweeteners are needed for this smoothie.

If a milk base is chosen for this recipe, almond is recommended: it blends well with fruits, low in fat and calories and has a pleasant, mild flavor that works with many different food combinations. The best almond milk to choose is unflavored and unsweetened, or it can be made from scratch by soaking one cup of almonds in four cups of water overnight and blending the next day. The basic ingredients of this recipe are as follows:

- One ripe banana
- 1 cup frozen or fresh berries (any variety or combination of strawberries, blueberries, blackberries and/or raspberries)
- 2 cups almond milk or freshly squeezed juice

Combine all ingredients in a blender and mix between 30-60 seconds. If the berries are frozen, a longer blend may be needed to ensure they combine well with all other ingredients. Alternatively, fresh berries and frozen chunks of banana can be used in this recipe.

Adding one tablespoon of green tea matcha powder is a great way to increase the antioxidants in this smoothie.

Watermelon and Mint Smoothie

The base of this smoothie is watermelon juice, which can be easily made by adding small, chopped (pit less) pieces of watermelon to a blender or food processor and blending into a juice. This smoothie is light and an excellent way to replenish your body with electrolytes, fiber and potassium. It's a good refreshment for a hot summer day and makes a good addition to a meal as a drink or dessert, though not sufficiently high in healthy fats or protein for a meal replacement.

Mint is added to this recipe due to its flavor, and how it complements the other tastes in this recipe. Fresh mint leaves should be finely ground in advance. In a pinch, dried mint leaves (or a small amount of natural mint extract) can be used as a substitute. The key ingredients are the antioxidants and vitamins contained in the following combined fruits:

- 2 cups watermelon juice (freshly blended into a juice from large slices, with rinds removed)
- 2 tablespoons freshly squeezed lime or lemon (or both)
- 4 tablespoons freshly ground mint leaves (or one teaspoon mint extract)

Combine all the ingredients in a blender and mix for approximately 30 seconds or until all items are evenly distributed. If needed, add more watermelon juice, lemon or water to aid in mixing the ingredients together. Ice cubes are another good option and best to add just before serving.

Mango and Yogurt Smoothie

This is a thick, nourishing and deliciously sweet recipe that combines fresh mangos with natural yogurt. Like the avocado and coconut smoothie, this recipe is suitable as a meal replacement, as it contains a good portion of protein, calcium, fiber and antioxidants. Adding a low carb sweetener and/or a dash of natural vanilla extract will add sweetness. Greek or Icelandic yogurt is recommended in its natural, unsweetened form.

Beware of yogurt brands that are "low fat" or "sugar-free," as they contain other additives. Monk fruit and/or stevia can be added in small amounts to enhance the sweetness, though mangoes, when very ripe, can provide a sufficient amount of natural sugar. Cardamom and/or crushed pistachio or almonds are a great addition to this smoothie for a twist on the flavor, similar to a mango lassi drink.

On its own, yogurt is thick and combining just the mangos and yogurt will not result in a smoothie, but rather a parfait-like dessert. To make a smoothie, almond, dairy or coconut milk is added:

- 1 cup full-fat yogurt, unsweetened and unflavored (Greek or Icelandic yogurt brands are best for their high protein and healthy fat content)
- 1 teaspoon vanilla extract
- 1 teaspoon cardamom powder
- 1-2 teaspoons monk fruit or low carb sweetener (optional)
- 1 teaspoon crushed pistachios or almonds (into a powder)
- 1 large or medium ripe mango, skin and pit removed, sliced
- ½ cup milk (dairy, almond or coconut)

In a large blender, add the yogurt, milk and mango and blend for 30 seconds. Add the remaining ingredients and continue to mix until all everything is evenly combined and serve. If cardamom is unavailable, cinnamon can be used as a substitute or omitted altogether. If you want to enhance the nutrient value of this drink, add a dash of turmeric along with the cardamom spice.

If mangoes are unavailable, peaches can be an excellent option, as they have a similar texture and blend similarly. Nectarines are another option. Kefir, a yogurt drink, contains a lot of beneficial bacteria and can substitute yogurt in this smoothie. Since it tends to be thinner than yogurt, kefir may not need to be supplemented with milk if used, or with less than ½ cup of milk. Plain, unsweetened and unflavored kefir, like yogurt, is recommended for this recipe.

Dark Chocolate and Peanut Smoothie

This smoothie works as a breakfast or a dessert. The high protein content in peanut butter and antioxidants and flavonoids in chocolate also create the perfect after-work out treat. In a pinch, this can be a meal replacement. If you have an allergy to peanuts, any nut butter can be used as an alternative: sesame (tahini) butter, hazelnut, almond or cashew butter.

Adding a tablespoon of coconut oil or MCT oil increases the portion of healthy fat in this smoothie and is recommended if this will replace a meal. The extra healthy fat is a good choice to enhance your brain's performance before taking an exam or another challenging task that requires exceptional focus and concentration. Milk is used as a base for this smoothie and this may include any dairy or non-dairy option. Adding a banana is a good way to get your fiber out of this recipe, thus increasing the nutrient value:

- ½ cup cocoa powder (or melted dark chocolate, unsweetened)
- 1 cup milk (coconut, almond, soy or dairy)
- 2-3 tablespoons peanut butter (smooth, unsweetened)
- 1-2 tablespoons low carb or natural sweetener
- 1-2 tablespoons MCT or coconut oil (recommended)
- ½ ripe banana (optional)

Combine the milk, peanut butter and cocoa/dark chocolate into the blender and mix for 60 seconds. Add the sweetener, MCT or coconut oil and banana (optional) and continue to blend for another 30 seconds. Add more milk if thinning is needed. An extra tablespoon of oil can also be added if desired.

Build Your Own Smoothie

There are numerous ways to create smoothies when considering the different ingredient options and flavors. The options are limitless and fun and can result in new favorites for your diet. The following basic steps will help you design your own custom smoothie:

1. Choose your base: milk, water or naturally squeezed juice
2. Choose your fiber/fruit option(s): avocado, banana, berries, mangoes, peaches, kiwi, pumpkin puree, etc.
3. Choose your protein: Nut butter (peanut, hazelnut, sesame, cashew or almond). Other options include whey or plant-based protein powder, such as hemp, pumpkin and soy proteins
4. Choose your fat: coconut oil, MCT oil, avocado oil
5. Other options for flavor:
    a. Low carb sweeteners
    b. Spices: cardamom, cinnamon, turmeric
    c. Vanilla extract (other options – mint, almond extract)

Adding vegetables to your smoothie are also a great way to increase the micronutrients. A juicer can be a handy appliance to create kale, spinach and ginger juice, combined with fresh apple. If a juicer is not available, dark leafy greens can be finely chopped or ground before adding to a blender to a fruit-based smoothie. Wheatgrass, ginger and apples are nutritious options to supplement the value of your fruit-based smoothie.

Breakfast Bowls

Breakfast is considered one of the most important meals of the day. It is the first meal of the day, and whether it is a highly nutrient-rich smoothie or fully prepared meal, it's important to include as many nutrients as possible. To keep your breakfast easy and simple, think of this meal as a "bowl" or combination of foods that work well together for brain function and taste. Anyone can prepare fried eggs with toast and bacon, though adding more to meet the daily requirements of vitamins, minerals and other nutrients is the focus of these recipes.

Egg Breakfast Bowl

Scrambled eggs serve as the base of this dish, and can be prepared with two or three eggs in a skillet, with salt, pepper and turmeric. Turmeric is good to add to as many meals as possible, due to its positive effects on mood elevation. Eggs are added to a plate or bowl, and "topped" with the following options:

- Fresh spinach (finely chopped)
- Cucumber (diced into small ½ inch squares)
- Cherry tomatoes (sliced in half)
- Onion (half of a small onion, finely diced)
- Basil (optional)
- Shredded cheese (sharp cheddar, or any variety as desired)
- Balsamic dressing (2 teaspoons)

The suggested toppings can be combined in a separate bowl and tossed with the balsamic dressing. To create a quick dressing add 3 tablespoons lime or lemon juice with 1 tablespoon vinegar and 1 tablespoon olive or coconut oil. Mix and combine as a dressing with the vegetables and serve over the scrambled eggs.

If you prefer to add meat to your breakfast, sauté a small number of bacon strips (or turkey bacon), sausage or another preferred breakfast meat, then slice and add to the toppings. Avoid creamy ranch dressings or sauces available in packages, as they are rife with additives and sugar. Balsamic and oil-based dressings are the best option for a natural, whole-food-based meal.

Tofu Scramble

This is an excellent breakfast dish for vegans as it perfectly substitutes eggs with tofu, a very nutrient-rich source of protein and vitamins. Tempeh, fermented soy, is another good option in place of tofu. Tempeh, like miso, contains B12, which is an important vitamin contained in red meat and a good way to include in a vegan or vegetarian diet. Tofu is prepared the night before by soaking one block in a container with vegetable broth, mixed with salt, pepper and turmeric. Tempeh can be similarly prepared as tofu. When ready, drain the broth and retain at least ½ cup to fry in the skillet:

- 1 block extra firm tofu or tempeh
- 2 cups of vegetable broth (bone broth can be prepared and used if there are no restrictions on animal products or foods)
- 1-2 tablespoons turmeric powder
- 1 tablespoon crushed garlic (optional)
- Salt and black pepper (pink Himalayan or sea salt is recommended)

To prepare the broth before marinating, combine the salt, pepper and turmeric and stir into the broth. Add chili pepper, paprika and other spices if desired. Pour the broth over the block of tofu or tempeh in a container, seal and refrigerate. Marinate the tofu or tempeh in a sealed container overnight in the refrigerator and remove the next morning. Drain the tofu and retain at least ½ cup of the liquid. Heat a skillet on medium heat with 1-2 teaspoons olive oil and mash the tofu or tempeh with a fork until it resembles a scrambled egg consistency. When the skillet is ready, add tofu or tempeh, frying consistently on low-medium heat, adding small amounts of the liquid gradually. Not all of the broth needs to be used, just enough to keep the food moist and flavored. Additional spices can be sprinkled over the tofu to increase the strength of the flavor. As the tofu or tempeh is sautéed, there are other ingredients that can be added:

- Diced onions (any variety)
- Sliced green peppers
- Spinach
- Kale (finely chopped)
- Dried basil, dill and oregano

There are many options to add to this dish, which can vary each time it's prepared. Similar to the egg breakfast bowl, scrambled tofu can be topped with a variety of fresh, raw vegetables.

Yogurt Parfait

Yogurt is an excellent source of protein and calcium, both of which are essential in building strong bones and muscles. The bacterial cultures in yogurt provide a healthy gut lining and aid indigestion. This dish is a great dessert or breakfast, and as a small meal or snack when there is little to no time to prepare a full meal. The parfait is layered in a bowl or large dessert glass to combine various tastes and textures, along with many nutrients:

- Bottom layer: 1 cup of fresh berries, mangoes, peaches, kiwi or any fruit sliced into small pieces
- Middle or second layer: Plain, full-fat Greek yogurt. Icelandic yogurt is another good option. Kefir can be used in place of yogurt, though it tends to be thinner
- Topping options: Chia seeds, pumpkin seeds, coconut flakes, cocoa powder and/or dark chocolate chips, slivered almonds, cashews, pistachios

There are many variations for this recipe, including blending spices and/or fruits directly into the yogurt instead of a bottom fruit layer or adding both options. Chia seeds can be soaked in the yogurt or kefir, instead of a topping. Flaxseeds and hemp hearts are also nutrient-rich toppings.

Salads and Platters

When salads come to mind, the traditional Ceasar salad or Waldorf variety may be the first thought. There are many options for salads and they are increasingly becoming main dishes, thanks to the popularity of vegan, plant-based and low carb diets. Platters, like salads, offer a dish full of dietary requirements and options all combined into one meal.

The Complete Meal Platter

This dish aims to include as many healthy, "brain" foods and micronutrients as possible, where the flavors complement each other when eaten together. The following options for this dish are not obligatory, though more of a guide on which types of foods to include according to their respective nutritional value:

- Bowled or devilled eggs
- Dill pickles
- Sliced carrots, celery, green peppers (also red, orange and yellow peppers)
- Baked turkey slices
- Smoked tofu or salmon and/or bacon
- Avocado slices
- Olives (black and green)
- Pickled beets
- Raw or sautéed shrimp

Other options for this platter include the addition of cheese, homemade guacamole (to replace the avocado slices) and a side of fresh fruit. Turkey slices can be wrapped and stuffed with capers, black olives and cream cheese. Celery stalks can be topped with shredded cheese and/or guacamole. Shrimp can be wrapped in bacon or turkey slices.

Kale and Goat Cheese Salad

This salad can serve as a convenient side dish or a main feature. The goat cheese provides protein and calcium, while the kale adds antioxidants, iron and vitamins. Kale gets a lot of attention for its numerous nutrients and health benefits; while it's a bitter-tasting vegetable, it works well in combination with many flavors. The main challenge in working with kale is removing the stems and slicing the leaves into small, fine strips. Any variety of kale will work with this recipe, and several types can be combined into this salad if desired. Use at least one small to a medium-sized bunch of kale.

This will produce at least two ample servings or three smaller portions. Kale is the foundation for this recipe. Once chopped, sprinkle lightly with sea salt and spray with a squeeze of lemon to help neutralize the bitterness of the leaves, then set aside and prepare the ingredients:

- Dried fruits: cherries, berries, and other small, sliced dried fruits, such as apricots and/or prunes. These can vary, though dried cherries and blueberries are recommended, due to the contrast in flavor with kale and other ingredients
- Roasted, slivered almonds. Raw almonds can be lightly roasted on the stovetop, or added raw in slivered or chopped.
- Walnuts, pecans and brazil nuts are other options that can be ground up and added as a topping for this salad
- Crumbled goat cheese is the final topping, along with a vinaigrette or balsamic dressing.

There are some options to consider if some of the ingredients are unavailable. Spinach or arugula can be used in place of kale or combined with kale to change the flavor. Fresh sprouts, such as alfalfa, bean sprouts and pea sprouts, are great additional ingredients to this dish. Roasted or grilled eggplant, portobello mushrooms, fried onions and/or melted brie cheese are tasty options for expanding the potential of this salad. In its original form, this salad also works well as a side dish or a light meal.

Healthy Snacks and Sides

In this category of recipes, snacks and sides, these recipes are suitable for a light meal on their own or as an integral part of a fuller meal. They serve as a good option in between meals, a boost during a busy, draining and stressful day or simply a source of energy for a workout or meeting. While these are smaller meals in size, they still pack a powerful punch of nutrients and satisfy hunger as well. They are excellent for advance preparation and can be portable for commuting or long trips.

Almond Protein Bars

These bars are an excellent source of plant protein and healthy fats, making this snack ideal for vegans, ketogenic diets and a good way to boost your brain's health just before writing an exam. Another advantage of this recipe is how quickly they can be made and no baking is required. These bars only need to be refrigerated for one or two hours (or overnight for best results).

Almond butter is used in this recipe, though any variety of nut butter can be substituted as desired if almond butter is unavailable. Protein powder is also added, and this ingredient is left as an "open" option for several reasons: vanilla flavored protein powder is complimentary for the recipe, though substituting chocolate protein powder is another option.

Whey protein is just one type of protein, which is dairy-based, though for a plant-based protein, choose soy, hemp seed or pumpkin seed-based protein powder. Some options may not provide the same flavoring options, though it is good to experiment with different types of protein supplements to determine which one fits your preference best.

Coconut and cocoa ingredients make up a good portion of this recipe, to ensure enough fats are included and to infuse a pleasant combination of flavors, which compliment almond (or any variety of) nut butter. Coconut oil in this recipe may be substituted with MCT oil to boost the healthy fat content:

- 1 cup of almond butter
- 2 portions of measured coconut oil: 3 tablespoons, plus another 1 teaspoon (MCT oil may be used instead)
- 4 tablespoons of maple syrup, honey or a low carb sweetener (monk fruit is recommended)
- 1 teaspoon vanilla extract
- Dash of salt (pink Himalayan salt)
- ½ cup protein powder (vanilla or chocolate flavor is recommended, whey or plant-based)
- 2 tablespoons shredded, unsweetened coconut flakes
- 2-3 tablespoons cocoa or dark chocolate chips or shavings

Prepare a baking sheet or loaf pan with parchment paper. In a medium to large-sized bowl, combine the almond butter, 3 tablespoons of coconut oil and sweetener and mix thoroughly. If the coconut oil is solid, melt on the stovetop or in the microwave prior to mixing. Add the vanilla extract, salt, protein powder, shredded coconut and chocolate or cocoa shavings/chips. Continue to mix thoroughly until all of the ingredients are evenly combined. Pour the mixture onto the parchment paper-lined pan and press down evenly to spread the dough across the pan. If desired, sprinkle extra cocoa powder and/or coconut shredding over the top, and refrigerate for at least two hours.

Chia Seed Pudding

There are many variations of the chia pudding recipe, which is an excellent source of nutrients packed into a small, snack-sized treat. Chia pudding is also a great breakfast on the go or dessert. Chia seeds are small, usually black or brown in color, that absorb and soften when soaked in liquid.

The key to create a pudding-like texture with milk (dairy, almond, coconut or another variety of milk) is to soak the seeds overnight or for a few hours prior to preparing the recipe. Plain, natural and unflavored almond or coconut milk works best for most diets, as these non-dairy milks are vegan (plant-based), low in carbs and calories. They also thicken well when mixed with chia seeds.

The most common and simple form of this recipe is a vanilla chia pudding, which tastes and resembles rice pudding (only without the carbs!) The following ingredients are mixed together and blended with a whisk in a medium to large-sized bowl. This recipe yields 3-4 servings (reduce in half for smaller portions or less servings):

- 2 cups coconut, almond or dairy milk
- 1 cup of full-fat whipping cream or coconut cream
- ¼ cup low carb sweetener
- ½ cup chia seeds (any variety)
- 1 tablespoon vanilla extract

Combine the sweetener and chia seeds in a separate, small bowl or measuring cup, prior to mixing with the liquid ingredients and vanilla. Stir all of the items gently and thoroughly, to make sure the chia seeds are evenly distributed. It is common for some of the seeds to stick to the fork or whisk, even after all of the ingredients are completely blended. Refrigerate for at least two hours, or overnight, and serve for breakfast or as a snack within the next 1-2 days. If possible, stir the chia seeds after 30 minutes of refrigeration, to prevent the seeds from clumping together.

There are many toppings that make a delicious to chia pudding. For this vanilla flavor recipe, sprinkling cinnamon or cocoa powder is a simple and tasty option. Fresh fruit, either during the mixing process or as a topping just before serving, make an excellent boost in nutrients. Berries, kiwi, banana, mango and peaches are all good options. If you use coconut milk as a base for the chia pudding recipe, the coconut flavor can be further enhanced by adding a light layer of toasted coconut flakes on top.

Avocado and Banana Pudding

This is an easy to make snack that can also be served as a dessert. The combination of banana and avocado provide a good source of nutrients for energy and renewal at any time of the day, from morning to evening. It is prepared raw, within a few minutes of mixing. Due to how quickly avocados and bananas ripen, this dish is best served immediately after it is prepared:

- 1 ripe avocado
- 1 ripe banana
- 2 teaspoons coconut or MCT oil (optional)
- ¼ cup cocoa powder or dark chocolate (powder or melted)
- 2 tablespoons low carb or natural sweetener
- ¼ cup coconut or full-fat dairy cream (optional)

In a small or medium-sized bowl, mash the banana and avocado, either together or separately, and combine with coconut or MCT oil, cocoa powder or chocolate and natural sweetener. Continue to mash and mix all of the ingredients until they are evenly dispersed and ready to serve. As an option, pour ¼ cup of coconut or dairy cream over the pudding and serve. Other toppings to add include toasted sesame seeds, almonds and chocolate or cocoa powder sprinkled on top.

Easy Lunch and Dinner Meals

Lunch meals tend to be quick and light, while dinners are traditionally large meals with more ingredients and preparation. With a fast-paced and ever-changing schedule in modern life, creating elaborate meals can elevate stress, especially following a long day at work. The best way to reduce stress is to focus on simpler, faster meals that don't take long to make, though can be savored and enjoyed at your own place. Your evening meal can be the onset of relaxation, enjoyed after a satisfying workout or before reading, meditation or relaxation.

Curried Cabbage Stir Fry

Cabbage is a cruciferous vegetable that contains a lot of vitamins and supportive of brain health. It is often associated with cabbage rolls and stews, though cabbage can be used in combination with other meals. As a raw vegetable, it is very strong in flavor, though becomes mild when steamed, baked or fried. In this recipe, sliced cabbage is curried and added to delicious skillet meal instead of rice or noodles, which are traditionally served with stir fry meals.

This dish can be served with or without meat, depending on your dietary needs and preference. Turmeric is added to the curry due to its nutritional benefits. Curry paste or powder are both options. To add more spice to this dish, chili pepper flakes or cayenne pepper can be added and mixed with the curry:

- ½ head of cabbage, sliced into strips or small pieces (bite-sized)
- 1 small stick of butter
- 20 oz of ground beef, pork, lamb or tempeh
- 2 crushed garlic cloves
- 2 teaspoons of salt
- 1 teaspoon onion powder
- 1 teaspoon black pepper
- 1 teaspoon chili or cayenne pepper (optional)
- 1 tablespoon white wine vinegar
- 2 tablespoons of curry paste or powder
- ½ small onion, diced in small pieces
- ½ cup of cilantro or parsley
- 1 cup plain, unsweetened yogurt

To prepare the cabbage for this recipe, slice thin, long pieces with a knife lengthwise, then chop horizontally for smaller pieces (or keep the cabbage in longer strips if desired). The cabbage can be easily chopped in a food processor as another option. Heat the skillet on medium heat and add the butter.

As the butter melts, reduce the heat slightly, so that it is closer to medium-low and add the cabbage and fry until it becomes tender, which takes approximately 5 minutes. The vinegar and spices, including the salt, can be added. Continue to stir and fry all of the ingredients for another 5-6 minutes, then remove and set aside in a pan or bowl.

Prepare another skillet (or the same skillet), with butter and melt for 2-3 minutes. Add the ground garlic cloves, chopped onions and curry powder. Mix the ingredients gently, so that the onions and garlic are coated in the curry, then add the meat or tempeh and continue to sauté.

Cook until the meat is done and most (not all) of the liquid is used up. Gradually add the cabbage back into the skillet, stirring it in with the curried meat, adding more salt. Once cooked, serve with fresh cilantro as a topping and a dollop of yogurt or sour cream on top or the side.

Cheesy Cauliflower and Broccoli Casserole

This is a filling and satisfying dish served as a main meal or in addition to a lean meat, salad or soup. Both cauliflower and broccoli contain high amounts of antioxidants and fiber and are applicable to many diets, including the ketogenic diet and similar low carb eating plans.

This recipe includes dairy cheese, which can be substituted for vegan replacements. When choosing a non-dairy cheese keep in mind that soy-based "cheese" products do not melt, and many varieties of vegan cheese, both soy or vegetable-based, may contain a lot of additives.

Choose the brand with the least amount of added ingredients and if possible, source from local shops and markets for the best results. Vegetable-based cheese products melt easier, similar to their dairy counterparts, making them the best substitute.

The broccoli and cauliflower are best fresh, though frozen works as well. Check to ensure the vegetables are not discolored, as this can impact the taste. If bought fresh use within one or two days for best results and flavor. Sharp, old cheddar, parmesan and other strong-flavored cheeses are best for this recipe. The ingredients for this recipe are fairly simple to find and assemble for the casserole:

- 1 medium-sized broccoli, chopped into small, one- or two-inch bite-size pieces
- 1 medium cauliflower, sliced the same as the broccoli
- 1 cup of grated old cheddar
- 1 cup of grated mozzarella
- ½ cup of grated or dried parmesan cheese (as a topping)
- 2-3 teaspoons olive oil
- Pink Himalayan salt to taste (add as much as desired)
- 2 teaspoons black pepper
- 2 teaspoons paprika
- 3 tablespoons almond flour (optional)

Preheat the oven to 350 degrees Fahrenheit and grease a medium loaf or square pan no larger than 9 inches. Grease the pan lightly with olive oil (coconut oil can be used instead, if preferred). In a large bowl, combine the chopped broccoli and cauliflower florets and mix in salt, black pepper and paprika.

In a separate medium bowl, combine the shredded cheese and at least one tablespoon of olive oil. Thoroughly mix the ingredients, and pour onto the baking pan, so that all the florets cover the entire surface. Sprinkle the shredded cheese over the vegetables. For more moisture add ½ cup of plain, unsweetened almond or dairy milk to the shredded cheese and oil in a small bowl before mixing into the broccoli and cauliflower.

Before placing in the oven combine the almond flour, paprika, black pepper and salt (and dried parmesan cheese, optional) in a small bowl and mix with a spoon. Scoop the mixture and sprinkle over the top surface of the casserole, then drizzle lightly with olive oil. Bake for approximately 25-30 minutes, until cheese is melted, the top layer is slightly crispy and the vegetables are tender.

There are a few variations that may be considered for this recipe: adding brussels sprouts and/or replacing one or both vegetables with them. Baking brussels sprouts in the same manner, with more parmesan and less melted cheese, is a delicious meal or side dish on its own.

Zucchini Lasagna

This recipe puts a twist on the traditional lasagna dish, by replacing the noodles with zucchini slices. Many of the other ingredients remain the same: cheese, tomato sauce, meat (or tempeh), spinach and other ingredients. Lasagna is an excellent casserole that provides a lot of options to vary the types of vegetables and meats used. Zucchini is used in place of noodles, in order to reduce the carbohydrates.

Tomato sauce can be prepared homemade, by stewing tomatoes with a handful of spices, or by adding a can of unsweetened, natural pureed tomato sauce. Be sure to read the ingredients to avoid hidden sugars and preservatives often used in sauces:

- 4-5 zucchinis, sliced very thin, lengthwise
- 2 cups of grated cheese (any combination of mozzarella, cheddar, parmesan, or vegan cheese)
- 2 tablespoons olive oil
- 2 crushed cloves of garlic
- 1 medium can of pureed or crushed tomatoes (unsweetened)
- 1 cup of artichokes, sliced
- ½ cup of basil leaves
- Sea salt and black pepper
- 1 onion, sliced into thin pieces

Preheat oven to 350 degrees and prepare a casserole dish with olive oil (to grease). Slice the zucchini and coat each piece lightly in salt (on both sides), and set aside for approximately 15 minutes, then rinse and drain in a colander. Layer the casserole dish evenly with the thin slices of zucchini until the first layer coats the bottom of the dish. If some slices do not fit, they can be sliced into smaller pieces to fit any gaps. Add a thin coating of tomato sauce over the zucchini, spread equally across all of the slices.

For the next layer, add a thin coating of shredded cheese, followed by a layer of garlic, onions, artichokes, evenly distributed across the casserole dish. Add a few basil leaves and coat again with tomato sauce, followed by a thin layer of zucchini. Repeat the layers until all of the zucchini is used and the top layer is cheese. Bake in the oven for 25-30 minutes, until all vegetables are tender and serve.

This recipe is vegetarian, though it can be modified to include fried ground beef, lamb or pork into the layers of the casserole. Meat can be prepared by frying on a skillet with olive oil, salt, pepper and chili flakes, then set aside and added to the artichokes or as a layer on its own.

Miso Soup with Greens

This is a simple soup recipe that can serve as a hearty lunch or light dinner, in combination with a main meal or salad. Miso soup is available in most grocery stores, usually as a paste or powder in packets. For best results, a paste is the best option, and it is usually sold in small jars, which can be refrigerated for up to one month. Miso soup is prepared by boiling water, then adding and stirring the paste so that it dissolves and spreads throughout the water to create the base.

Salt can be added, though miso usually contains enough salt for flavor. Any variety of miso paste is good. Generally, the darker the color, the bolder or stronger the flavor, as red miso is fermented for years, while white and yellow miso varieties are fermented for several months.

To create the soup base, add approximately one tablespoon of miso paste for every cup of boiling water. Mix well with a whisk to make sure all of the miso is dissolved and dispersed into the water, leaving no lumps. Once the soup base is ready, reduce heat to medium, and prepare to add the following:

- Kale: at least ¼ or ½ bunch of kale leaves, with stems removed, sliced into long, thin strips, then added to the soup
- Green onions, chopped in ½-1-inch pieces
- Half a block of firm tofu, sliced into cubes
- 1 cup of sliced swiss chard or arugula (spinach is another option)
- 1-2 sheets of nori (seaweed)
- 4 cups of vegetable broth

Once all of the above ingredients are added, continue to stir the soup on medium heat, until the vegetables become tender and tofu is cooked. To infuse more flavor into the tofu, marinate the cubes in a small sealed container covered in vegetable broth and miso paste overnight for at least one hour. Serve with sushi or salad.

Miso soup is a popular base for ramen soups and beef stews, in addition to low carb, vegan meals. Adding bone broth, stewing beef cubes, carrots, celery, red peppers and other vegetables are all great options to consider. This soup base is a good foundation to build many hearty meals, especially during colder winter months.

Burrito Bowl

This dish is a quick and easy way to enjoy a burrito-inspired meal without the added flours and sugars of the wrap and tortilla shells. The base is combined with fresh kale and spinach, tossed with olive oil and lime, with beans, brown rice and spices. Ground beef, pulled pork or seasoned chicken can be added as a topping. Seasoned tempeh is a vegan option. Cheese can be added or omitted altogether (it is optional):

- 1 bunch of kale, chopped into small, bite-sized pieces, and tossed in a large bowl with 3 tablespoons olive oil and ¼ cup lime juice (freshly squeezed). Set aside and allow to marinate for 15 minutes
- 1-2 jalapenos, thinly sliced
- 2-3 black olives, thinly sliced
- 1 teaspoon cumin
- ¼ teaspoon sea salt
- Black pepper and chili flakes to taste

Add all of the ingredients into a large bowl with the marinated kale, once it has soaked in the lime and olive oil for at least 15 minutes. Mix thoroughly, to ensure all kale leaves are adequately coated with spices and set aside to prepare the remaining parts of the recipe: guacamole and beans.

Guacamole:

- 1 large or medium avocado, ripe
- ½ cup salsa
- ½ cup parsley or cilantro leaves, dried for fresh

- 2 tablespoons lime juice
- Salt and pepper to taste
- 1 tablespoon olive oil

Combine all of the ingredients into a small bowl, mashing the avocado first, then adding the oil, salt, pepper, lime and remaining ingredients. All of the ingredients can be mixed in a blender or food processor to ensure they are evenly mixed. Once thoroughly mixed, set aside to prepare the beans:

Spicy Beans:

- 2 cans of black beans, already cooked, rinsed and drained
- 1-2 small onions, thinly sliced into small pieces
- 2 cloves crushed garlic
- 1 teaspoon chili powder
- 1 teaspoon cayenne powder
- ½ teaspoon turmeric

Mix the beans in a medium bowl with the spices, making sure all of the beans are well coated.

To prepare the burrito bowl, which serves approximately 3-4 portions, scoop the marinated kale into a medium serving dish or bowl, add the beans next and top with the guacamole. Other options for this dish include adding brown rice (approximately one or two cups of cooked brown rice) to the beans to increase the fiber and carbohydrates if desired. Cheddar and/or crumbled feta cheese make excellent toppings, along with cherry tomatoes and cilantro or parsley.

Curried Butternut Squash Soup

This soup is an ideal meal to keep you warm and satisfied during colder weather. Butternut and other squash varieties have a calming effect and contain a lot of vitamin A, beta carotene and other nutrients. Adding curry to this dish compliments the naturally mild and pleasant flavor of squash:

- 1 tablespoon olive oil
- 1-2 two small onions, diced in small pieces
- 1-2 cloves garlic, crushed
- 5-6 cups cubed butternut squash (baked in an oven for 15-20 minutes on 350 degrees with olive oil to soften the squash, prior to slicing)
- 2 teaspoons curry powder
- ¼ teaspoon salt
- Black pepper to taste
- 1 can coconut milk
- 2 cups vegetable broth

Heat a large pot on medium, and add the olive oil, onions, garlic and spices. Fry for approximately two minutes, then add the butternut squash, plus a dash of salt and black pepper. Add in the curry powder and any other spices and continue to cook for another 5-6 minutes. Pour the vegetable broth and coconut milk and stir all of the ingredients together, reducing the heat to low.

Remove from the heat in batches, allowing the soup to cool and blend in a food processor until the entire mixture is smooth and all ingredients are included and combined. Return the soup to the pot and bring to medium heat, until it is ready to serve. There are options to garnish this soup with parsley, cilantro (fresh or dried), toasted pumpkin seeds or a dollop of yogurt or sour cream.

If butternut squash is not available, any variety of squash can be used in this recipe. Pumpkin puree, in the same proportion as squash, can also be used to create a curried pumpkin soup and include the same ingredients. If you want to get adventurous with the flavors, combine squash and carrot, or carrot, ginger and squash, or any variety of vegetables the soften similarly to these vegetables.

4-Week Meal Plan for the Anti-Anxiety Diet

Once the shopping list is prepared, and foods purchased, the next step is to prepare a realistic, week-by-week meal plan that fits your lifestyle while ensuring you get all the nutrients needed. This section provides a four-week plan as a guide to start and continue with preferred modifications and customizations.

There are four weekly tables in total, creating a one-month starter guide for implementing a new diet. Each table lists each day and the main meal. Snacks are not included, though may be added in between meals or in place of them in a pinch, when necessary.

The first week of the anti-anxiety diet plan focuses on simple meals to start with. Some meals are just a few items combined for a quick fix and focus on the nutrients. The guides take into account the possibility for leftover, especially if at least two servings are created from one recipe. For example, preparing a zucchini lasagna on Sunday for dinner can result in leftovers for lunch on Monday. Some meals referenced in the guide are generic and can include any ingredients that are suitable for an anti-anxiety, whole food diet.

Stir fry and skillet meals are examples of dishes that can be easily improvised based on the foods you have available on hand. These meals can be as simple as stir-fried chicken, soy sauce, spinach, carrots and snow peas served with brown rice, or on a bed of shredded kale. Fried ground beef with sautéed mushrooms, arugula, bell peppers, garlic and onions are another example of a skillet meal. These dishes are a great way to get creative, yet practical and making use of leftover ingredients found in the fridge, pantry or freezer.

The second week builds on the first, adding more options and taking into consideration different combinations of foods.

The third and fourth weeks continue to combine similar foods, allowing for more creativity, with a focus on keeping the idea simple. For example, building your own smoothie and creating a salad bowl for stir fry provide an opportunity to expand with additional toppings and ingredients: roasted yams, goat cheese, eggplant, portobello mushrooms, etc.

Week 1	Monday	Tuesday	Wednesday	Thursday	Friday	Saturday	Sunday
Breakfast	Chia seed pudding	Tofu scramble with spinach	Fresh berries and yogurt	Tofu Scramble	Avocado and coconut smoothie	Egg breakfast bowl	Yogurt parfait
Lunch	Burrito bowl	Burrito bowl + rice	Boiled eggs (2) with dill pickles	Baked salmon + cup of miso soup	Stir fry (leftovers)	Miso soup with greens	Zucchini lasagne
Dinner	Miso soup with greens	Squash soup	Platter – olives, greens, smoked salmon and cheese	Stir fry with chicken or tempeh and vegetables	Bone broth or vegetable soup	Curried cabbage and spicy ground beef	Yogurt and mango smoothie

Week 2	Monday	Tuesday	Wednesday	Thursday	Friday	Saturday	Sunday
Breakfast	Peanut butter and chocolate smoothie	Watermelon and mint smoothie + cup of Greek yogurt	Tofu scramble + greens	Build your own smoothie	Avocado and coconut smoothie	Egg breakfast bowl	Yogurt parfait
Lunch	Burrito bowl	Burrito bowl + rice	Boiled eggs (2) with dill pickles	Baked salmon + cup of miso soup	Stir fry (leftovers)	Miso soup with greens	Curried chickpeas
Dinner	Stir fry with chicken and spinach	Carrot and ginger soup	Platter – olives, greens, smoked salmon and cheese	Stir fry with chicken or tempeh and vegetables	Kale salad with dried fruits, walnuts	Curried cabbage and spicy ground beef	Yogurt and mango smoothie

Week 3	Monday	Tuesday	Wednesday	Thursday	Friday	Saturday	Sunday
Breakfast	Avocado and coconut smoothie	Build your own smoothie	Egg breakfast bowl + roasted squash	Build your own smoothie	Avocado and coconut smoothie	Egg breakfast bowl + grilled eggplant	Tofu scramble
Lunch	Burrito bowl	Burrito bowl + rice	Platter – devilled eggs, avocado, dill pickles	Miso soup with kale and seaweed	Curried broccoli and chicken leftovers	Kale salad with dried fruits, walnuts	Curried lentil soup
Dinner	Stir fry with chicken and spinach	Roasted squash and baked salmon	Stir fry with ground beef, peppers, onions, garlic, and spinach	Curried broccoli and chicken	Yogurt cup with banana	Curried cabbage and spicy ground beef	Grilled portobello mushrooms + salad

Week 4	Monday	Tuesday	Wednesday	Thursday	Friday	Saturday	Sunday
Breakfast	Build your own smoothie	Build your own smoothie	Yogurt parfait	Build your own smoothie	Tofu scramble	Eggs poached with asparagus	Eggs and vegetable skillet
Lunch	Egg breakfast bowl + curried chickpeas	Cucumbers, boiled eggs, and smoked salmon	Miso soup with kale, tempeh, and seaweed	Squash soup + side salad	Cheesy casserole leftovers	Burrito bowl	Cream of mushroom soup
Dinner	Stir fry with chicken and spinach	Roast beef with pickled beets	Stir fry with ground beef, peppers, onions, garlic, and spinach	Cheesy cauliflower and broccoli casserole	Yogurt cup with banana	Kale salad with dried fruits, walnuts, goat cheese	Grilled portobello mushrooms + salad

Each week contains some variations that resemble the previous week, along with some additions and/or replacements. In reality, we are often left with odd amounts of different foods that may not be considered ideal for a recipe. In these cases, they can be combined into recipes and concoctions that work on a budget and within a short period of time.

A typical example may include the following odds and ends you find in your fridge on a weekend or midweek when you have no plans of grocery shopping for another few days:

- Half an onion
- 2-3 kale leaves
- Half a carton of Greek yogurt
- 1/3 cucumber
- ½ pound ground beef

Whether it seems like it or not, these few items can combine to make a tasty recipe. One key "ingredient" to making leftovers work is to keep a healthy supply of spices, herbs and dried goods, which can easily supplement and support these creative meals. For these ingredients, heat a skillet and add olive oil, followed by ground beef, spices (turmeric, curry, salt, pepper, etc.), then add kale (sliced thin), onion and any other leftover vegetables that combine well in a stir fry. On the side, serve the yogurt and top with sliced cucumbers.

When there is leftover milk, yogurt and/or kefir in the refrigerator, these can be combined and blended with fresh or frozen fruits for a quick smoothie. If only yogurt is available, blend with bananas and/or mangos or other fruits that thicken, for an easy and tasty dessert. Keeping a good stash of nuts and seeds is important, as these can serve as a quick protein and healthy fat "fix" when preparing a full meal is neither economical nor time-efficient.

CHAPTER 9

Exercise and Diet: Why Keeping Active Combats Anxiety

Exercise and diet are linked to good health, including the prevention of anxiety and related mood disorders. In general, all forms of exercise provide benefits. As cardio, weightlifting and endurance sports becoming more popular, many people do their best to fit their exercise routine into a busy schedule. Yoga, Pilates and stretching can benefit the body and mind by increasing calmness, reducing stress and bringing a sense of well-being and restfulness.

High impact interval training (HIIT) is a great way to gain the benefits of high impact exercise within a relatively short period of time. Research on this type of exercise indicates positive results after merely a half-hour of intense training in one- or two-minute intervals, separated by very brief rest period in between (about 30 seconds). The impact of these workouts includes faster metabolism and increased energy, lasting nearly twenty-four hours following a workout. There are also positive benefits on the brain, including a stable mood and feeling well. Based on the findings of this type of exercise, only four to five HIIT workouts each week would yield significant improvements in mood, anxiety, and overall health.

Yoga, Pilates and exercises that focus on breathing, mindfulness and balance can improve depression and anxiety by reducing their effects drastically. Other benefits of these forms of exercise include lower blood pressure, improved sleep, respiratory function and a significant reduction in joint and muscle pain. These classes are often guided by an experienced instructor that can provide the necessary modifications and enhancements to make the experience not only beneficial but enjoyable and relaxing.

Long-term forms of exercise, such as marathons, cycling, swimming and other activities that focus on endurance and strength, are equally beneficial for your mind and body. Studies often link the reduction of depression, anxiety and stress to regular exercise, whether it's high or low impact. Regular exercise and a healthy diet also prevent mood disorders.

How to Approach Exercise: From Inactive to Low or Moderate Activity and Beyond: How Increasing Your Efforts Makes a Big Difference in Your Mind and Body's Health

If exercise is not already a part of your routine and your lifestyle is sedentary, it's best to gradually introduce yourself to simple forms of movement and activity to get started. One of the best ways to get started is walking and stretching. Start with a short, brisk walk of fifteen minutes and increase more each day. Daily physical movement is recommended and will shift your metabolism into working more efficiently.

Most studies on the benefits of exercise suggest a minimum of thirty-minute sessions at least three times per week. This is a good start, that can be increased to longer periods of exercise and more frequency, to four or five sessions weekly.

Swimming and cycling are excellent ways to lose weight and build lean muscle. Aquatic exercise is a great option for people who suffer from arthritis and chronic joint paint. When your body moves in the water, it doesn't feel the same resistance, making movement easier and available, where it would otherwise be too difficult and challenging. Aqua fit classes are usually open to the public or for a nominal fee in many local community centers and gyms.

They are enjoyable classes, usually accompanied by music and an enthusiastic instructor, with participants of all ages and levels of ability. These classes are also beneficial for people who have more severe mobility restrictions, as there is usually supportive equipment available for accessibility.

Dancing and movement to music is a great way to boost your mood and feel good. It's a great way to release stress and to "escape" from a difficult situation. Often when we are stressed, we vent our emotions or crawl inward, suppressing our feelings, which only makes us feel worse.

If possible, combat these negative reactions by getting active right away: slip on your headphones go for a walk, jog or engage in simple stretching. Any movement, minimal or enduring, releases endorphins, as well as serotonin and dopamine, which help us feel good, giving us the sensation of receiving an award for our efforts.

The combined benefits of an anti-anxiety diet with exercise include sustainable, long-term weight loss and management, better overall focus and energy.

CHAPTER 10

Long-term Benefits of Implementing the Anti-Anxiety Diet into your Lifestyle

Adapting to any new diet or way of eating takes time and effort, though by easing into new foods and trying recipes with healthier options, you will begin to notice significant changes over time. In some studies, switching to an anti-anxiety diet produces results within a week, such as a calmer disposition and stable mood, along with a renewed sense of energy. In the longer term, over a period of a month or more, a nutrient-rich diet will eradicate a lot of symptoms you may experience from chronic conditions and diseases.

If you are already active, improving your diet will help with recovery from sports and other activity-related injuries. In everyday life, there are helpful tips for keeping your diet and lifestyle on track, to gain the most out of the anti-anxiety diet:

Q: How can I stick to this diet when it's challenging to find some of the ingredients for recipes?
A: There are a lot of substitutes available for foods that are not readily available. The key to eating well is keeping as many options open as possible and including them in your shopping lists. Maintaining a versatile pantry full of spices, dried goods and soups is one way to stay prepared.

Q: How can I build a healthy, nutritious pantry on a budget?
A: Buy in bulk as much as possible and use reusable containers. Some local shops and food co-ops will provide a discount or other incentive when reusable containers are returned or exchanged for other options. Some small, local stores will charge less for certain goods that are easy to supply. For imported spices and goods, it may be a challenge, though shopping online for a reputable supplier is a good option.

Q: What sort of foods are good for long road trips and traveling?
A: Energy bars that combine nut butter with seeds, cocoa, natural sweetener and chia seeds are best for providing ample nutrients on your travels. An even simpler idea is to combine mixed nuts and dried berries together for a "trail mix" snack. If you bring a cooler, be sure to include fresh fruits and yogurt for nourishment, especially if you are taking a long trip. Drinking water with freshly squeezed lime or lemon will increase the electrolyte production in your body, keeping you hydrated and reducing stress in hot or humid climates.

Q: How can I implement an anti-anxiety diet when everyone else I live with eats differently?
A: There are several options available: you can introduce your family and/or roommates to your new way of eating and offer to make some meals together. If there is a lack of interest, simply calculate the portion size to fit your individual budget and do your best to stick with that. They may eventually see the benefits (in mind and body) and choose to try it out someday!

Q: Are there any foods that should be avoided completely, not even to be consumed in moderation?

A: All foods, once in a while, are not harmful, as long as the majority of your diet is based on healthy, natural whole foods. One major ingredient to avoid is trans fats, or the "bad" fat, which leads to many diseases, including cancer, heart disease and obesity. Even on occasion, trans fats will have little effect, so the danger lies in eating bad foods regularly. Some of these foods can become addictive or habit-forming, which makes them best to avoid always.

Overall, the anti-anxiety diet is beneficial for everyone, from all ages, lifestyles and stages in life. It's not so much about counting calories or tracking specific levels of nutrients, as it is about maintaining an abundance of as many nutrient-rich foods and varieties as possible. In just weeks, you'll feel and look better, benefitting the value of good foods from the inside out for a sustainable, long-term mental and physical well-being.

Finally, if you found this book useful in any way, a five star review is always appreciated !

DISCLAIMER :

The author is not a licensed practitioner, physician, or medical professional and offers no medical diagnoses, treatments, suggestions, or counseling. The information presented herein has not been evaluated by the U.S. Food and Drug Administration, and it is not intended to diagnose, treat, cure, or prevent any disease. Full medical clearance from a licensed physician should be obtained before beginning or modifying any diet, exercise, or lifestyle program, and physicians should be informed of all nutritional changes.

The author/owner claims no responsibility to any person or entity for any liability, loss, or damage caused or alleged to be caused directly or indirectly as a result of the use, application, or interpretation of the information presented herein.

CPSIA information can be obtained
at www.ICGtesting.com
Printed in the USA
BVHW081448150321
602550BV00007B/662